REA

Cold Warriors

Contemporary American History Series
William E. Leuchtenburg, General Editor

Cold Warriors

Eisenhower's Generation and
American Foreign Policy

H. W. Brands, Jr.

Columbia University Press
New York   1988

Columbia University Press
New York   Guildford, Surrey
Copyright © 1988 Columbia University Press
All rights reserved
Printed in the United States of America

Library of Congress Cataloging-in-Publication Data
Brands, H. W.
  Cold Warriors

  (Contemporary American history series)
  Bibliography: p.
  Includes index.
  1. United States—Foreign relations—1953–1961.
2. Eisenhower, Dwight D. (Dwight David), 1890–1969.
I. Title.   II. Series
E835.B684   1988   327.73   87-17900
ISBN 0-231-06526-4

Clothbound editions of Columbia University Press are Smyth-
sewn and printed on permanent and durable acid-free paper

Book design by Ken Venezio

I would like to thank especially Robert Divine and William Leuchtenburg.

Contemporary American History Series
William E. Leuchtenburg, General Editor

Lawrence S. Wittner, *Rebels Against War: The American Peace Movement,*
1941–1960. 1969

Davis R. B. Ross, *Preparing for Ulysses: Politics and Veterans During World*
War II. 1969

John Lewis Gaddis, *The United States and the Origins of the Cold War,*
1941–1947. 1972

George C. Herring, Jr., *Aid to Russia, 1941–1946: Strategy, Diplomacy, the*
Origins of the Cold War. 1973

Alonzo L. Hamby, *Beyond the New Deal: Harry S. Truman and American*
Liberalism. 1973

Richard M. Fried, *Men Against McCarthy.* 1976

Steven F. Lawson, *Black Ballots: Voting Rights in the South, 1944–*
1969. 1976

Carl M. Brauer, *John F. Kennedy and the Second Reconstruction.* 1977

Maeva Marcus, *Truman and the Steel Seizure Case: The Limits of Presiden-*
tial Power. 1977

Morton Sosna, *In Search of the Silent South: Southern Liberals and the Race*
Issue. 1977

Robert M. Collins, *The Business Response to Keynes, 1929–1964.* 1981

Robert M. Hathaway, *Ambiguous Partnership: Britain and America, 1944–*
1947. 1981

Leonard Dinnerstein, *America and the Survivors of the Holocaust.* 1982

Lawrence S. Wittner, *American Intervention in Greece, 1943–1949.* 1982

Nancy Bernkopf Tucker, *Patterns in the Dust: Chinese-American Relations*
and the Recognition Controversy, 1949–1950. 1983

Catherine A. Barnes, *Journey from Jim Crow: The Desegregation of Southern*
Transit. 1983

Steven F. Lawson, *In Pursuit of Power: Southern Blacks and Electoral*
Politics, 1964–1982. 1985

David R. Colburn, *Racial Change and Community Crisis: St. Augustine,*
Florida, 1877–1980. 1985

H. W. Brands, Jr., *Cold Warriors: Eisenhower's Generation and American*
Foreign Policy. 1988

Marc S. Gallicchio, *The Cold War Begins in Asia: American Foreign Policy*
and the Fall of the Japanese Empire. 1988

Melanie Billings-Yun, *Decision Against War: Eisenhower and Dien Bien*
Phu, 1954. 1988

Contents

Introduction

People make policy, and understanding policy requires examining the people who make it. In the case of the Eisenhower administration and American foreign policy of the 1950s, historians and other students of the period have concentrated on the president and Secretary of State John Foster Dulles; their investigations have pursued the question that gave title to one of the earlier works of what has become a revisionist school: "Eisenhower and Dulles: Who Made the Decisions?"[1] Most contemporary observers believed that Dulles held the balance of diplomatic power in the administration; the revisionists have thrown the weight of recent scholarship to Eisenhower's side of the scale. The received view required modification, to be sure, but in redefining conventional wisdom the revisionists have perpetuated the impression that administration diplomacy was a one-man show; their accomplishment has been to place a new man in charge.[2]

Such an emphasis distorts reality. Eisenhower and Dulles were certainly the major players in the diplomacy of the 1950s, but formulating and implementing foreign policy required a supporting cast that collectively often exerted as much influence as they did on that policy's final form. In any administration, most decisions are made below the level of the president and the secretary of state; the sheer mass of issues demanding attention would force the policy process to a halt were this not so. Moreover, the manner of putting decisions into effect frequently counts no less toward their success or failure than their intrinsic wisdom or folly. These observations apply with special force to Eisenhower's administration, for with the possible exception of Ronald Reagan, Eisenhower consciously apportioned responsibility to trusted subordinates to a greater degree than any president in the last half-century.

Eisenhower acquired the delegating habit during the most formative period of his career, the years of World War II, when George Marshall singled him out for command and ultimately glory. Shortly after Pearl Harbor, Marshall summoned Eisenhower to the War Department. The chief of staff told the junior officer of the difficulties he encountered in converting a peacetime army to a war-fighting machine; he dwelt especially on the paralysis induced by excessive deference to higher-ups. "Eisenhower," Marshall said, "the Department is filled with able men who analyze their problems well but feel compelled always to bring them to me for final solution. I must have assistants who will solve their own problems and tell me later what they have done."[3] Eisenhower never forgot this meeting; as his career progressed he emulated Marshall's leadership style and adopted his criteria for choosing subordinates.[4] When he became president, he continued to spread responsibility. Eisenhower's White House staff secretary, Andrew Goodpaster, characterized his boss as "a man who (a) knows how to delegate, and (b) when he delegates, expects the people to carry out the responsibility that he had delegated to them."[5]

The present study aims to broaden understanding of Eisenhower's foreign policy by placing the president and the secretary of state in the context of several of the individuals to whom Eisenhower delegated authority. The nine men sketched here are grouped into four categories, according to their roles in the administration and their connections to the president. In the first, innermost group, are John Foster Dulles, Milton Eisenhower, and Allen Dulles. Foster Dulles was unquestionably the president's most influential diplomatic adviser, a distinction he achieved by his long experience in international affairs, his eventual warm relationship with Eisenhower, and his sensitivity to the political overtones of foreign policy decisions. Milton Eisenhower had only modest official duties in the administration, but unofficially he served as his brother's alter ego and chief confidant. Milton's counsel covered a broad range of topics, domestic and foreign; in the diplomatic realm, his greatest influence was in the shaping of administration policy toward Latin America. CIA Director Allen Dulles was not close to Eisenhower personally, but the sensitive nature of the intelligence agency's activities and the president's willingness to use covert methods when others failed dictated that he would be near the center of the policy process.

In a second, rather different, category are Walter Bedell Smith and Robert Murphy. Eisenhower valued the analytical ability of the two men, especially Smith, but their primary function lay in executing, not devising, policy. Eisenhower had worked with Smith and Murphy during World War II, and he had developed great confidence in their capacity to make the best of difficult situations. During his presidency, he again turned to them to help him out of tight spots. The high point of Smith's relatively brief tenure as undersecretary of state was the Geneva conference of 1954; for Murphy, the American landing in Lebanon in 1958 provided the climax to a series of trouble-shooting assignments.

The third rank comprises three men who served as policy agitators, keeping the decision-making process from congealing prematurely, and as agents of influence with groups Eisenhower could not satisfy fully, but which he did not wish to alienate. C. D. Jackson, an associate of Henry Luce at *Time* magazine and an active member of various right-wing organizations, was the administration's gadfly, continually seeking support for the psychological warfare activities that fascinated him. Harold Stassen argued the case for disarmament; his role as hopeful counterweight to the gloomy Foster Dulles was intended to demonstrate to audiences at home and abroad the president's commitment to arms control. In addition, Eisenhower sought to use Stassen as a bridge to young moderates in the Republican party. Henry Cabot Lodge acted as defender of the faith at the United Nations; his denunciations of communist perfidy generated politically potent headlines. At the same time, Lodge became something of a lobbyist for the third world in administration councils, and he opened channels to newly independent nations that might otherwise have remained closed.

Eisenhower receives a section of his own, not simply because he was president and therefore stood apart from his advisers, but because he embodied and in a sense encapsulated many of the traits and attitudes of the men he appointed—which is only natural, since he would not have chosen individuals whose philosophy he rejected. The characteristic feature of Eisenhower's, and his administration's, approach to international relations was a mixture of an almost unthinkingly anticommunist ideology with a remarkably practical reluctance to translate that ideology into action. Nearly all presidents discover that they can do less in office than they hoped; the constraints of political life made no exception for Eisenhower.

But in Eisenhower's case, the tempering of ideology with practicality deserves special note, for it antedated his White House years and reflected influences deeper than politics. Eisenhower's understanding of the relationship between principle and power was forged in the crucible of World War II; with the others of his generation he sought, not fully consciously and not always successfully, to apply the lessons of the world war to the cold war.

In what follows, the emphasis is on the people who made the policy of the Eisenhower administration. Some of those portrayed here would occupy places on any list of central figures of Republican diplomacy of the 1950s; the positions of others might be argued. The more challengeable ones owe their inclusion sometimes to being in the right place at the right time, sometimes to demonstrating distinctive elements of Eisenhower's diplomatic style, sometimes to representing roads not taken. Smith, for example, had little effect on administration policy after 1954, but his part in the Geneva conference helped shape the American response to one of the landmark negotiations of the postwar years. Murphy's frequent missions abroad exemplify Eisenhower's habit of relying on individuals he had seen tested under fire—literally—for delicate foreign assignments. Jackson enjoyed relatively small success in promoting psychological warfare, but examining Jackson's failure illuminates the path Eisenhower *did* choose to follow. In general, individuals appear here because their experiences reveal something significant about the administration's approach to international affairs. A similar criterion determines which parts of each person's activities receive treatment. Stassen, to cite one illustration, played an important role in the development of Eisenhower's foreign aid policy, but for the present purpose his work in arms control is more instructive.

Throughout, the emphasis is on the personal factor in the development of Eisenhower's foreign policy. Who were the people involved? To what and to whom did they owe their positions? What attitudes and beliefs did they bring to their diplomatic tasks? What did the president expect from them? How did they fit into the decision-making process? How did they interact with each other? What did they hope to accomplish? Why did they succeed, and why did they fail? And finally, what do their experiences tell us about the policy they fashioned?

I
Inner Circle

1

John Foster Dulles: Speak Loudly and Carry a Soft Stick

John Foster Dulles enjoyed the reputation of principal ideologist in the Eisenhower administration. His deeply held and frequently voiced beliefs regarding the morality of America's purpose in the world and the immorality of the designs of America's foes set the tone for the nation's diplomacy during most of the 1950s. At the same time, though, Dulles was the administration's chief pragmatist. The secretary of state understood that neither communism nor Soviet power would wither away in the near future, and he knew that rash attempts to rush the issue might bring on the conflict that, above all, had to be prevented. Such were the limits of power in the international realm. At home, Dulles paid no less attention to the limits of politics. He recognized the potential for obstruction that lay with the professional anticommunists of the Republican right, and he sought, on the whole successfully, to neutralize this potential by keeping his own anticommunist credentials in unimpeachable order.

On February 19, 1920, Dulles received a letter from his uncle, Robert Lansing, who had just resigned his position as Woodrow Wilson's secretary of state. Lansing's resignation had been a long time coming; he had chafed for many months at the fact that Wilson heeded his advice less than that of Edward House. "You are sufficiently intimate with the inside events during the past year," Lansing wrote his nephew, "to know the increasing difficulties of my position."[1]

Lansing went on to describe some of the details of the events that had convinced him that he could no longer remain in the Wilson administration. Dulles no doubt paid close attention; one as attuned as he was to diplomacy and the making of foreign policy could hardly do otherwise. In later years, as the possibility of Dulles' assuming the secretaryship grew stronger, Lansing's example would remind him of what ought not to happen between a president and his secretary of state.

That Dulles remembered the Lansing affair seemed clear to many who served in Eisenhower's State Department. Robert Murphy, who worked closely with Dulles during the latter's entire tenure, later recalled of Dulles that "the history of the Lansing-Wilson thing was very vividly on his mind." Murphy added that Dulles "was determined that that was not going to happen" to him in his relationship with Eisenhower.[2] Roderic O'Connor, Dulles' administrative assistant, said, "I'm quite sure that he had the impression that his uncle, Robert Lansing, had had his effectiveness severely diminished by Colonel House and other people who were close to Wilson."[3]

Dulles' associates could not help noticing the effect of Lansing's unfortunate experience on Dulles; the familial tie alone rendered the connection inevitable. Certainly it played a central role in shaping Dulles' attitudes. However, another aspect of the events Lansing described, though less noted by Dulles' contemporaries, must have made a deep impression on the future secretary as well.

Through Lansing, Dulles gained an inside view of what undoubtedly seemed the decline and fall of Woodrow Wilson. For Dulles, Wilson had represented nearly all that was right with America and most of what ought to be right with the world. Dulles could identify with much in Wilson. Each had a Presbyterian minister father; partly in consequence, each considered diplomacy a suitable field for the expression of an ethical and moral view that distinguished the United States from its international rivals. Princeton figured prominently in the life of each; Dulles passed under Wilson's tutelage in the political science department there and later declared, "The major benefit I got from Princeton was participating in Woodrow Wilson's courses where I gained my interest in public affairs."[4] Wilson's example, later reinforced by what Dulles' brother Allen described as the Democratic president's "inspirational call for joining public service,"[5] strongly influenced the decision of Dulles, then a promising young New York lawyer, to forsake Wall Street for Washington.

Dulles embraced Wilson's wartime policies, applauding the Fourteen Points as giving to the war effort "the character of an idealistic crusade," and he joined Wilson in enthusiastic advocacy of the League of Nations.[6] Dulles narrowly missed witnessing Wilson's victorious entry into Paris— he was on a ship making the crossing from America—but he arrived before the cheers faded, while Wilson still embodied the hopes of much of humanity for a just and enduring peace.

Thus it must have been with especial dismay that Dulles watched Wilson's designs for a better world run afoul of the cynicism of European diplomats who contested to see how loudly the German pips could be made to squeak. To save his beloved League, Wilson sacrificed much of his plan for a humane postwar order to these cunning men. And then he returned to the United States, only to be bested by politicians more clever than he. In the end, Wilson lost all that he had fought for—and Dulles had hoped for—by his inability to meet his foes on their own ground.

In the February 1920 letter from Lansing to Dulles cited above, Lansing described the sad condition of the president. Wilson had suffered a stroke the previous autumn on an exhausting tour of the country in defense of the peace treaty and the League. Lansing suspected that the stroke had affected Wilson's reasoning powers. "I really fear he is less sound mentally than we have been led to suppose." The former secretary of state also commented on the low level to which public support for Wilson had fallen. In particular, he mentioned an incident in a movie theater at which his own picture had been thrown onto the screen at the end of the performance, to "loud applause," while that of the president had evoked only a reaction "weak and without heart."[7]

In reading Lansing's remarks, Dulles certainly recognized that they came from a man defending his own actions. Still, he must have been struck by the contrast between the feeble and ineffective Wilson described in 1920 and the dynamic and inspirational leader of only one year before. Perhaps at that time, and undoubtedly later, Dulles must have reflected on the tremendous gap that often existed between intentions and results in the conduct of American foreign affairs. Wilson, whose desire to shape the world according to certain moral and philosophical principles would be paralleled by Dulles', had been singularly unsuccessful in translating his noble intentions into reality. Wilson's rigidity doomed his designs; he did not understand that in the diplomacy of a democracy the shortest distance between two points is not always a straight line, but often a crooked and devious route. When it became Dulles' turn to formulate American policy, he would not make the same mistake.

The repudiation of Wilson had been for Dulles an early lesson in the politics of diplomacy. Three decades later, he received another lesson. This time Dulles himself played a central role.

In 1948, the Republican party eagerly awaited its chance to run a candidate for president against someone other than Franklin Roosevelt for the first time in twenty years. Domestic dislocations, the failure of real peace to follow the war, and general dissatisfaction with the Truman administration made a Republican victory appear likely, if not certain. John Foster Dulles had become by this time a foreign policy authority on the Republican side, and when his close friend and associate Thomas Dewey won the party's nomination for president, Dulles received, for all intents and purposes, the nomination for secretary of state.

So confident were the Republicans of victory that they decided to wage a cautious and statesmanlike campaign, one chosen to protect Dewey's lead in the polls and to avoid harsh feelings that might encumber a Dewey administration. Restraint especially prevailed in the realm of foreign policy. Arthur Vandenberg, the most important Republican in the Senate on international affairs and the chief architect of postwar bipartisanship, urged Dulles to avoid attacks on Truman's handling of diplomacy, for fear of permanently alienating Democrats. "I keenly feel that it is very important that 'foreign policy' should be handled with highly intelligent skill lest we do more harm than good," Vandenberg told Dulles. "It is to be ever remembered that the next Republican Secretary of State is going to need Democratic votes in the Senate just as badly as the present Administration has needed Republican votes." Vandenberg concluded, "It is peculiarly our job—yours and mine—to see that bipartisan liaison in the next Congress does not become impossible. Otherwise November will represent a pyrrhic victory."[8]

Dulles had been personally involved in American diplomacy since World

War II, as part of the Truman administration's effort to gain Republican support for its foreign policy, and so he did not find uncongenial the tone recommended by Vandenberg. Indeed, Dulles' Republicanism had hardly been evident to those with whom he had worked. Robert Murphy said of Dulles' participation in a London conference in early 1948, "He might as well have been a career Foreign Service officer."[9] Throughout the campaign, Dulles passed up numerous opportunities to criticize Truman's policy on topics like Berlin, Palestine, and China. One result was a contest in which foreign affairs played little part. Another result—also attributable to Republican circumspection, or so Republicans later interpreted matters—was Dewey's defeat.[10]

Through this defeat, which snatched from the would-be secretary of state, at the age of sixty, the office he had sought for many years,[11] Dulles learned the limits of speaking softly in the political hubbub surrounding American foreign policy. The election of 1948 marked a turning point in Dulles' understanding of democratic politics and diplomacy. He gained an appreciation of the importance of reinforcing good diplomatic ideas with popular support, and he discovered the consequent necessity of actively managing the public relations of foreign policy.

After 1948, and throughout the years of his direction of the State Department, Dulles put into action the knowledge and experience he had gained through Wilson's failure in 1919–1920, and his own and Dewey's failure in 1948. In contrast to Wilson, Dulles was flexible and cautious, carefully weighing his diplomatic options for feasibility, in terms both of what American power would bear and what the American public would support. In contrast to his own actions in the campaign with Dewey, he did not again neglect the cultivation of public opinion. The rhetoric he used to advance the policy of the Eisenhower administration, and thus to promote what he conceived to be the interests of the United States, was often overblown and overdramatic. It commonly tended toward the moralistic, which, while honestly reflecting an important aspect of Dulles' temperament, also contained a strong element of calculation.

This combination in Dulles of the shrewd practitioner of political diplomacy with the moralizing preacher of American righteousness was easier on his own psyche than it sometimes was on his reputation. Dulles had no great difficulty reconciling the two roles he had to play; if the success of administration policies required overselling them, that was something that came with the territory. Dulles' critics, however, observed the discrepancy between what Dulles preached and what he practiced, and pronounced him a hypocrite. To a certain extent, they were right—if it makes sense to talk about hypocrisy in the conduct of foreign affairs. One does not have to accept the dictum that the function of diplomats is to lie for their country, to recognize that a gap often exists between what the representatives of a government feel obliged to say and what they feel required to do. Dulles saw the gap clearly, and he determined not to let it swallow him.

The part of his political education acquired in the 1948 election showed its effects before another year had passed. In July 1949, New York senator Robert Wagner retired for reasons of ill health, and Governor Dewey, having been unable to give Dulles the position to which he most aspired, offered the vacant Senate seat to his erstwhile foreign policy adviser. At the time Dulles accepted the post, he had no plans to run for election in his own right in November of that year. After a taste of Senate life, however, he changed his mind.

Dulles leaped into his contest against the popular Democratic former governor Herbert Lehman with a zest that must have astonished observers who expected a repeat of the moderation of 1948. From appearing above the fray in the campaign with Dewey, Dulles switched to an enthusiastic courting of public opinion, employing various of the tricks of innuendo and deception that made politics in the late 1940s an entertaining, if often battering, business. At a time when the communists-in-government issue was just gathering momentum, Dulles lashed Lehman for insufficient opposition to subversion. He opened his campaign with a speech in which he asked rhetorically, "The half million Communists and fellow travelers who last year voted for Henry Wallace, who will they vote for now?" He distributed leaflets with the message, "The Reds Will Register and Vote. Will You?" He welcomed, and repeated in case some people had not heard, a statement allegedly made by Soviet diplomat Andrei Vishinsky that Dulles ought to be thrown into chains. He rounded out the campaign in the final week by claiming, "If I am defeated in this election, the greatest rejoicing will not be in New York or Washington but will be in Moscow."[12]

Although these attacks failed to overcome a heavy Democratic majority in New York City, Dulles made a strong showing. He lost the election, but he had not expected to win, and as he pointed out to Robert Murphy in a December post-mortem, he had carried fifty-seven of the state's sixty-two counties.[13] Contemplating the results, and comparing them with the come-from-ahead defeat in 1948, Dulles must have been convinced of the advantages of an aggressive style.

When his next opportunity to gain high office came in 1952, Dulles demonstrated, this time with greater success, his political skills in support of his foreign policy goals. By 1952, of course, most of the bipartisanship of the early cold war had dissolved. Indeed, so heated and incessant had the criticism of Truman and Secretary of State Dean Acheson grown that foreign policy inevitably became a major issue in Eisenhower's campaign for the presidency. Dulles led the way for the Republicans in castigating Truman and his advisers for their "defeatist" attitude in confronting the communist challenge. Dulles understood that foreign policy defied definition in simple slogans, but he also recognized the political effectiveness of stating positions in arresting terms. In contrast to the Truman policy, which itself had been oversimplified by the rubric "containment," Dulles advocated "liberation."

Liberation had been a Dulles theme since 1949. In the wake of his Senate defeat, Dulles had written to an acquaintance that the "eventual liberation" of countries under communist control ought to be "an essential and enduring part" of the foreign policy of the United States. Dulles advocated no specific action, but he said, "Dictatorships always look formidable until they collapse," and he added that "there will develop pockets or centers of resistance." Dulles suggested that "in the light of what happens, further steps can be taken."[14]

When Dulles made a point of the "eventual"—which seemed to imply peaceful—aspect of liberation, his statements evoked few objections. But with his talk of "further steps" to be taken, presumably to aid the "centers of resistance," his declarations lost much of their moderation and sounded uncomfortably like a call to arms for Eastern Europe. In the next few years, until the election of 1952, Dulles would increasingly slur over the qualification that liberation should be eventual and peaceful. Before long, he was talking as though freedom for the satellite states awaited only a Republican victory.

By the early part of 1951, Dulles was going public with his demands for liberation and his criticism of the Truman containment policy. In May of that year, Dulles gave a radio address in which he said, "Liberation is a goal we must never relinquish. . . . It is the goal which, if we are resolute, we shall attain."[15] In this speech, as in all of his statements on the subject, Dulles avoided specifying just how liberation would come about; his vagueness demonstrated the degree to which he had adopted the political campaigner's practice of saying what his listeners wanted to hear, without committing himself to anything that might be refutable or embarrassing later on.

When the campaign of 1952 began in earnest, Dulles' attacks on containment and his demands for liberation gained emphasis. "We must abandon the 'containment' policy and, above all, the defeatist, appeasing mood which gives it birth," Dulles told an audience in September 1952. Later in this address, Dulles cautioned that any action taken in the direction of liberation "should only be peaceful action,"[16] but he was not always so careful. At least once, Eisenhower felt obliged to warn Dulles against promoting liberation without making clear that such liberation must only be by peaceful methods.[17]

Candidate Eisenhower was not alone in thinking that Dulles' rhetoric might be getting the better of his judgment. Dean Rusk, a Far Eastern specialist in the State Department whom Dulles had known from negotiations on the Japanese peace treaty, commented on a draft of an article by Dulles that appeared in *Life* magazine in May 1952.[18] To a statement by Dulles that seemed to promise support for an Asian version of liberation through what was often called the "unleashing" of Chiang Kai-shek, Rusk responded, "The idea that Formosa might somehow threaten or attack the mainland without U.S. participation is . . . somewhat quixotic." Rusk objected to other passages with the comment, "It sounds as though you have a lot of concrete steps ready to 'spring' on the world if given the chance." Questioning the prudence of Dulles' remarks, Rusk asked, "Can't you moderate this language?"[19]

With the White House for Eisenhower and the State Department for himself so near at hand, Dulles would not soften his language conspicuously. In the months before the election, he did not worry about the fact that little substance lay behind the rhetoric of liberation. Emmet Hughes, then foreign affairs editor for *Life*, worked with Dulles on his May 1952 article. During their period of collaboration, Hughes repeatedly asked

Dulles what liberation meant in the way of action. As often as Hughes asked, Dulles failed to provide an answer.[20] Dulles had had his fill of moderation and statesmanlike conduct in the election of 1948. In 1952, Dulles turned sixty-four; he could not reasonably expect another chance to gain the office he had coveted for so long. If his campaign rhetoric caused problems for him after Eisenhower's victory, he would deal with those problems when he took control of the State Department. What mattered at the moment was gaining control.

During the campaign of 1952, Dulles acted much like a candidate running for office. That indeed was what he was doing, for although Eisenhower considered others for secretary of state, Dulles certainly led the field of contenders. Eisenhower and Dulles had become acquainted during the former's term as president of Columbia University. The two men had discussed foreign affairs and had discovered a similarity of views. During one dinner visit to the Dulles household, Eisenhower had suggested to his host that he write a book setting down his thoughts on America's relationship to the world; Dulles took the advice and produced *War or Peace* a short time later.[21] Few observers expressed surprise, therefore, when Eisenhower designated Dulles as secretary of state only a few weeks after the election.[22]

Like many another successful candidate, Dulles soon demonstrated that the practices of the officeholder differed from the promises of the office seeker. His outspoken criticism of the Truman-Acheson containment policy diminished, and liberation came increasingly to be treated as something more hoped for than actually pursued. The fact, of course, was that containment had not been chosen by the Truman administration so much as it had been forced on the United States by a lack of desirable alternatives. Dulles understood this, as did those who became Dulles' subordinates at the State Department. Alexis Johnson, for example, a veteran of State's Far Eastern division, later remembered Dulles' arrival and the little serious diplomatic attention the new secretary paid to the themes of the 1952 campaign. Regarding the "unleashing" of Chiang and the Chinese Nationalists, Johnson recalled that Dulles "made it clear that he thought this was good domestic politics." Liberation, as well, had been designed for an American audience. "Foster Dulles was a realist and knew the world well," Johnson said, "and I think the 'liberation' theme that he adopted was for domestic political purposes more than out of any genuine conviction with regard to international affairs."[23] Dulles himself admitted privately that campaign oratory would not determine policy; at a CIA briefing shortly after the November election he said that the "unleashing" of Chiang would be primarily a symbolic action.[24]

Dulles insisted, however, that the retreat from the themes of the campaign be an orderly withdrawal, and he made it clear that he would set the pace. After the election but before he began to hint that freedom for Eastern Europe might not top the list of the new administration's priorities, senior diplomat George Kennan delivered a speech criticizing liberation. Kennan had early articulated the containment idea, and naturally his remarks gained a wide hearing. Kennan's candor brought down Dulles' displeasure; before long the secretary showed him the State Department door.[25] Dulles did not object to Kennan's views on liberation; indeed, as Dulles' actions would soon demonstrate, his own approach to relations with the communists differed little from Kennan's. But Dulles could not tolerate Kennan's public questioning of the liberation concept. To suffer Kennan's presence in the State Department after such criticism would greatly complicate Dulles' task of backing away from liberation at a measured tempo. That the content of Kennan's views was not the problem was demonstrated by the secretary-designate's response to Charles Bohlen when the latter told Dulles that he, as State Department counselor, had cleared Kennan's speech. Bohlen told Dulles that if Kennan was not acceptable, then neither, presumably, was he. Dulles brushed aside Bohlen's conclusion, saying that he had kept his differences to himself.[26]

Kennan's ouster stirred concern among the diplomatic corps. Bohlen thought Dulles exuded suspicion; he later said, "The Republicans came into the State Department rather like a wagon train going into hostile Indian territory, and every night they'd group their wagons around the fire."[27] Dulles did not diminish this impression in his first meeting with career officials in February 1953, when he told the assembled group that he expected their "positive loyalty." Dulles did not define "positive loyalty," but with Joseph McCarthy on the loose, his reputation largely the result of attacks on the State Department, such words sounded sinister.

Alexis Johnson considered the emphasis on loyalty part of the public relations package that included liberation and the "unleashing" of the

Chinese Nationalists. It was designed, he believed, for domestic political consumption.[28] Bohlen concurred in this judgment, describing Dulles' motivation in more forceful terms. According to Bohlen, Dulles "was a man who really had one obsession: to remain Secretary of State"; consequently he went out of his way to appease the McCarthyites. "Mr. Dulles throughout his entire life had really been pointing toward the Secretaryship of State, and he had it, and he was concerned lest the right wing of the Republican Party might mount a campaign against him which might cause him to leave the office."[29]

Bohlen disliked Dulles and doubted his integrity,[30] but his assessment of Dulles' motivation, even if overstated, contains a solid core of truth. Dulles had seen what the career anticommunists had done to Dean Acheson, and he did not intend to let them do the same to him. A less than spotless—from the subversive-hunters' perspective—record heightened his sensitivity to right-wing criticism. In the early postwar years, Dulles had been a close associate of Alger Hiss, and he had stood by Hiss as rumors began to circulate of the latter's communist affiliations and activities. Dulles had helped Hiss gain appointment as president of the Carnegie Endowment; he had dismissed reports of Hiss' checkered past by saying, "I am confident that there is no reason to doubt Mr. Hiss' complete loyalty to our American institutions."[31]

What had appeared in the late 1940s to be a commendable expression of loyalty seemed to Dulles in 1953 a source of potential embarrassment or worse. Knowing that many on the Republican right distrusted him for connections with Dewey, with Truman, and with internationalist opinion, and knowing that the conservatives would be happy to cause him trouble, Dulles sought to minimize potential sources of conflict. At the cost of the morale of the State Department, he declined to defend diplomats John Carter Vincent and John Paton Davies against charges of disloyal complicity in the "loss" of China. Dulles tried to finesse the security issue by firing Vincent and Davies for bad judgment rather than subversion, but the message seemed clear to Dulles' subordinates. Bohlen thought the secretary "very anxious to keep his lines of communication sweet" with the conservatives; this seemed his chief priority.[32]

Dulles may have worried particularly about Vincent and Davies because of an earlier affront to the China lobby. In 1950, Dulles had corresponded with Henry Luce, probably the most prominent of the Nationalist sympathizers in the United States, regarding American policy toward China. At that time, Dulles had said that the United States ought not to shun China simply for its communism. Regarding recognition of Beijing and membership in the United Nations, Dulles rejected an ideological test. He said that the primary consideration ought to be the Communists' ability to govern effectively. Dulles told Luce, "I would not think it wise to lay down the principle that the United States would use the veto power to prevent the seating of a government which had proved, over a period of time, its ability to govern without domestic violence merely because that government was Communist."[33] Dulles changed his opinion on China to one more acceptable to conservatives after the outbreak of the Korean War, but Luce could be expected to remember Dulles' previous position.

The secretary had reason to fear obstruction by the Republican right, but his public relations problem ran deeper. The people who elected Eisenhower in 1952 had been promised—so they thought—a basic change in the direction of American foreign policy. Dulles knew that no such change impended; consequently he feared a backlash by a disappointed electorate.

Dulles sought to avert this reaction by a campaign of distraction. He understood that the Eisenhower administration could not *act* much more forcefully than its predecessor; the facts of nuclear life dictated caution. But the administration could, and through Dulles it would, *speak* more forcefully. Dulles would focus the attention of the public on what he said, rather than on what the administration did. By this means, the secretary hoped to divert attention from the fact that what the Eisenhower administration did differed little from what the Democrats had done.

Speaking often and in a manner likely to attract attention came naturally to Dulles. He considered public addresses a means of enforcing personal intellectual discipline. In 1948, Dulles wrote his son, "I have always found for myself that the principal advantage of undertaking to speak is that it forces me to think things out for myself."[34] Speeches and statements also served to keep the secretary in the public eye. By the frequency of his press conferences alone, Dulles would have been a constant source of news and a center of attention.

But Dulles' specialty, and the heart of his policy of distraction, was the intentionally provocative statement. The liberation device of the 1952 campaign fell into this category; so also his comment in late 1953 that failure by France and Germany to approve the European Defense Community would impel the Eisenhower administration to an "agonizing reappraisal" of its strategic policy toward Europe.[35] The latter statement, of course, was designed for shock value on the continent, but it also had the aim of presenting the administration as tough-minded and willing to risk the displeasure of the allies for the sake of American interests. Of all of Dulles' remarks, however, none sparked such controversy, and thus served so well as camouflage for a cautious pragmatism, as those introducing and defending the strategy of "massive retaliation" and the related notion of "brinkmanship."

Dulles had broached the idea of massive retaliation in his 1952 campaign piece for *Life*. At that time, responding to widespread dissatisfaction over the course of the Korean War, Dulles sought to demonstrate how a Republican administration would avoid getting itself into such a hopelessly stalemated situation. The key, he argued, was to convince the communists that aggression would bring down atomic destruction, not only on the area attacked, but on the directing headquarters—meaning Moscow and Beijing. Dulles advocated the creation of a "punishing force known to be ready and resolute to retaliate, in the event of any armed aggression, with weapons of its choosing against targets of its choosing at times of its choosing."[36]

In 1952, the point of such language had been to offer a dramatic alternative to the "treadmill policies" of the Democrats. In 1954, the same language still commanded headlines, but it also provided a convenient rationale for an important shift in America's defense posture. For reasons primarily of economics, the Eisenhower administration decided during 1953 to place greater reliance on nuclear forces; in October of that year, the president approved a policy paper authorizing his war planners to assume that the United States would use nuclear weapons even in limited-war situations. The result was the so-called New Look in American strategy.[37]

In January 1954, Dulles went before the Council on Foreign Relations to explain the administration's policy. Dulles spoke of the desire to achieve "a maximum deterrent at a bearable cost," and he stressed the need for "a selection of military means instead of a multiplication of means." The most noticed part of his address, however, dealt with the way military economies related to strategy. In a slap at containment, he said, "If an enemy could pick his time and place and method of warfare—and if our policy was to remain the traditional one of meeting aggression by direct and local opposition—then we needed to be ready to fight in the arctic and in the tropics; in Asia, in the Near East and in Europe; by sea, by land and by air; with old weapons and with new weapons." On the other hand, the innovative approach of the Eisenhower administration relied on "massive retaliatory power" and followed from a "basic decision . . . to depend primarily upon a great capacity to retaliate, instantly, by means and at places of our choosing."[38]

Thus Dulles launched the doctrine of "massive retaliation"—a phrase that fit news heads better than the secretary's wording. Immediately the concept met resistance as forcing the United States into an atomic corner, for it seemed to imply that the administration would risk the incineration of tens of millions, Americans included, to prevent peripheral aggression similar to that which had occurred in Korea or was gaining momentum in Indochina.[39] Two years later, despite intervening events to the contrary—the Viet Minh victory, for instance—Dulles claimed that this implication was essentially correct.

In January 1956, Dulles prepared another article for *Life*, though this time his authorship extended only to what he told the magazine's interviewer. Like the 1952 piece, this was a campaign statement; not coincidentally, Eisenhower would soon announce his candidacy for a second term. Dulles defended the foreign policy accomplishments of the administration, and in doing so he claimed that they had been possible only through the willingness of the president and the secretary of state to take risks—in Korea, in Indochina, and in the Formosa Strait. "You have to take chances for peace," he said, "just as you must take chances in war." Dulles went on to describe, in matter-of-fact tone, how closely the United States had come to war. "Some say we were brought to the verge of war. Of course we were brought to the verge of war." He pointed out how the coolness and resolve of the administration had averted disaster and preserved American interests. "The ability to get to the verge without getting into war is the necessary art. If you cannot master it, you inevitably get into war. If you run away from it, if you are scared to go to the brink, you are lost." Lest any doubt linger regarding the courage and ability of the administration, Dulles concluded, "We walked to the brink and looked it in the face. We took strong action."[40]

As an attention-getter, Dulles' statement on what quickly became known as "brinkmanship" surpassed anything he had said to date. Cries of indignation and outrage arose that the fate of the country and the world lay in the hands of a person who seemed to enjoy rolling nuclear dice. Critics declared that even if what Dulles described had indeed happened—many questioned this—he was a fool to announce the fact. Certainly America's allies would not rest easily knowing that they were chained to a government willing to risk the destruction of the West for something as inconsequential as two small island groups off the China coast. Columnist James Reston, no Dulles admirer in the best of circumstances, remarked that the secretary had introduced a new technique into "the art of diplomatic blundering . . . the planned mistake." Dulles, Reston said, "doesn't stumble into booby traps; he digs them to size, studies them carefully, and then jumps."[41]

Reston hit the mark in saying that Dulles' comments were planned, but he missed the point in declaring them a mistake. Brinkmanship was not a mistake at all—not from the secretary's perspective. It represented simply another part of Dulles' continuing effort to surround administration diplomacy with an aura of dynamism and boldness. By this measure, massive retaliation succeeded admirably. Each editorial decrying the manner in which Dulles drew the United States close to nuclear war granted, implicitly or explicitly, the secretary's basic contention—that the administration "took strong action" to protect American interests. With the 1956 election approaching, Dulles asked little more.

Less spectacular than Dulles' remarks on nuclear war, but notorious in their own right, were some comments the secretary made in the spring of 1956 on the nonalignment of third world nations. Dulles and other members of the administration worried that many of the newly independent countries of Asia and Africa were choosing to distance themselves from both the Soviet Union and the United States. This policy struck a blow at the American system of alliances by undermining the principle of collective security against communist aggression, and Eisenhower and Dulles sought to discourage its spread. Accordingly, Dulles, in a 1956 address at Ames, Iowa, denounced neutrality as "an increasingly obsolete conception." He added that it was almost always "immoral and short-sighted."[42]

Dulles believed unquestioningly in the rectitude of the United States in its struggle with communism. "Moral law . . . ," he declared, "decides our foreign policy."[43] Yet, even granted this conviction, he seemed to go out of his way to cast American actions, and those of other nations, in moralistic terms that struck many observers as excessive. Branding nonalignment as "immoral" was a case in point. To Dulles' critics, gratuitous attacks on the motives of important third world countries like India which were already predisposed to question America's sincerity seemed wrongheaded in the extreme.

Again the critics were right, in one sense, in claiming that the secretary's statements made the task of American diplomacy more difficult. Dulles' public self-righteousness won few friends for the United States. But again the critics missed the real message. Dulles had seen too much of the world to think that claims of morality or charges of immorality influenced power politics. Dulles' ethical posturing was intended for a domestic audience, to convince potential obstructionists on the American right that the administration remained staunch in opposing communism and anything related to it. Nonalignment, of course, was not communism, but many in America, including Dulles at times, believed that the one frequently led to the other. By attacking nonalignment, Dulles gave a new twist to the old redbaiting theme. In doing so, he maintained an image of unyielding opposition to America's foes, and he again drew attention away from the essential pragmatism that lay at the heart of administration policy.

Dulles had reason to be pleased with his public relations work. Popular approval of the administration's handling of foreign affairs ran consistently high, as Dulles noted in close scrutiny of opinion polls. In early 1957, for instance, the secretary sent Eisenhower some charts he had drawn up, demonstrating that satisfaction with foreign policy was twice as high for Eisenhower-Dulles as it had been for Truman-Acheson. "You might get some amusement out of the enclosed," Dulles commented to the president.[44]

Behind the smoke screen of his provocative rhetoric, Dulles approached the problems of American diplomacy in a careful fashion. The distinction between the public Dulles and the private Dulles was evident not only to those who worked with him in the State Department, as noted above, but also to diplomats from abroad. Charles Malik, the Lebanese foreign minister, described the manner in which the secretary's style masked the substance of his diplomatic skills:

In the case of Mr. Dulles, he spoke rather categorically, stiffly—in terms of black or white, in terms of good or evil, in terms of God and Satan, and all that sort of thing. That's quite true. But few men, I tell you, had as much flexibility, as much power of nuance, of making nuances, as Mr. Dulles did.[45]

For Dulles, flexibility and the "power of nuance" held the key to diplomatic success. He did not believe that caution and compromise involved the abandonment of principle to expedience, although observers might have gathered as much from his public statements. Indeed, Dulles the diplomat, as opposed to Dulles the politician, would have considered the contraposition of principle and expedience a misleading dichotomy. In the firmness of his belief that the principles represented by the "free world" were superior to those of the communist bloc, he yielded to no one; this conviction made his denunciations of the communists so persuasive. But whatever the domestic value of uncompromising rhetoric, strong talk was not diplomacy; it could only create the political preconditions for diplomacy. Diplomacy itself—the effort to put American principles into practice—called for compromise, for a sense that the desirable was not always the possible and that, in a world of contending and powerful interests, progress toward American goals would necessarily come only in small steps. If Dulles were ever tempted to try, at one blow, to force reality to conform to his desires, he only had to remember the tragic fate and, more to the point, the failure of Woodrow Wilson to regain his caution.

Dulles' pragmatism governed his actions from the moment he took office. In March 1953, Stalin's death prompted some in the Eisenhower administration to think that the time had come to act on the liberation theme of the 1952 campaign. Dulles, however, counseled circumspection, and the administration confined itself to an address by Eisenhower advocating peace. Later in the year, riots in East Germany again brought calls for putting liberation into practice. Again Dulles, recognizing the inability of the United States to take meaningful action against the Soviets in Eastern Europe without incurring the danger of general war, stood firmly against anything beyond moral support.[46]

The autumn of 1956 brought the *coup de grâce* to liberation. As Soviet armor crushed the rebellion in Hungary, the United States offered the insurgents only words. Liberation had fallen on hard times after the administration's initial manifestations of indifference, but in case anyone still harbored hopes that liberation was a serious policy, the Hungarian affair sank them. With Hungary's suppression, it became perfectly obvious that the administration was not about to risk war with the Russians for marginal interests like the independence of Eastern Europe.

Long before the Hungarian revolt, Dulles had dropped liberation as a public relations device in favor of massive retaliation. Here again, Dulles's closet realism belied the hype of his public utterances. In the interview that gave birth to the term "brinkmanship," the secretary of state claimed three specific victories for the massive retaliation approach: in the Korean truce talks in 1953, at the siege of Dien Bien Phu in 1954, in the Formosa Strait in 1955. Each time, he declared, fear of atomic punishment had deterred the Chinese from aggression.

In a narrow sense, Dulles correctly interpreted these events. Each instance involved a warning from the United States that provocative actions by the communists might lead to American intervention or escalation, including, perhaps, the use of nuclear weapons. In each instance, the warning had been followed by a favorable response, or what the administration chose publicly to interpret as a favorable response. In Korea in 1953, the Chinese had resumed negotiations on the crucial issue of prisoner repatriation. In Indochina in 1954, Beijing had refrained from openly joining the Viet Minh attack against the French. In the Formosa Strait in 1955, the communists had decided against an invasion of Quemoy and Matsu.

No doubt the threat of atomic attack influenced Chinese leaders' decisions to refrain from the actions against which they were warned. But the facts hardly justify Dulles' assertion that these three cases demonstrated the efficacy of massive retaliation. In Korea, the death of Stalin and uncertainty over future support from Moscow probably influenced the Chinese as much as threats from Washington.[47] Regarding the Quemoy-Matsu affair, such victory as the administration achieved mattered more in neutralizing the China lobby in the United States than in preserving the strategic balance in East Asia. As for Indochina, the crisis there demonstrated a lesson precisely opposite the one Dulles claimed for it. If Dien Bien Phu proved anything at all, it proved the hollowness of the all-or-nothing approach. Perhaps the administration had succeeded in keeping the Chinese out of the battle for northern Vietnam, but the communists won anyway. Had massive retaliation been a policy of conviction rather than a pseudopolicy of diplomatic and economic convenience, it should have brought down an American attack on the Chinese or the Russians, whom the administration considered responsible for Viet Minh aggression. But Dulles never considered such action.

In the early spring of 1954, as the predicament of the French in Indochina worsened, members of the Eisenhower administration pondered how to prevent a communist victory. Some of the president's advisers favored military intervention; foremost of these was Arthur Radford, the chairman of the Joint Chiefs of Staff, who supported an air strike, code-named Operation Vulture, against the communist forces investing Dien Bien Phu.[48] Dulles opposed such an aggressive response, believing the hazards outweighed the likely benefits. In a memorandum to Eisenhower written on March 23, 1954, Dulles pointed out the dangers of committing America to overt military support of the French.

If the United States sent its flag and its own military establishment—land, sea, or air—into the Indochina war, then the prestige of the United States would be engaged to a point where we would want to have a success. We could not afford thus to engage the prestige of the United States and suffer a defeat which would have worldwide repercussions.[49]

Dulles worried that the American people, so soon after Korea, would not support the commitment necessary to achieve the required success. A meeting with congressional leaders as April began reinforced his concern. In a note recording the session, Dulles described the "unanimous" feeling of the senators and representatives that they wanted "no more Koreas with the United States furnishing 90% of the manpower." When Dulles told the group that the administration did not intend to introduce American ground troops, the lawmakers responded that "once the flag was committed the use of land forces would inevitably follow."[50]

Dulles had no desire to challenge Congress; on the contrary, he consistently sought to keep the legislators happy. In the secretary's opinion, congressional reluctance regarding Indochina killed the possibility of unilateral American action, and it closely circumscribed action of any other sort as well.[51] On April 6, he told the National Security Council that it would be "impossible" to get Congress to go along with a solely American rescue mission. On the basis of his discussions with influential lawmakers,

Dulles predicted that Congress would insist on three conditions for American involvement in Indochina: the active cooperation of other Southeast Asian nations and the British Commonwealth, the acceleration of France's schedule for independence for the Associated States of Indochina, and agreement by the French not to pull out and leave the United States to fight alone. Military considerations aside, these political conditions constituted "a plain fact which the Council could not overlook." Absent their fulfillment, the administration would find the effort to persuade Congress a "hopeless fight."[52]

Some of Eisenhower's other advisers did not share Dulles' deference to Congress. Vice President Richard Nixon thought Eisenhower had more influence with the legislature and the American people than Dulles gave him credit for; Nixon told the president that he ought not to underestimate his powers of leadership. According to Nixon, "Congress would do what the National Security Council felt was necessary."[53]

Dulles preferred not to test the vice president's prediction. Eisenhower agreed with Dulles, and the conditions the secretary said Congress would require became the conditions the president accepted as prerequisite to intervention. When the British and the French failed to respond favorably in time to do any military good, these requirements kept American forces on the sidelines while the Viet Minh seized control of northern Vietnam.

Dulles' reaction, and that of Eisenhower, to events in Indochina in 1954 demonstrated the emptiness of massive retaliation. Neither the secretary nor the president doubted that Beijing and ultimately Moscow were behind the communist insurgency against the French. If Dulles had been serious about massive retaliation, the administration ought to have warned the Chinese and the Russians to call off their Vietnamese allies or face nuclear destruction. But neither Eisenhower nor Dulles ever contemplated anything so drastic.

Critics of massive retaliation rightly argued that the fundamental premises of such a policy were specious. After the Soviet Union had broken the American nuclear monopoly, Moscow could counter in kind an American threat of an atomic strike. Besides, the Kremlin's post-Stalin actions indicated that the Russians were shifting their energies from military confrontation to political and economic competition. In light of this transformation in the nature of the cold war, the United States would not likely face the type of clear-cut challenge that alone supplied credibility to massive retaliation. Eisenhower himself pointed out this weakness to Dulles as early as 1952, following his preview of Dulles' article for *Life*. "What should we do," Eisenhower wrote, "if Soviet *political* aggression . . . successively chips away exposed portions of the free world?" If this occurred, he said, the result "would be just as bad for us as if the area had been captured by force." Eisenhower concluded, "To my mind, this is where the theory of 'retaliation' breaks down."[54]

Eisenhower's objection to massive retaliation was unanswerable, and by itself it would have sufficed to discredit the theory, had the major purpose of massive retaliation been strategic. Even more damaging ought to have been the failure of the administration to take strong action in Indochina against what was undeniably a direct military assault by communists. But the concept survived, for the reason that it was and always had been primarily a matter of politics and public relations.

Dulles' failure to support liberation in Eastern Europe and his refusal to apply the theory of massive retaliation to Indochina paralleled a similar discrepancy between pronouncement and practice in his prescriptions for the third world. Regarding nonalignment, for example, the secretary's private correspondence reveals a latitudinarianism at odds with his widely publicized opinion that the idea was immoral. Dulles recognized that in Asia and Africa the outcome of the cold war would turn, not on ideology, but on the relative abilities of West and East to provide the material necessities of life. He described his views to C. D. Jackson:

I have become personally convinced that it is going to be very difficult to stop Communism in much of the world if we cannot in some way duplicate the intensive Communist effort to raise productivity standards. They themselves are increasing their own productivity at the rate of about 6% per annum, which is about twice our rate. In many areas of the world such as Southeast Asia, India, Pakistan and South America, there is little, if any, increase. That is one reason why Communism has such great appeal in areas where the slogans of 'liberty,' 'freedom' and 'personal dignity' have little appeal.

To counter communism's attractions, Dulles believed, the United States would have to increase its foreign aid program. Characteristically, however, he declined to challenge congressional reluctance to increase economic assistance, telling Jackson that such a move was "not practical."[55]

Dulles' comments on foreign aid indicate a realistic sense of the forces at work in the developing world. On another topic—third world nationalism—Dulles displayed equal pragmatism. During Eisenhower's first term, the secretary noted the growing strength of nationalism, especially in Africa, and he realized that it offered an opening to communists who would encourage the nationalists to dump the United States on the same ash heap of history as they had the colonial powers. The colonial issue, of course, had made the Indochina affair especially difficult for the administration; not surprisingly, in the aftermath of Dien Bien Phu Dulles began to consider how to avoid another such predicament. At a meeting with Eisenhower in June 1954, the secretary asserted that nationalism would sweep through Africa in ten to fifteen years, with the result that most of the continent might well be lost to the West. Despite the fact that it would certainly antagonize the British and French, and without specifying details, Dulles argued that the only solution in the long run lay in America's taking the side of the nationalists.[56]

Had he lived to write them, Dulles' memoirs would have made interesting reading—especially his thoughts on the relationship between his persona and his policies, and his judgment regarding the effectiveness of his management of the politics of diplomacy.

At one level, he would certainly have been pleased at his ability to maintain good relations with Republicans in Congress. Through his solicitude for the sensitivities of the right wing, he avoided alienating those who might have paralyzed him diplomatically as they had paralyzed Dean Acheson. Through his respect for congressional opposition to activities like unilateral intervention in Indochina, and by his cultivation of Congress generally, Dulles gained the support of moderate members as well. Senator H. Alexander Smith of the Foreign Relations Committee later commented on the beneficial effect of Dulles' numerous personal appearances before the committee. Smith appreciated the fact that Dulles took upon himself the task of informing the committee about administration policy. Unlike Acheson, said Smith, "he didn't delegate it."[57] Alexander Wiley, another member of the Foreign Relations Committee, kept a count of the number of times Dulles appeared before the committee. Wiley described Dulles' forty-eight appearances as "very helpful" to the committee, and he contrasted Dulles' attitude to that of Acheson. The latter, said Wiley, "came when he was called." Dulles, on the other hand, "was always the one who recognized that through understanding much can be accomplished—and through a friendly approach."[58]

At the broader level of relations with the American public, Dulles was hardly known for his "friendly approach." On the contrary, he possessed a reputation as a grim, unyielding, moralistic ideologue. He was an ideologue, certainly, but his forbidding demeanor was by design. If he caught criticism for being too much of a hard-liner, all the better; such criticism was not the kind that would cause him trouble. Attacks from the other direction were the ones he feared. Charges of softening his opposition to communism and of compromising with the enemies of the United States would be dangerous because they would hit closer to the truth than allegations of excessive rigidity. They might reveal him for what he was: a realist who recognized that America could not impose its will on the world, but must pursue its purposes a little at a time. Such a revelation might be politically damaging, perhaps fatal, for the American people had not in recent years demonstrated their ability to accept such an unpalatable truth.

At the level of policy, as distinct from public relations, Dulles' assessment of his term as secretary of state would have been complicated by the fact that he never acted autonomously in important matters. Despite the contemporary view that Eisenhower had turned control of foreign policy over to Dulles, the secretary never would have claimed that he decided policy himself. He influenced policy; he managed policy; but the president decided policy. Dulles never forgot that he was hired help. At times, though, it served Eisenhower's purpose to let Dulles appear to be directing foreign policy; on controversial or unpleasant issues, the president preferred to keep his own popularity untarnished. Indeed, Eisenhower conspired, if only by acquiescence, in Dulles' whole approach to public relations. With the secretary playing the role of brinkman, Eisenhower could don the mantle of peace-minded statesman.

Knowing that his influence flowed from the president, Dulles worked hard at matching Eisenhower's pace, step for step. Robert Murphy described Dulles as "assiduous in his efforts to adapt himself to Eisenhower's personality and methods of work."[59] Andrew Goodpaster, one of Eisenhower's closest aides, later recalled of Dulles that there "was never any hesitation on his part in following the direction that he received from the

President." Goodpaster added further, "When we got into an issue which was really of profound significance to the security interests of the United States, he would quite regularly say to Eisenhower, 'Mr. President, you've got to tell me what to do.' "[60]

More important than Dulles' care in following the president's lead was the fundamental compatibility of views of the two men. Both believed firmly in America's moral ascendancy over the Russians, but neither held any illusions that moral superiority would soon lead to a major shift in the global balance of power. The cold war would not yield to genuine peace in the foreseeable future; in the meantime, necessity dictated a cautious, incremental approach in dealing with the communists.

2

Milton Eisenhower and the Coming Revolution in Latin America

Closer to the president than John Foster Dulles—closer indeed than any-one else—was Eisenhower's brother, Milton. A veteran of a quarter-century of Washington politics before Ike entered the White House, Milton contributed to the Eisenhower administration an experience of the federal bureaucracy unmatched among the president's close advisers. More important, Milton brought to his many and detailed conversations with the president a sympathetic ear and a critical intelligence. With no one else could Ike be so free in testing out new ideas; from no one else could he expect such candid and disinterested opinions.

The president leaned heavily on Milton's counsel on topics ranging from executive organization and management to public relations and party lead-ership. On no subject, though, did Ike consult Milton's opinion more closely than on United States relations with Latin America. Milton served as the president's personal representative to Latin America, traveling ex-tensively throughout the region and reporting back his impressions regard-ing the present condition and future prospects of Central and South Amer-ica. Milton described an area vexed by economic, social, and political problems. Through eight years, he became increasingly convinced that Latin America was on the verge of dramatic and far-reaching changes, and he grew ever more certain that the administration must act quickly and forcefully to ensure that these changes were for the better, both for Latin America and for the United States.

Milton came to his role as Latin American adviser with solid credentials. Following World War I, which he missed only because a high-school teacher dissuaded him from lying to an army recruiter about his age, he had gained appointment to a Foreign Service post in Scotland. Edinburgh was not especially exotic, but to a young man from Abilene, Kansas, it provided a window to a whole new world. A call from Washington, however, cut short the budding diplomat's career: one of Milton's college professors had been named secretary of agriculture by Calvin Coolidge, and he needed an able assistant.[1]

Milton filled the position with a flair, soon acquiring a reputation as an accomplished and well-connected civil servant. He weathered the shift from Republicans to Democrats after the 1932 election, and by the mid-1930s, he acted as the number-two man at the Agriculture Department. He became a presidential adviser—a role he would fill for forty years—when his new boss at Agriculture, Henry Wallace, discovered Milton's skill at penetrating the cloud of jokes and anecdotes that Franklin Roosevelt often threw up to put off visitors with unwelcome news.

As an informal liaison between the Agriculture Department and the White House, Milton observed how corridor politics could frustrate the best-designed plans for administrative reform. In a preview of the type of resistance he would later meet trying to modify the policy of the Eisenhower administration toward Latin America, Milton watched with dismay as entrenched interests opposed and quietly smothered a program for streamlining Agriculture that he had developed with Roosevelt's support.

Milton impressed Roosevelt, though, and on the eve of Pearl Harbor the president asked him to set up the Overseas Information Agency. In December 1941, FDR shifted Milton to the thankless but seemingly necessary task of directing the removal of Japanese-Americans from the West Coast. Milton had decidedly mixed emotions about his three-month stint at the War Relocation Authority,[2] but before his doubts had time to sink in, he was transferred again, this time to the Office of War Information.

While with OWI, Milton first professionally encountered his increasingly prominent elder brother. Late in 1942, Roosevelt enlisted Milton's services to defumigate the malodorous Darlan deal. Despite the savings of Allied lives that the arrangement with Darlan made possible, General Eisenhower was excoriated on both sides of the Atlantic for tainting Allied purposes by cooperating with the Nazi-collaborating admiral. For a moment, it looked as though Eisenhower's bright career as commander of Allied forces might end before it had fairly begun. Although FDR publicly stated his approval of Eisenhower's action, Milton thought he ought to go further. He urged Roosevelt to send someone recognized as close to the president to North Africa to demonstrate official support for General Eisenhower. Milton suggested Harry Hopkins, but the president tapped Milton instead.

Milton's goals in North Africa, like those he would pursue more than a decade later in Latin America, combined service to country with fraternal loyalty. Officially, his task was to stamp the Darlan deal with the White House seal of approval. This he accomplished merely by his presence and his known connections to Roosevelt. Less officially, he sought to shield Ike from further criticism. Outraged at charges in the media that his brother was a "fascist" for his continued toleration of Darlan and other former Vichy officials, Milton determined to lessen Ike's exposure to such attacks. Upon his arrival in Algiers, he called on Robert Murphy, then General Eisenhower's military attache, and demanded immediate and drastic measures to remove some of the more obnoxious of the French leaders. "Heads must roll, Murphy!" Milton declared. "Heads must roll!"

Milton soon discovered that getting rid of French officials with checkered backgrounds was not as easy as he thought. However, he did manage to accomplish part of the task. One aspect of the problem confronting the Allies in North Africa involved a continuing flow of misinformation regarding Allied aims from territory under Darlan's control. Once Milton had located the source of many of the erroneous reports in a particular radio station in Morocco, he consulted Ike on the best method of handling the matter. Ike decided that Milton ought to go talk to Darlan; he telephoned the French admiral and arranged an interview. In this first opportunity to test his diplomatic aptitude under pressure, Milton succeeded thoroughly. He explained to Darlan the difficulties Radio Moroc created for the United States, and he requested that the offending personnel be fired. Darlan consented, and by the next day, Milton began staffing the station with OWI people.[3]

The situation at Radio Moroc did not become entirely satisfactory until a full-time psychological warrior, C. D. Jackson, took charge in early 1943. By then, however, Milton had returned to Washington, where his attention was drawn in another direction—one that would attract him increasingly for the next two decades. In April 1943, Henry Wallace, then vice president, made a tour of Latin America to promote hemispheric solidarity. Milton followed Wallace's travels closely, corresponding with his old chief and writing of the "unusual interest" with which he studied Wallace's activities in Central and South America.[4] For the moment, however, and indeed for the next several years, Milton's interest in Latin America remained avocational. Shortly after he wrote this letter to Wallace, Milton decided to leave government service and accept an offer of the presidency at his alma mater, Kansas State College.[5]

Milton did not forsake government for long; in late 1945 he began serving in a part-time capacity in various positions in the Truman administration. The post he found most interesting was the chairmanship of the American commission of the United Nations Educational, Scientific and Cultural Organization. In conjunction with UNESCO work, Milton spent six weeks in Mexico in 1946.[6] This visit further sparked his interest in Latin America, and during the late 1940s and early 1950s he read, as he later said, "essentially every book and article that had been written" on the region.[7]

When Dwight Eisenhower entered the White House, Milton became, as Ike noted in his diary, his "most intimate general adviser."[8] For eight years the White House often served as Milton's weekend home, a circumstance facilitated by certain changes in his personal affairs. In 1950 he had left Kansas State for a new job in the East, as president of Pennsylvania State College. Through most of his brother's first term, Milton made the four-hour commute from State College to Washington; in 1956 another career move, this time to Johns Hopkins in Baltimore, reduced his travel time. On a more somber note, the death of his wife in mid-1954 made Milton more available to the president than he otherwise would have been.

The relationship between the two brothers combined an affection made easy by the relatively wide gap in their ages with a mutual admiration enhanced by the success of the two men in their separate fields of endeavor. From the time when Milton wept to see his nine-year-older brother leave home in Abilene for West Point,[9] to the April day in 1952 when he felt "immense pride" on learning that Ike would probably be a candidate for president,[10] Milton's attitude mixed warm respect and hero worship. Ike displayed his feelings toward Milton in a diary entry in 1953:

I have no hesitancy in saying I believe him to be the most knowledgeable and widely informed of all the people with whom I deal. He is a great character and personality, a humanitarian, and a truly capable organizer and leader. So far as I am concerned, he is at this moment the most highly qualified man in the United States to be President. This most emphatically makes no exception of me.[11]

Dwight Eisenhower was not given to self-deprecation; such comments were high praise indeed. Foreign affairs, particularly, the president considered his forte, with good reason. He had seen a large part of the world; he personally knew many of the world's most powerful leaders; and for more than a decade of world war and cold war he had played a central role in shaping and executing American foreign policy.

Latin America, however, represented a comparative gap in Dwight Eisenhower's experience of the world. In the early 1920s, he had spent three years stationed in the Panama Canal Zone, but the greatest benefit he derived from that tour of duty was an increased knowledge of American and European military history and the advice to try for an assignment under George Marshall if the opportunity ever arose—both courtesy of his commanding officer, Fox Conner.[12] Occasional visits to Mexico, and a brief good-will trip to several Latin American countries after World War II, provided little more in the way of deep understanding of the region and its problems.[13] The simple fact was that Eisenhower, with most of his generation in the United States, had generally overlooked Latin America. The world crises of his adult life had taken place in Europe and Asia; Latin America, by comparison, seemed uninteresting and unimportant.

However, Eisenhower as president recognized that the Eurasian tilt of United States policy might cause problems; these he sought to avert. In one of his first major speeches on foreign affairs, Eisenhower told the Organization of American States in April 1953 that he was appointing his brother Milton to be his personal representative to Latin America. Milton would visit the region and report "on ways to strengthen the bonds of friendship" between the United States and its hemispheric neighbors to the south.[14]

Whether the president intended substantive changes in policy toward Latin America or merely wanted to improve appearances, Milton was a logical choice. For one thing, Milton knew more about the region than anyone else among Eisenhower's close advisers. For another, if policy changes did seem advisable, Milton's experience of administrative politics in Washington would help implement them. Furthermore, the president had witnessed in North Africa, if only briefly, Milton's skills as a diplomat, and he recognized that most of Milton's career success resulted from his ability at handling people. Finally, as the president's brother, Milton would enjoy a stature unavailable to regular State Department officials, especially in countries where politics was often a family affair, and he would lend a prestige to U.S.-Latin American relations that had often been lacking in the past.

Regarding the administration's intentions, certainly it was not coincidence that six weeks before the president's announcement of Milton's trip, the Arbenz government of Guatemala had inaugurated a plan for expropriating a quarter-million acres from the American-based United Fruit Company, with compensation that the company and the Eisenhower administration considered grossly inadequate. Administration officials debated whether Arbenz was a communist; the eventual consensus held that if not, he would "certainly do until one came along."[15] Over the course of the next year, the administration grew convinced that the cold war was infiltrating the Western Hemisphere through Guatemala. In response to this perceived threat, the administration devised a two-pronged counteroffensive. One prong, managed by the CIA, resulted in the overthrow of Arbenz and the installation of a more manageable replacement.[16] The other prong comprised the work of Milton Eisenhower, of which the first manifestation was his 1953 tour of Latin America.

From beginning to end, the administration promoted Milton's trip as assiduously as it covered up the activities of the CIA. Whether Ike and Dulles scheduled the "fact-finding" tour by the president's brother partly to draw attention away from American efforts to destabilize Arbenz is difficult to determine. This might have been a side effect, but diversion was not the tour's primary purpose. However effective CIA action in Guatemala might be, such covert operations were merely stopgap measures. Milton's assignment was to make recommendations for a long-term policy that would render such intervention unnecessary.

Five days after the president's speech, Milton described strong support throughout the United States for his upcoming trip. "In all parts of the country," he wrote, "it was top-head news. Editorials from the newspapers in conservative Kansas have been as favorable as those from California and New York." Milton added that the "tremendous importance" a great many people were placing on his trip made it imperative that he do his job well. He requested assistance from the State Department, in the form of "a couple of its best analysts and writers," so that on his return he might be able to give the president "a report of some significance."[17]

The president provided more support than his brother requested, and when Milton left Washington on June 23, 1953, his entourage included John Cabot, the assistant secretary of state for inter-American affairs; Tapley Bennett, the deputy director of the office of South American affairs; and assistant secretaries from the Treasury and Commerce departments. In order to give Milton sufficient time to get some work done between the ceremonial duties incumbent on a president's brother, Milton and Ike decided to limit the trip to South America. Even then, the journey lasted five weeks before the group returned to Washington at the end of July.

While Milton found the entire tour intensely interesting, two countries—Bolivia and Argentina—especially drew his attention. A steep slide in the world price of tin, Bolivia's major export, had hit that country hard. In late 1952, the Bolivian government had nationalized the properties of the country's three largest tin producers, an action that aroused suspicion in the new Republican administration and, as events proved, did little to relieve Bolivia's economic distress. The State Department expressed concern that Bolivia might be following Guatemala's example; John Foster Dulles warned of "the danger that Bolivia would become a focus of Communist infection in South America."[18]

Milton Eisenhower acknowledged the seriousness of Bolivia's problems, and upon his departure from that country he reported to the president, "Conditions in Bolivia are unbelievably bad, thus creating a situation of grave concern to the entire hemisphere."[19] But he took pains to register his belief that the threat to Bolivia was primarily economic, not political, and that communism posed little imminent danger. Ten days after his first report, Milton elaborated:

The situation in Bolivia is exceedingly bad. All of us are convinced that the present government, while restless in tendency, is by no means communistic. Should the present government fall, it seems probable that it will not be succeeded by a communist government. . . . Rather, a period of chaos would set in.[20]

The State Department received Milton's opinion regarding the noncommunism of the Paz regime with doubt; the CIA was more skeptical still. Following his return to the United States, Milton corresponded with Allen Dulles on the nature of Bolivia's problems. Milton repeated his contention that the Bolivian government was not communist; to this, Dulles replied, "I am frank to say that there are different points of view regarding the leadership [of Bolivia]."[21]

If opinions in the administration varied regarding Bolivia, Argentina was even more puzzling. President Juan Peron's peculiar mixture of fascism and Marxism lent itself to assorted interpretations. On one hand, Peron's advocacy of a "third position" between the United States and the Soviet Union seemed an attack on hemispheric unity, and his violent denunciations of the United States appeared to be, in Foster Dulles' words, "straight Commie line."[22] On the other hand, Peron gave intermittent indications of interest in rapprochement with Washington, and he claimed to have the Communist party in Argentina firmly under control. To bolster this claim, Peron went so far as to offer to the American ambassador in Buenos Aires police dossiers on Argentine Communist leaders.[23]

At the time of Milton's departure from the United States, Dwight Eisenhower and Foster Dulles still had not decided whether Milton ought to visit Argentina. To do so would be to invite criticism for consorting with dictators, of which Peron was commonly considered a prime example; to fail to do so risked missing an opportunity for an improvement in Argentine-American relations. Dulles chose to accept the argument that the most vitriolic of the attacks on the United States had been the work of "the extreme nationalists and crypto-Communists in Peron's entourage," rather than of Peron himself, and he suggested to the president that Milton include Argentina in his itinerary. Eisenhower approved the suggestion.[24]

Peron rolled out the red carpet, literally, along with military bands and honor guards, for Milton's visit. "To say that I was amazed at the reception Peron staged," Milton later wrote, "is a gross understatement." So friendly was the Argentine president that the American ambassador, Albert Nufer, concluded, in a remark to Milton, "Peron has decided that his third force is a failure. He's been looking for an excuse to reverse his policy and is seizing upon your visit as that excuse." During the two days of Milton's visit, Peron certainly did seem intent on working for better relations with the United States; as a gesture of friendship he relaxed restrictions on American correspondents and news agencies in Argentina.[25]

Milton, however, questioned the sincerity of Peron's conversion. Milton had a general suspicion of dictators and, more to the point, a hesitancy about allowing them to get close to the Eisenhower administration. Peron, especially, seemed to promise trouble for the United States because of his individual volatility. On Milton's return to the United States, he told his brother, "We should not deceive ourselves as to the nature of the Government with which we are dealing or as to Peron's personalist and emotional type of leadership. He could turn against us as dramatically as he has turned toward us." Milton advocated a steady policy, neither friendly nor hostile. The administration, he said, must continue to discourage Peron's third-force proclivities, latent though they might be at the moment. "Our primary aim in Argentina should be to counter the Argentine tendency toward neutralism on the great East-West issues, and to align Argentina firmly on the side of the West."[26]

Generating good will for the United States and for the Eisenhower administration was one purpose of Milton's tour; a reliable evaluation of conditions and important leaders in South America was another. For three months after his return to Washington, Milton discussed with various knowledgeable persons what he had seen and heard on his trip, and at the end of October 1953 he submitted his official report and recommendations to the president.

Much of the report was predictable. Milton emphasized the economic and political interdependence of North and South America and the continuing need for understanding between the peoples of the two continents. He gave the expected nod to the "unique" record of the American nations in "settling disputes by peaceful means." At the philosophical level, he noted the shared Judeo-Christian background of Americans north and south. Regarding culture, he declared the diversity among peoples of the Western Hemisphere to be a source of strength rather than of division: "The predominantly Anglo-Saxon culture of the United States and the predominantly Latin cultures of the other American republics, the latter often blended with strong and proud Indian influences, are today cross-fertilizing each other, to their mutual enrichment."[27]

Despite the Good-Neighborly tone of much of Milton's report, the cold war informed its substance. Milton specifically reaffirmed and updated the Monroe Doctrine, giving that hoary principle a meaning that leaders of certain countries, notably Guatemala, could not miss:

If the arguments to justify it were strong in 1823, they are truly mighty in the shrunken world of today. The possible conquest of a Latin American nation today would not be, so far as anyone can foresee, by direct assault. It would come, rather, through the insidious process of infiltration, conspiracy, spreading of lies, and the undermining of free institutions, one by one. Highly disciplined groups of communists are busy, night and day, illegally or openly, in the American republics, as they are in every nation of the world. . . . One nation has succumbed to communist infiltration.[28]

Milton asserted that the communists of Latin America were making common cause with "ultra-nationalists," as he labeled individuals who carried their nationalism to the point of what he considered xenophobia. In contrast to a "praiseworthy" nationalism, "ultra-nationalism" was "a major retrogressive influence" in a number of countries. Especially harmful to the people of Latin America, in Milton's opinion, were the claims of the "ultra-nationalists" that foreign investment constituted imperialism. Such allegations, he said, made it difficult for Latin American nations to attract the foreign capital that the region desperately needed.[29]

Milton's report contained further remarks along similar lines. In this respect it followed Republican anticommunist orthodoxy; Milton could easily have written it without leaving the United States. In his final few pages, however, he offered recommendations that diverged from the party line. Here the report became more interesting.

The most important of these recommendations stated that the Eisenhower administration ought to provide public funds "on a substantial scale" for economic development projects in Latin America.[30] Milton recognized that private capital would continue to play a leading role in the development of the hemisphere. While his report was still in preparation, he had written to Ike regarding the needs of Brazil specifically, but his comments applied generally. "Brazil desperately needs capital, and you and I know that the bulk of that capital—no matter how much the International and Ex-Im banks are prepared to do—must come from private sources."[31] Private capital, however, would not be forthcoming for many necessary projects that would yield returns to the United States in other than financial terms and whose payoff might not occur for decades. Brazil again was the example, but Milton might have been speaking about any of several Latin American nations. "It is vital that she be tied to us, in firm economic, cultural, political, and military cooperation. We must therefore take the long view. We must be prepared to run some risks. Investments which may not be profitable for the next five years can pay great dividends over a twenty-five year period."[32]

Milton's argument for public funding of development projects in Latin America directly contradicted the 1952 Republican campaign slogan, "Trade not aid." To the budget balancers at the Treasury Department, the notion of a "substantial" new assistance program, even when aid took the form of loans, as Milton recommended, rather than grants, seemed a repudiation of the purposes for which the Republicans had been elected. Milton knew that certain persons in the administration would not welcome this suggestion; perhaps this knowledge was what prompted him to bury his aid proposal halfway down a list of nine recommendations, of which no other was so controversial or expensive.[33]

Most of the controversy would come later; in October and November 1953, Milton's report elicited enthusiastic praise from the State Department and the president. Dulles arranged a propaganda blitz for the paper's release, ordering its publication in Spanish and Portuguese as well as English and its mass distribution throughout Latin America.[34] Ike declared in a congratulatory letter that he was "more than delighted" with the report, and he stated with uncharacteristic hyperbole that it "ought to be studied by every man, woman, and child in North and South America."[35]

A second letter to Milton reiterated the president's satisfaction; it also revealed the combination of affection and admiration Ike felt for his younger brother:

Had your South American trip been undertaken and the report on it written by anyone else, I should, of course, have gone to great pains to write a glowing letter of appreciation and thanks. In your case this does not seem appropriate, for several reasons. In the first place, I feel a bit diffident about complimenting anyone on a task where his competence in the particular field is so clearly superior to mine. In your knowledge of South America and your ability as a writer, I would not be bold enough to claim equality with you. In the second place, one of the purposes of a letter of commendation is to leave a record of the recipient's accomplishments in the public service. I doubt that your own record could possibly be embellished by a compliment from me. Finally, how does anyone go about the writing of a commendation for his own brother; that is, for a man who knows all the writer's failings, foibles, idiosyncracies, and even stupidities?[36]

Milton Eisenhower had been in the practice of government long enough to realize that enthusiasm in the White House and at the State Department did not necessarily mean that changes in policy would swiftly follow. Too many other people with potentially conflicting priorities had a hand in diplomacy for change to come quickly, and when the ranks of the opposition included individuals as formidable as George Humphrey, it remained an open question whether change would come at all.

Humphrey's reluctance to dip into the public purse for development loans was well known. Within months of the installation of the Eisenhower administration, Humphrey had managed to persuade Congress to place the Export-Import Bank, the source of most such American credit, almost entirely under his control at the Treasury Department. He then had proceeded to cut the bank's lending by four-fifths in one year.[37] Thus Milton was hardly surprised when Humphrey, the most fiscally conservative member of a conservative administration, registered something less than support for Milton's proposed aid program for Latin America.

Within weeks of the delivery of his report to the president, Milton began to detect the resistance of the treasury secretary to his loan plan. A meeting of the American republics was scheduled for March 1954, and Milton hoped that the administration would unveil a program demonstrating that the opinions he had solicited in South America the previous summer had had an effect in Washington. Indeed, he hoped that the president would announce such an aid program himself; Milton told Ike that it would be "tremendously fortunate" if he could take the time to fly to Caracas to address the conference.[38] But the aid plan moved distressingly slowly. Milton wrote to the president in mid-January expressing dismay that with the conference only six weeks away, the administration had not yet settled on an agenda. Part of the delay resulted unavoidably from concurrent concern in the State Department regarding the more imminent Berlin conference; much, however, of the procrastination seemed to originate in the Treasury. "I am strongly of the impression," stated Milton, "that Secretary Humphrey is prepared to stand out against certain actions which in my opinion must be taken . . . if we are to make real progress in our relations with several of the key Latin American countries."[39]

Normally, Milton could have counted on the backing of the secretary of state in arguing for a liberalized economic policy toward Latin America. As noted in the previous chapter, Dulles considered economic development essential in halting the advance of communism in the third world, and if this called for American aid, he supported it. In March 1954, however, as he prepared for the Caracas conference, Dulles worried more about lining up the American republics for action against Guatemala than about discussing economics. Dulles did not object, as he told the cabinet a few days before leaving for Venezuela, to giving the Latin Americans certain economic reassurances, but he intended to concentrate his efforts on persuading the conference to denounce communism as an international conspiracy.[40]

As a result of Humphrey's hostility and Dulles' distraction, Milton Eisenhower's hopes for an economic initiative at Caracas came to nothing. Dulles' anticommunist declaration required all the secretary's energy; the conference deferred consideration of economic matters until later in the year.[41]

But for the delay, Milton might have been cheered by the news that a conference devoted principally to economic and social issues had been scheduled for Rio de Janeiro for November 1954. As the Rio meeting approached, however, it became evident that most of the Latin American countries, taking Dulles at his word that there would be serious discussion of economic matters, were planning to be represented by their finance ministers. The Eisenhower administration felt compelled to follow the lead of the Latin Americans and send its finance minister, Humphrey. This turn of events disheartened Milton. To Dulles he described Humphrey's appointment as "tragic";[42] to the president, who was closer to Humphrey than was the secretary of state, Milton spoke in terms more measured but no less clear.

Milton believed that Humphrey would try to sabotage efforts to use a more generous loan policy to improve relations with Latin America, despite the fact that this policy represented a stated goal of the administration, hammered out through long meetings of the National Security Council. "I realize that I may be mistaken," Milton wrote to Ike, "but I am persuaded that George is not friendly to a cooperative effort toward Latin American development, and I do not believe he will be a good soldier and carry out orders in the spirit of an agreed-upon program." As an indication of Humphrey's attitude, Milton cited a speech that the treasury secretary had recently delivered to a group of business executives, in which he had declared his disapproval of a more generous lending policy. Milton thought that nothing good would come of the Rio conference with Humphrey representing the United States, and he said that he wished to withdraw his offer to attend the conference himself. "I would not want such little prestige as I have in Latin America to be identified with the ill consequences that I fear would flow from the general Humphrey attitude."[43]

Milton's complaints about Humphrey got some results. In his reply, Ike admitted the obsolescence of Humphrey's attitude, and he indicated that he would speak to the treasury secretary.[44] A short while later he did so, telling Humphrey just before the latter left for Rio what the administration expected of him. The president reminded Humphrey that the Latin American policy of the United States followed from a more general approach to the cold war; he pointed out that the United States was not merely "doing business" in Latin America, but was fighting a battle against communism. And he told Humphrey that he cared less for agreement at Rio on any single agenda item than for the creation of a "good climate of opinion."[45]

Milton could not help being pleased with the president's response, although he continued to worry that Humphrey's narrow fiscal calculus failed to allow sufficiently for the significance of amicable relations with Latin America. Milton admitted that Humphrey might be heading in the right direction, but the going seemed slow. "Basically," he told Ike, "George is an isolationist who is learning that isolationist policies won't work."[46]

By the end of 1954, efforts within the administration for a liberalized foreign aid program were moving forward—but not in the direction of Latin America. Awakened to the cold war significance of financial help to third world nations by the "economic offensive" of the Soviet Union in Asia and the Middle East, the Eisenhower administration began to realize that an excessive concern with budget tightening might result in the United States' being squeezed out of much of the nonaligned world. This conversion to a belief in the necessity for economic assistance largely resulted from the Russians' activities; not surprisingly the administration focused its attention regarding aid on Asia and the Middle East, where the immediate danger of Russian penetration seemed greatest.

Milton Eisenhower did not begrudge aid to potential trouble spots in the Eastern Hemisphere, but he worried that Latin America would be forgotten. As had so often been the case in the past, and seemed to be true again following the toppling of Arbenz in Guatemala in the summer of 1954, Latin America was being overlooked because it was not the center of crisis. At least that was the impression Latin Americans would get from an American aid plan for Asia, approved while Milton's recommendations for assistance to Western Hemisphere nations continued to languish. In communications with the president in the last two months of 1954, Milton argued that Latin America ought to be included in any aid program the administration presented to Congress. He pointed out the relative insignificance of the money involved; he argued, for example, that a $100 million package in the works for Pakistan alone would last Latin America five years.[47] In reacting to an aid proposal by Foreign Operations Administration chief Harold Stassen, Milton spelled out his concerns in greater detail:

What troubles me most now is the possible Latin American reaction to Harold Stassen's suggestion that we should have a new economic aid program for Asia. We could justify the omission of Latin America from the Marshall plan, for that aid was intended primarily to help rebuild productive resources destroyed by war. We could justify the omission of Latin America from most of the subsequent military-aid program, for it was designed primarily to help rearm nations directly threatened by communism (of course Latin America isn't immune from this). But if we now develop an economic program of fairly generous proportions for Asia, and offer Latin America primarily an alteration in Export-Import bank policy, I think we can be certain that our relations in this hemisphere will deteriorate.[48]

Dwight Eisenhower's reply to this letter confirmed Milton's misgivings about the direction of administration policy. The president conceded that the public unveiling of Stassen's plan could have been handled in a manner less likely to give offense in Latin America, but he held that there existed a basic difference between the necessity for economic assistance to Asia and similar needs in the Western Hemisphere:

We should not forget . . . that countries like Burma, Thailand, and the remaining parts of Indo-China are directly open to assault [by communism]. This does not apply in South America. . . . The difference between South America and Asia, in my own mind, is this. In the case of South America we want to establish a healthy relationship that will be characterized by mutual cooperation and which will permanently endure. This will apply whether or not the Communist menace seems to increase or decrease in intensity. In Asia we are primarily concerned with meeting a crisis, establishing firm and friendly governments, and making certain that the critical area of Indo-China and the surrounding islands and adjacent portions of the mainland do not fall into Communist hands. If the Communist menace should recede in the area, we would consider ourselves still friendly, but we would feel largely relieved of any obligation to help them economically or militarily.[49]

Milton Eisenhower could not disagree that the administration faced a crisis in Asia in 1954 and 1955, but he remained convinced—and his conviction deepened during the next few years—that the United States confronted a crisis of even greater proportions in Latin America.

Between 1954 and 1956, various events in Milton's and Ike's personal lives circumscribed Milton's activities relating to Latin America. The death of Milton's wife had a delayed but decided influence on his assessment of his position at Penn State; in 1956 he decided to move to Johns Hopkins, partly to gain a fresh start and partly to be closer to Washington.[50] The president's heart attack in 1955 required frequent shuttling to Denver while Ike convalesced there,[51] and it created inevitable concern until recovery was assured.

In the latter half of 1956, however, Milton resumed his activities as the president's special ambassador to Latin America. In September of that year he hosted a conference of top-level representatives from the American republics; in 1957 he visited Mexico. The following year he traveled throughout Central America and the Caribbean, completing the fact-finding tour of Latin America he had begun in 1953. Upon his return, he presented to the president an updated edition of his earlier report.

Milton's 1958 assessment of U.S.-Latin American relations differed from his 1953 estimate primarily in that the later version stressed that the time of reckoning drew near. "I reaffirm essentially all I said in my report of 1953," Milton wrote, "but now I must add a note of urgency."[52] Troubles that had threatened five years earlier crowded ever closer. "Latin America is a continental area in ferment."[53] Milton argued that while the economies of many Central and South American countries had improved in the previous half-decade, in part through United States assistance, "unprecedented" population growth jeopardized economic gains. Poverty, illiteracy, and disease remained the lot of the common people of the region. "But the people generally, including the most humble of them, now know that low standards of living are neither universal nor inevitable, and they are therefore impatiently insistent that remedial actions be taken."[54]

Milton found some of the remedies insisted upon by Latin Americans to be based on false conceptions of the United States and its role in the world economy. Many Latin Americans, he said, thought that the resources of the United States were virtually unlimited. "This leads them to conclude that their failure to obtain credit in the desired volume is either sheer perversity or discrimination on our part." Another notion he deemed mistaken was the idea that the United States conspired to fix prices on the world market for various commodities on which Latin American economies depended heavily. The worst of the erroneous beliefs he attributed to leftist propaganda. "Based on a distortion of facts, a false impression is now held by certain misinformed individuals and is also being cleverly fostered by communist agitators. Despite our adherence to a policy of nonintervention,[55] we are charged with supporting Latin American dictators in the face of a strong trend toward freedom and democratic government." Milton added, "It is ironic that this charge is insidiously spread by international conspirators who represent the most vicious dictatorship in modern history."[56]

Mistaken though he thought them to be, Milton admitted that many Latin American convictions about the United States had acquired a political momentum that transcended their invalidity. If only for this reason, the Eisenhower administration needed to take notice and take action. Milton did not think the United States manipulated prices of coffee, tin, and other Latin American exports, but Latin Americans did; the administration, then, ought to help Latin American exporters raise and stabilize prices, even to the extent of encouraging cartels among exporting nations. He did not believe that the United States supported dictators, but Latin Americans did; the administration, therefore, without ostracizing any countries, should adopt a policy of friendliness toward representative rulers and cool politeness toward autocrats: "an 'abrazo' for democratic leaders, and a formal handshake for dictators."[57]

Most important, he strongly recommended that the administration increase economic assistance, and in a conspicuous manner, to combat the impression that the rich Yankees cared little for Latin Americans. His argument for greater aid was part of the battle he had been fighting for five years; now new urgency demanded novel tactics. Where Milton before had advocated stepping up assistance through existing organizations, this time he favored the creation of something different: an Inter-American Development Bank, a high-profile organization to be headed by a Latin American, designed with the express purpose of making loans for Latin American projects that were not being funded by currently operating credit agencies.[58]

Though Milton did not mention it in this report, the major purpose behind his proposal for a lending institution nominally controlled by Latin Americans was to force Latin Americans to get their economies and societies in order. In his discussions with leaders from Central and South America at the Washington conference in 1956, and on his tour of Central America and the Caribbean in 1958, Milton had been struck by the dual nature of the crisis in Latin America. The stability of the hemisphere was challenged both by an aggregate economic deficiency, which depressed average living standards, and by social and political inequities in most Latin American countries, which channeled what little wealth did exist into the hands of a tiny fraction of the population. By the late 1950s, Milton had come to believe that the sociopolitical side of the problem posed just as great a threat as did the economic to the future of Latin America and the United States.

Milton described the double danger in a letter to Ike written shortly after Fidel Castro took power in Cuba in 1959:

Throughout Latin America there is a serious revolutionary spirit on the move. Its appeal is two-fold. First, there is rising resentment against established social orders which find a thin layer of prosperity and a vast sea of misery. The Castro Revolution is popular solely because it initially represented to these people a revolt against things as they are. . . . The second element has to do with the need for massive amounts of development capital.[59]

The United States could meet the requirement for development capital, Milton believed, without straining the American economy. The administration should provide funds, both "hard" loans, repayable only in dollars, and "soft" loans, repayable in local currencies and hence preferred by the borrowing countries. Milton suggested a figure of $150 million per year, an amount he considered a wise investment in terms of hemispheric stability. "Things are moving awfully fast. If extreme left-wing governments sprang up in a number of the [Latin American] nations, we would find ourselves with problems that would call for vast expenditures, whereas right now I believe the situation can be taken care of with hard and soft loans."[60]

The other contributor to communism's appeal in Latin America—hostility toward the prevailing social order—presented a more delicate problem. Milton recognized that the United States could not start preaching to the oligarchs of Latin America to mend their ways and spread their wealth. Such meddling would produce more resentment than reform, for in the absence of violent revolution, the avoidance of which was the raison d'être of Eisenhower administration policy, the oligarchs represented the instrument with which the administration had to work for change.

The way around this difficulty lay through the Inter-American Development Bank. Headed by a Latin American, and receiving contributions from Latin American nations as well as from the United States, the bank would appear sufficiently removed from Washington's control to be able to mandate social and political changes in return for loans. "We cannot very well tell these countries to reform, as a condition of our extending credit," Milton commented to Ike. But he added, "The Inter-American Bank can do so, and should do so."[61]

The most important single development in U.S.-Latin American relations in the late 1950s was, of course, the rise of Castro in Cuba. Available documents do not make clear the extent of Milton's influence in shaping administration policy toward the charismatic dictator. What *is* clear, however, is that Castro's seizure of power gave added effect to the arguments Milton had been making for half a decade. The Latin American crisis seemed to be coming to a head, and the administration finally began to move quickly on Milton's proposals.

Early in 1959, the United States signed an agreement establishing the Inter-American Bank; by September of that year, the administration had sanctioned an international scheme for stabilizing the price of coffee through export limitations and had begun work on similar plans for other Latin American exports. In 1960, the president made a personal good-will visit to South America, where he went beyond Milton's advice on handshakes and *abrazos* by avoiding dictators entirely.[62]

In the summer of 1960, the president sent to Congress a $500 million aid package targeted at promoting social reform in Latin America, especially improvements in housing, education, and land use. Congress approved the proposal, just in time for a September meeting of the Organization of American States in Columbia, where administration representatives worked successfully for a proclamation known as the Act of Bogota. The act, which combined with the just-approved aid program to form the basis of what John Kennedy would christen the Alliance for Progress, called for a cooperative effort to better the social and economic condition of common people throughout Latin America.[63]

Three months before his brother left the White House, Milton Eisenhower offered a summary of his impressions regarding the accomplishments of the administration with respect to Latin America. He commended the increased sensitivity of the administration to the problems of Central and South America, and he expressed satisfaction at the administration's good start at solving these problems. But it was only a start, and the problems continued to grow. As he had said before, the people of Latin America had learned that their poverty and degradation were not inevitable, and they were demanding a change. Reform would come, by one means or another. "This reform will either be peacefully achieved," Milton wrote, "or violence will be resorted to in an effort to bring it about." He believed that the fate of democracy in Latin America hung in the balance. "The failure to achieve reasonable social reform is the main reason for the spread of communism in some countries."[64]

The future, Milton thought, could go either way: to peaceful change along lines marked out by the Act of Bogota, or to violent revolt like that which had brought Cuba Castro. In this letter to the president, Milton mentioned plans to write a book about his Latin American experiences after Ike left office. The opening passage of that book captured Milton's deep concern about Latin America more clearly than the circumspect and hopeful statements he often felt constrained to make while his brother occupied the White House. "There is absolutely no doubt in my mind that revolution in Latin America is inevitable," Milton wrote. Latin Americans were angry, and they had resolved to take their future into their own hands, changing it to suit their own needs and desires.

How will they change it? The enlightened among them—the good leaders, most intellectuals—call for a peaceful revolution, a series of sweeping reforms to topple the oligarchists, the corrupt, the dictators. But there are loud and insistent voices demanding violent revolution. The Communists and their fellow travelers feed the fury of the underprivileged with half-truths and false promises. They nourish a lust for revenge and a cynical conviction that only blood will wash away injustice. The choice between these two courses is awesome. Cuba has succumbed to the lust for blood and violence. The remainder of the hemisphere teeters precariously on the verge of revolution—peaceful or violent.[65]

Milton Eisenhower had worked for most of a decade to push the revolution in a peaceful direction. He had managed, after considerable effort, to enlist at least some American resources on the side of nonviolent change. But he recognized that whether his efforts would meet success, only Latin Americans could decide.

3

Allen Dulles and the
Overthrow of Clausewitz

If Milton Eisenhower's aid plan for Latin America failed to stem the advance of radicalism in the hemisphere, there remained another string to the administration's bow. During the same period when Milton was persuading the president to fund the social reform of Latin America, Dwight Eisenhower also approved a CIA plan for training Cuban exiles to overthrow Castro.

In Eisenhower's use of covert operations to wage the cold war, ideology and pragmatism met. Ideology demanded that the United States carry on the struggle against communism; pragmatism required that the struggle be conducted by means other than direct confrontation with the Soviet Union. Covert operations seemed ideally suited to the task. Never has the Central Intelligence Agency been more influential than during Eisenhower's administration. The toppling of governments in Iran and Guatemala marked the extreme points of a campaign of secret activities that also included the acquisition of Khrushchev's "secret speech," the development of the U-2 spy plane, preparations for an invasion of Cuba, and plans to assassinate or otherwise "eliminate" troublesome individuals like Castro and the Congolese leftist leader, Patrice Lumumba.

In part, the free rein Eisenhower gave the CIA reflected the administration's ideological assurance. So morally self-confident were Eisenhower and his advisers that they willingly countenanced, with little apparent soul-searching, activities that under circumstances other than those of the cold war they would have found repellent.

In equal part, the freedom the CIA enjoyed reflected Eisenhower's confidence in the agency's director, Allen Dulles.

Allen Dulles would later be identified with the forces of counterrevolution, but he began political life, at a tender age, as an indignant liberal. Discussions of world affairs were unavoidable in the Dulles household, with three former or future secretaries of state in the family,[1] but even in this diplomatically saturated atmosphere, Allen was precocious. At eight years old, he became outraged on learning of the harsh nature of British imperialism in South Africa. Following months of research, Allen committed his indignation to paper, producing a small book entitled *The Boer War: A History*, profits from the sale of which he dedicated to the Boer Relief Committee.[2]

Allen followed brother Foster, five years his elder, to Princeton, where he encountered more consistent success in the social realm than in the academic.[3] The summer following graduation found Allen in France with some Princeton companions, taking in the annual running of the Grand Prix at Longchamp.[4] From France he trekked to India on a tour of adventure financed by the result of a last-minute burst of intellectual energy at Princeton: a cash prize for a senior essay in philosophy.[5]

The year was 1914, and as Europe went to war Dulles continued across Asia, writing home occasionally regarding the war's effects on India, Ceylon, China, and Korea.[6] Upon his return to the United States, he enlisted in the New Jersey National Guard. Allen nearly saw action, not in Europe but on the Mexican border; however, as his messmates prepared to head south, Allen received an invitation to join the American legation at Bern.

Considering his family background, a decision to enter government work came naturally. The fact that a fellow Princetonian occupied the White House provided further encouragement. Clinching the matter was the additional fact that Allen's uncle, Robert Lansing, headed the State Department and offered his nephew an interesting post.[7]

Dulles certainly found his new job interesting. War, of course, was serious business, even in neutral Switzerland, but for Allen Dulles it was also a great adventure. Throughout the war, Switzerland served as a vital listening post for the major powers; it gained a reputation for harboring more spies per square kilometer than any other country in the world. From the moment of his arrival, Allen reveled in the excitement of using his wits and personality to gain secret or otherwise difficult-to-obtain information, and he acquired a taste for the game that he never lost. He wrote enthusiastically to Foster of his intelligence-gathering activities,[8] and to "Uncle Bert" of his idea to draft scholars to study the European political problems that would face the United States after the war.[9] He even dabbled in psychological warfare, describing various ways by which the United States might exacerbate tensions within Germany.[10] Dulles impressed his fellow diplomats; Robert Murphy, who did not bestow compliments lightly, later characterized the twenty-four-year-old third secretary as "brilliant."[11]

On at least one occasion, however, Dulles slipped. In the early part of 1917, he received an invitation to a reception hosted by an eccentric Russian exile in Zurich. Dulles declined the offer, in favor of a tennis date with a young lady. "Two weeks later," Dulles recalled many years after the fact, "the eccentric, who turned out to be Nikolai Lenin, returned to Russia in the famed sealed railway carriage." Dulles used this tale in his remarks to new agents at the CIA; he concluded, "Since then I've never refused to see anybody."[12]

After the war, Dulles was transferred to Constantinople. Although the Turkish city did not live up to its Byzantine reputation for intrigue, it did offer an opportunity to observe the incipient decline of one empire, and the growing pains of another. Dulles, retaining some of his youthful distrust of Britain, wrote to the now-retired Lansing of the cynicism of the British in prodding Greece to continue "an entirely unjust war" in Turkey for lands "to which they had no just claim."[13] At the same time, he described with interest the efforts of the Bolsheviks in the Soviet Union—"Bolos," he called them—to maintain their grip on Georgia and the Caucasus.[14] Somewhat later, Dulles made note of a factor that seemed of growing importance in the struggles for the Middle East: oil.[15]

In 1926, Dulles decided to leave the practice of diplomacy for the more remunerative realm of law. "Although I had not exhausted my curiosity about the world," he wrote afterward, "I had exhausted my exchequer."[16] He joined Sullivan and Cromwell, his brother's firm in New York, where he remained until the beginning of American involvement in World War II. He managed to keep in touch with international events, however, through Sullivan and Cromwell's extensive affairs in Europe and through his own participation in various arms limitation conferences as the American legal adviser.[17] He visited Germany a number of times in the early 1930s, acquiring through personal contact a respect for the strength, if not the motives, of the Nazi movement and of its strangely fascinating leader, Adolf Hitler.[18]

On the whole, though, a lawyer's life failed to quench Dulles' thirst for adventure. Consequently, when a friend from New York, William Donovan—the legendary "Wild Bill" of the Fighting Irish 69th Division—asked him to participate in the organization of the Office of Strategic Services, he accepted with delight. Donovan initially wanted Dulles to accompany him to London to set up OSS operations there, but Dulles persuaded Donovan to let him go to Switzerland, where his World War I experience could be put to use—and where, Dulles undoubtedly thought, he could operate more freely.[19]

Within days of his return to Bern, Dulles found himself on his own. His journey to Switzerland had coincided with the Allied landings in North Africa; Hitler, provoked by the complicity of French officers in the Allied operation, ordered the occupation of France completed and access to Switzerland cut off. Dulles turned out to be one of the last Americans allowed through by the Vichy government, and he almost failed to make it.[20]

As in the earlier war, Dulles thrived in the real-life cloak-and-dagger atmosphere of espionage and support for underground movements. Dulles devoured spy stories; he later edited two volumes' worth.[21] During World War II, he had the opportunity to write his own scripts. He established an espionage network that blanketed France, Italy, and Austria and stretched from Portugal and North Africa to the Baltic.[22] The best-known of his roles—because he authored books about them afterwards—involved acting as liaison with the German resistance to Hitler, culminating in the unsuccessful bomb plot of July 1944, and as mediator in Operation Sunrise, the secret negotiations that led to the surrender of Nazi forces in Italy.[23]

Even as the war continued, Dulles began to think about the status of intelligence in the period to follow. Trapped inside Switzerland, he could do little to promote a peacetime version of the OSS, but he did correspond with Donovan on the subject. He shared Donovan's sentiments, and a copy of Donovan's letter, when the OSS chief wrote to Roosevelt of the need for postwar intelligence gathering: "We have now in the Government the trained and specialized personnel needed for the task. This talent should not be dispersed."[24]

The talent was dispersed, however, as the OSS disbanded after the war. Allen Dulles went back to Sullivan and Cromwell in 1946. But this time his departure from the spy game lasted only a short time. The world seemed more threatening after the second great war than after the first; besides, Dulles could not shake the espionage habit. Not that he tried; in the years after the war, he remained in close contact with Donovan and others of professional acquaintance.[25] Those who strove to salvage something from the scuttling of the OSS welcomed his attention; Richard Helms, later one of Dulles' lieutenants at the CIA, wrote in 1946, "May I say that your continuing interest in our work is to many of us a decided benzedrine lift."[26]

In some respects, Dulles' interest reflected personal motives as much as professional. Following VE-Day, he spent several months in occupied Germany trying to locate former contacts in the anti-Hitler underground who had survived the Gestapo sweep following the failed assassination attempt.[27] Dulles possessed a strong sense of loyalty, heightened, quite naturally, by shared dangers during the war. For the next few years, he often acted as a patron for former agents who wanted jobs, help with visa problems, or merely recognition for services rendered.[28]

By 1947, the Truman administration had decided, in line with its conversion to a belief in the necessity for a firmer policy toward the Soviet Union, to reverse the disintegration of America's intelligence capabilities. Truman considered deficient the information he received from the State Department; he later wrote to an acquaintance, "There were a large number of people in the State Department when I took over, who were certain I did not know what was going on in the world and they tried to keep me from finding out."[29] The Democratic president brought Dulles, whose wartime work he had admired and decorated,[30] to Washington to help frame the legislation that created the CIA in 1947. The following year Truman appointed Dulles to head a committee to review the work of the new organization, especially its relations with other offices engaged in intelligence work. The resulting report[31] contained fifty-seven conclusions and recommendations for strengthening the CIA; it included provisions for reinforcing covert operations capabilities, found to be particularly deficient, and a strong suggestion that the agency's director always be a civilian. Despite support from the State and Defense departments, the report met the fate of many such reorganizational blueprints.[32] In Dulles' words, it was "duly read and pigeon-holed."[33]

Yet two years later the Truman administration once more called on Dulles. Truman judged the surprise attack by North Korea on South Korea more surprising than necessary; in the shakeup of American intelligence that followed, the new director of the CIA, Walter Bedell Smith, invited Dulles to implement the ideas of his 1948 report. Perhaps the summary treatment given his 1948 report had offended him; in any event, Dulles liked the idea that the Truman administration was coming to him again. When his consulting post turned into a permanent position, Dulles wrote to a friend, "I must admit that I did not expect to be back on the old job, but with developments in the world generally, persuasion from that direction was pretty strong and I succumbed to it."[34]

Another shakeup, this the result of the 1952 presidential election, landed Dulles in the director's office at the CIA. Bedell Smith went to the State Department as undersecretary; Dulles, at Foster's request and with Eisenhower's approval, took over Smith's post.

Beyond his experience in the intelligence game, Allen Dulles brought to his new job a number of gifts. In the first place, he had an engaging personality. The contrast with his brother could hardly have been more striking. Where Foster seemed to strain in many social settings, Allen was thoroughly at home on the cocktail circuit. Richard Bissell, who would head the CIA's U-2 operation, later described Allen as "much more informal . . . more outgoing . . . a much warmer person than Foster."[35] Even people who discovered faults in Allen's management of the CIA found the director personally appealing. Following the Bay of Pigs disaster, Dulles' removal from the Kennedy administration was inevitable. However, as Robert Kennedy averred afterward, hard feelings toward Dulles as an individual played no part in his firing. "The President was very fond of him, as I was."[36]

Again in contrast to Foster, Allen Dulles generated among his subordinates great affection and esprit de corps. In part, this loyalty followed naturally from the conspiratorial atmosphere surrounding the work of the CIA. For Allen, intelligence never lost the romance of the wartime underground—not least because he continued to work with underground types during the cold war. Beyond this, however, Allen accepted political responsibility for shielding CIA employees when they came under attack, as by Joseph McCarthy. He insisted on and succeeded in establishing the principle that agency officials would not testify before McCarthy's investigative committee. Dulles' assistant Cord Meyer characterized his boss as "a pillar of courageous strength inside the Eisenhower administration during the McCarthy era";[37] to Richard Bissell, Allen Dulles seemed "a courageous defender of his own people and a courageous adherent to principle."[38]

Dulles' orthodox perceptions of recent world history also accompanied him to the CIA directorship. With others in the Eisenhower administration, Dulles viewed the cold war through the prism of Munich. The Nazi movement had battened on the weakness and vacillation of leaders and peoples paralyzed by fear of war; acquiescence in aggression only postponed the deluge. In a radio interview in 1948, Dulles said, "Today we stand where we were ten years ago. . . . Ten years ago, appeasement and inaction brought war. Appeasement and inaction today will have the same result."[39]

Dulles did differ somewhat from most others in the administration in the activist interpretation he put on his antiappeasement philosophy. While Eisenhower and Foster Dulles began moving away from the liberation theme of the 1952 campaign almost as soon as they took office, events never convinced Allen that liberation was such a bad idea. In 1949 he had joined a delegation named by the National Conference of Christians and Jews to press Secretary of State Dean Acheson to work harder for religious freedom in Eastern Europe; at the same time he had participated actively in the liberationist National Committee for a Free Europe.[40] In 1950, Dulles had seen in recent events behind the Iron Curtain some cause for optimism. "There is a spirit of revolt in every one of those countries," he said, speaking for the NCFE, "and we hope that this spirit may bring about a liberation from Moscow's control by means of internal uprising."[41]

As director of the CIA, Dulles continued to support liberation. With kindred spirit C. D. Jackson, a former associate in the NCFE and Eisenhower's psychological warfare expert, he swapped ideas regarding ways to keep up the pressure on the Soviets. When the liberation idea grew moribund, Dulles and Jackson shared their dissatisfaction and frustration—although Dulles, because he retained a position of responsibility after Jackson left official Washington, could not vent his frustration so freely as Jackson. Sometimes Dulles felt compelled to remind Jackson of larger considerations that made unrelenting psychological warfare against Moscow inadvisable. A 1957 letter, in which Dulles responded to suggestions regarding the use of CIA-sponsored Radio Free Europe against the satellite states of Eastern Europe, was typical. "The developments following the Hungarian revolt and repression, and the more favorable trends in Poland, create a great opportunity for Radio Free Europe but also raise a series of difficult problems."[42]

Still, to the end of Eisenhower's term in office, Dulles concurred with Jackson in the need for keeping the Russians off balance. In 1959, while Nikita Khrushchev tried to make life difficult for the United States in Berlin, Jackson recommended a renewed psychological warfare offensive to foment unrest among the Soviet allies. Dulles replied, "I fully agree that we should move from the defensive to the offensive, and not let K. and company feel that they can push us around without stirring up some trouble in their own back yard."[43] Dulles believed that so long as the Soviet Union engaged in its own version of liberation—infiltration and subversion—the United States could ill afford not to do likewise. He refused to be lulled by various Russian "peace offensives." Of one such Soviet maneuver late in Eisenhower's tenure, Dulles wrote to Harry Truman, "Despite the coexistence formula of Khrushchev, there is no evidence that the Communists have abandoned their policy of 'wars of liberation.' "[44]

Although Dulles considered destabilizing action against the communists desirable, he hesitated to take the initiative in promoting changes in policy. In large part, this reluctance reflected care not to tread on his brother's toes. Robert Amory, one of Allen's top assistants at the CIA, later commented on the relationship between Allen and Foster. "You see he'd had to be so careful in the days when he and Foster were together in the thing not to one-up on his brother, and time and again I've heard him respond to Eisenhower, 'Yes, Mr. President, that's a tough question, but it's really up to the Secretary of State to answer it.' "[45]

The relationship between the two Dulles brothers placed Allen in the subordinate position on both professional and fraternal grounds. Allen deferred to Foster because of the latter's position as chief foreign policy adviser to the president, but also because of Foster's status as elder brother. Observers recognized clearly who carried more weight. Richard Bissell afterwards remembered having "no doubt that Foster during those years was the senior partner."[46] Apparently the fraternal factor mattered more, for after Foster died Allen assumed substantial policymaking responsibility. By the time Eisenhower left office, Allen had grown accustomed to the idea of operating on his own; an observer in the early Kennedy administration considered him a de facto secretary of state.[47]

In managing the CIA, Allen Dulles encountered the basic problems inherent in trying to keep secrets in an open society. Shortly after his installation as director, he discovered that confidentiality and security, in Washington especially, had limits. In early 1953, the headquarters of the CIA occupied a compound bearing the sign "Government Printing Office." The subterfuge fooled few; Washington cab drivers found the CIA offices with no trouble, and tour buses made it a regular stop. But those who did get confused included some who had official business there. One day Milton Eisenhower made an appointment with Dulles, and the president offered to drop him off. The two drove around the area for some time, looking in vain for Dulles' office. They only found the place after calling for directions. Following this incident, Dulles decided to erect a sign frankly marking his place of business.[48]

This incident might have struck all concerned as humorous, but it typified the fundamental operational dilemma in American intelligence: how at once to maintain security and accountability. In the immediate postwar years Truman had resisted establishing a permanent intelligence organization for fear it would evolve into an American "Gestapo."[49] Although Truman changed his mind, he continued to have reservations about the covert activities of the CIA; he later asserted, "I never had any thought that when I set up the CIA that [sic] it would be injected into peacetime cloak and dagger operations."[50] Truman's misgivings were shared by many Americans uneasy with a potentially powerful government agency not subject to democratic control.

This distrust of things secret created trouble for Allen Dulles. In an address to a gathering of lawyers, after five years as CIA chief, Dulles summarized the problem. "We must work with a great deal of anonymity, which is not a characteristic attribute of Americans."[51] At another time, in a background briefing for a few veteran Washington journalists, Dulles further explained the special obstacles confronting a director of American intelligence operations. "Intelligence here is a relatively new toy, its use made more difficult by the fact that it operates in a goldfish bowl." Dulles contrasted the experiences of Americans regarding the conduct of intelligence with those of the British. "England has the tradition for it, and is able to operate in some secrecy. That is not possible in this country." The American aversion to confidentiality, Dulles believed, handicapped the United States in its struggle against communism. Dulles did not advocate government controls on the freedom of the press, though he obviously hoped that the correspondents at this briefing would take the hint regarding their responsibility to American security. He did say that he would give "a good many million dollars" to acquire information about the Soviet Union analogous to that readily available about the United States in any large American newspaper.[52]

While Dulles worried about the inability of American society at large to operate under the security restrictions necessary for the successful management of intelligence activities, others in the Eisenhower administration thought the inability to keep secrets had a more specific source. In 1954, the president appointed General James Doolittle to head a committee to evaluate the work of the CIA and its director. In October of that year, Doolittle visited the White House to report his findings.

Doolittle had some strong words about Dulles. On the positive side, he found the director's principal strength to be his "unique knowledge" of his subject. Doolittle considered Dulles a man of "great honesty," and one who had invested "his whole heart . . . his life" in his work. Further, Dulles could count on the unquestioning support of his staff. But these beneficial attributes had their negative counterparts. Doolittle described an insufficient attention to discipline in parts of the CIA and a "complete lack" of security consciousness throughout the organization. Too much information, he said, leaked out at Washington parties.[53]

Doolittle believed the problem stemmed in part from the circumstances in which the CIA had developed. It "grew like topsy," with the result that sloppiness characterized its operation. Dulles did not help matters, in Doolittle's opinion, by surrounding himself with people chosen more for loyalty than for competence. The overly close tie between Allen Dulles at the CIA and Foster Dulles at the State Department compounded the problem. Doolittle asserted that the combination led to bureaucratic protection of each brother by the other and to excessive influence of one upon the other. The relationship, Doolittle said, damaged the administration.[54]

Eisenhower accepted some aspects of Doolittle's criticism of Allen Dulles and rejected or discounted others. The partnership of Dulles brothers at CIA and State did not bother him, he said, because he valued the confidentiality possible between Allen and Foster. Besides, he considered the work of the CIA an extension of the work of the State Department. Furthermore, Allen Dulles had contacts throughout the world that greatly benefited the United States. Doolittle had described the CIA chief as too emotional for his sensitive position; Eisenhower responded by saying that he personally had never observed the slightest disturbance in Dulles. Moreover, the intelligence agency was one of "the most peculiar types of operation" any government could have, and it probably took "a strange kind of genius" to run it. The president did find unacceptable the lack of security in the CIA; he commented that it was "completely frustrating" continually to find evidence that people were talking.[55]

On the whole, Eisenhower considered Dulles' performance more than satisfactory, and he accepted the bad with the good. "I'm not going to be able to change Allen Dulles," the president said. "I have two alternatives, either to get rid of him and appoint someone who will assert more authority or keep him with his limitations." In deciding on the latter course, Eisenhower declared, "I'd rather have Allen as my chief intelligence officer with his limitations than anyone else I know."[56]

The activities of the CIA under Allen Dulles ranged a spectrum from reading newspapers to toppling governments. In terms of intrusiveness, what Dulles later labeled "one of the major intelligence coups" of his tenure—the acquisition of Khrushchev's anti-Stalin speech of 1956—fell about mid-spectrum.[57] Khrushchev spoke to a secret session of the Communist Party Congress, but a general description of his remarks soon surfaced. Although Khrushchev had a reputation for extemporaneous long-windedness, American analysts thought he must have committed an address of this duration, detail, and importance to paper. Dulles sent out a call to all CIA stations to place top priority on obtaining a transcript. Various accounts exist concerning how the agency six weeks later came into possession of the desired document. By one version, a Polish contact of the Israeli intelligence bureau provided the paper; by another, a disaffected Italian communist served as the conduit.[58]

Once acquired, the question arose as to what to do with the text of Khrushchev's address. CIA officials involved in encouraging resistance to Soviet rule in Eastern Europe wanted to disseminate the speech a little at a time, in such a fashion as to maximize its divisive impact among the satellite states. Disinformation specialists advocated the circulation of a doctored version, modified from the original to include disparaging remarks about Chinese and Indian leaders made by Khrushchev on other occasions. More-moderate types, foreseeing problems of credibility with a document leaked under mysterious circumstances, urged that the address be turned over to the State Department and published openly. Allen Dulles, after listening to the various sides of the argument, compromised. He ordered the transmission of one version to the *New York Times* through the State Department; he directed that another, including Khrushchev's jabs at the Chinese and the Indians, be distributed secretly.[59]

After its successful end, Dulles did not mind acknowledging the Khrushchev-speech operation. In the first place, once the *Times* aired the text, the need for and possibility of secrecy disappeared. More important, though, only the most scrupulous could challenge the premises of the plot or its modus operandi. Straight intelligence, it involved no sordid deeds and compromised no country's right of self-determination.

The program of aerial reconnaissance that found form in the U-2 plane fell into a similar category. Sky spying was clean; the blood spilled in the aircraft's early years was mostly of the figurative sort and flowed in the halls of the Pentagon.[60] From a legal standpoint the U-2 did violate the sovereignty of the Soviet Union and other countries flown over without permission; but the infraction seemed to most Americans, after the flights became known, merely technical. Following the downing of Francis Gary Powers' plane in 1960, few in the United States criticized Eisenhower for a moral lapse. A diplomatic disaster, to be sure; but the morality of the case did not become a major issue. Once the administration discovered that it could no longer deny the fact of the flights, Eisenhower instructed Dulles to brief congressional leaders "fully but without apology" on the program. The president himself publicly defended the operation as necessary to the security of the United States and entirely justified.[61]

Other covert operations, however, received no public defense, because the administration managed to keep them secret—or at least deniable—and because they violated stated ideals of the United States. Notable among these were CIA-sponsored coups in Iran and Guatemala. The details of American involvement in deposing left-leaning leaders in those two countries have been told elsewhere;[62] in the present context it suffices to say that the administration suffered no more pangs of conscience over the toppling of Mossadeq and Arbenz than it did over the U-2 flights. The administration deemed any abridgment by the CIA of self-determination of Iranians and Guatemalans merely passing and inconsequential next to the permanent loss of autonomy it thought inherent in a communist take-over. Besides, American officials did not believe that people chose communism freely; countries went communist only through deception or force. From this perspective, American-led anticommunist coups did not so much violate self-determination as restore it. Other nations might not accept this line of argument; thus the United States kept its hand hidden. But in the moral reckoning of administration leaders, such operations amounted to nothing more than cold war analogues of the American rescue of democracy in Europe in two world wars.

In 1944, Allen Dulles had done his best to help the German underground trying to assassinate Hitler. Under normal circumstances, murder was no more a part of Dulles' ethical system than it was an accepted element of American diplomacy. War, however, was not a normal circumstance. The Nazis had declared their enmity toward America; Germany's policy directly opposed the ideals and security of the United States, and the elimination of Hitler offered the hope of saving tens of thousands, conceivably millions, of lives. In this light, attempts to kill Hitler seemed not only justified, but imperative.

When the war ended, of course, there had been no return to "normal" circumstances. Communism, not Nazism, constituted the new threat, but the arguments for taking all feasible action to disrupt the enemy's plans remained essentially the same. Communism had announced its hostility to the United States and all America stood for; communists claimed the right to pursue their goals by any means; communists worked through dictators whose elimination might keep the cold war from flaming into World War III.

Therefore, as in the war against Hitler, assassination seemed, in certain instances, a conscionable tool of American foreign policy. Whether it was attempted against communist leaders—or leaders thought to be pursuing the goals of communism—depended on practical, not ethical, considerations. Among these practical considerations, three counted most. First, would the elimination of an individual in question produce a change for the better in that individual's country? Or would someone equally undesirable pick up the reins? Second, did an assassination attempt have a reasonable chance of success? There was little point in wasting effort and resources trying to kill someone physically beyond reach. Third, could American involvement in the operation be kept secret? In this respect, the cold war differed from the world war, for while a design on the life of Hitler could be defended as falling within the compass of the rules of warfare, a discovered attempt on the life of a leader not at declared war with the United States would have damaging political repercussions outweighing its benefits.

By these criteria, certain communist rulers had little to fear. Stalin, for example, had he lived past 1953, would not have made a tempting target. Beyond the fact that there seemed little chance of penetrating his security curtain, few in the Eisenhower administration thought Stalin's death would portend a serious weakening of the decades-old grip of the Communist party on Russian life, or even the more recently established Soviet control of Eastern Europe.[63]

Leftist leaders in third world countries, on the other hand, faced greater risks. The personalist nature of government in many developing nations heightened the prospect that drastic alterations in policy would follow a change in leadership; slipshod security was often the rule; and amidst the civil wars and revolutions that convulsed many of these countries, assassinations might be thought to have numerous non-American sources.

Such considerations led the CIA, under Allen Dulles, to plot the assassination of leaders in at least two countries: Cuba and the Congo.

In Cuba, the agency targeted Fidel Castro, who seemed to American leaders during Eisenhower's last two years in office to be moving dangerously in the direction of Moscow. By early 1960, the CIA had begun organizing Cuban emigres opposed to Castro in preparation for an invasion of the island.[64] Even before this, Allen Dulles had approved a recommendation that "thorough consideration be given to the elimination of Fidel Castro." This recommendation, which originated with J. C. King, the head of the CIA's Western Hemisphere division, cited Castro's "mesmeric appeal to the masses" and noted the opinion of "many informed people" that "the disappearance of Fidel would greatly accelerate the fall of the present government."[65]

Following this early approval, however, Dulles cooled to the idea of an immediate attempt to assassinate Castro. In January 1960, Dulles told a meeting of the National Security Council's special group for covert activities that the CIA no longer planned "a quick elimination of Castro"; rather, the agency had shifted to a program with a longer time-frame, aimed at strengthening Cuban alternatives to Castro's leadership.[66] Aside from the delay imposed by the desire to reinforce Cuban opposition, CIA planners began to reconsider the effects of a mere decapitation of Castro's regime. J. C. King told a task force in charge of Cuban operations that Castro's brother Raul and associate Ernesto (Che) Guevara might well step into any breach left by a fallen Fidel. According to the minutes of a March 1960 meeting, King stated "that unless Fidel and Raul Castro and Che Guevara could be eliminated in one package—which is highly unlikely— this operation can be a long, drawn-out affair and the present government will only be overthrown by the use of force."[67]

A few days later, a White House discussion turned to the question of what might happen should the two Castros and Guevara "disappear simultaneously." One participant suggested that such a development would lead to even greater control by the communists, since they were the best-organized group in Cuba. Dulles thought such an outcome not entirely bad, since it would flush the communists into the open. An indisputably communist coup—Castro's declaration of allegiance to Marxism-Leninism remained eighteen months in the future—"might not be disadvantageous because it would facilitate a multilateral action by OAS [Organization of American States]."[68]

From early 1960 until the end of Eisenhower's tenure, covert attempts to destabilize the Castro regime emphasized an emigre invasion. Still, contingency planning for an assassination of Fidel Castro continued; in

September 1960 Richard Bissell, then chief of covert operations, briefed Dulles on CIA contacts with Mafia figures regarding a contract on Castro's life.[69] As Eisenhower's time in office ran out, though, the killing of Castro received only secondary consideration. The difficulty of the operation, the likelihood of an equally obnoxious successor regime, the sensitivity of election year politics, and the existence of an apparently more promising alternative in invasion combined to make delay of further action on the assassination appear prudent.[70]

In the Congo, on the other hand, delay seemed dangerous. The summer of 1960 brought trouble and violence to the Congolese, who were seeking to navigate the passage from colonial status to independence. A secessionist movement in the copper-rich Katanga province and murderous personal rivalries between Premier Patrice Lumumba, President Joseph Kasavubu, and Army Chief of Staff Joseph Mobutu complicated the transition. Cold war considerations entered the picture when an American-backed United Nations peace-keeping expedition ran up against Lumumba's threats to call in Soviet aid to strengthen his hand against Kasavubu.

In July 1960, the CIA dispatched a new station officer to Leopoldville to monitor the situation. A few weeks after his arrival, Victor Hedgman reported that with Lumumba's help the Congo was sliding rapidly in the direction of Moscow. A cable of August 18 summarized Hedgman's assessment:

Embassy and Station believe Congo experiencing classic Communist effort take over government. Many forces at work here: Soviets . . . [passage deleted upon declassification] . . . Communist party, etc. Although difficult determine major influencing factors to predict outcome struggle for power, decisive period not far off. Whether or not Lumumba actually Commie or just playing Commie game to assist his solidifying power, anti-West forces rapidly increasing power Congo and there may be little time left in which to take action to avoid another Cuba.[71]

Such reports strongly influenced top officials in Washington. In late July, Dulles told the NSC that Lumumba was "a Castro or worse"; he added, "It is safe to go on the assumption that Lumumba has been bought by the Communists; this also, however, fits with his own orientation."[72] In mid-August, at another NSC meeting, Eisenhower declared that it was "simply inconceivable" that the United Nations should be forced out of the Congo by Lumumba and his Russian allies. According to the minutes of the meeting, the president said, "We should keep the UN in the Congo even if . . . such action was used by the Soviets as a basis for starting a fight." Eisenhower laid the blame for the situation at the feet of Lumumba. "We were talking of one man forcing us out of the Congo; of Lumumba supported by the Soviets."[73]

A week later, Eisenhower's national security adviser Gordon Gray went from a conference with the president to a meeting of the NSC's special group on covert operations with the message that Eisenhower "had expressed extremely strong feelings on the necessity for very straightforward action" regarding Lumumba. The president had reviewed CIA plans for political subversion of Lumumba, including the arrangement of a no-confidence vote in the Congo's parliament, and he had expressed reservations "whether the plans outlined were sufficient" to neutralize Lumumba. When the special group reached the point of recommending action to implement the president's desire that something be done about the Congolese leader, it refused to rule out "any particular kind of activity which might contribute to getting rid of Lumumba."[74]

The next day Allen Dulles sent a cable under his own signature—a message format used in the CIA only for especially urgent or sensitive missives—to Leopoldville, stressing the importance of removing Lumumba from influence in the Congo.

In high quarters here it is the clear-cut conclusion that if [Lumumba] continues to hold high office, the inevitable result will at best be chaos and at worst pave the way to Communist takeover of the Congo with disastrous consequences for the prestige of the UN and for the interests of the Free World generally. Consequently we conclude that his removal must be an urgent and prime objective and that under existing conditions this should be a high priority of our covert action.[75]

Dulles went on to grant the CIA station officer in Leopoldville "wider authority" than before to seek ways of replacing Lumumba, "including even more aggressive action if it can remain covert." Dulles added, "We realize that targets of opportunity may present themselves to you," and he authorized the expenditure of up to one hundred thousand dollars "to carry out any crash programs on which you do not have the opportunity to consult [headquarters]." Dulles commented that these instructions had been approved at the "competent level" in the State Department, and he concluded, "To the extent that Ambassador might desire to be consulted, you should seek his concurrence. If in any particular case, he does not wish to be consulted you can act on your own authority where time does not permit referral here."[76]

In early September, Kasavubu dismissed Lumumba from the premiership, despite the latter's great popularity in the Congolese parliament. A power struggle ensued, which Lumumba lost, even as Mobutu pushed Kasavubu aside. Fearing for his life, Lumumba placed himself in the custody of the UN peace-keeping forces.

In Washington's view, this turn of events did not end the threat Lumumba posed to American and Western interests in the Congo. Douglas Dillon, the undersecretary of state, later recalled the administration's assessment of Lumumba's hold on the Congolese people. "He had this tremendous ability to stir up a crowd or a group. And if he could have gotten out and started to talk to a battalion of the Congolese Army, he probably would have had them in the palm of his hand in five minutes."[77] On September 21, Allen Dulles told the NSC that while Lumumba had lost for the moment, he "was not yet disposed of and remained a grave danger as long as he was not disposed of."[78] Three days later, Dulles telegraphed to Leopoldville, "We wish give every possible support in eliminating Lumumba from any possibility resuming governmental position or if he fails in Leop[oldville], setting himself up in Stanleyville or elsewhere."[79]

During this period, plans for effecting the elimination of Lumumba proceeded on two fronts. In the Congo, CIA operatives met with and encouraged some of Lumumba's opponents who were plotting an assassination. Victor Hedgman warned anti-Lumumba Congolese government officials of the possibility of a Lumumba-led coup, and urged the arrest or "more permanent disposal" of the ex-premier.[80] At the same time, the CIA set in motion its own assassination schemes. Richard Bissell arranged for one of the agency's biological warfare experts to select a pathogen to send to the Congo. If all went as planned, Lumumba would be exposed to the microorganism and would then succumb to a disease that would either kill him or incapacitate him so severely that he would be "out of action."[81] The material reached the Congo, and CIA agents attempted to find a means of getting it into Lumumba's food or onto his toothbrush—"anything he could get to his mouth."[82] Hedgman apparently questioned the likelihood of success by the germ technique; he later remembered something about "suggesting" that Lumumba be shot instead. Hedgman received orders to use his own judgment in the matter, as long as the method he chose met one requirement. "It had to be a way which could not be traced back . . . either to an American or the United States government."[83]

The inability to guarantee that American connections to an assassination would remain hidden delayed the implementation of CIA plans. Further, Lumumba, aware that he was a marked man, remained inside his residence and out of sight. In mid-November, Hedgman cabled to Washington, "Target has not left building in several weeks." Hedgman went on to explain the problems involved in gaining access to Lumumba. Congolese troops loyal to Mobutu surrounded the house Lumumba occupied to prevent his escape; inside the ring of African soldiers, UN forces prevented the Mobutu partisans from seizing their leader's primary rival. Further, Lumumba had dismissed all but his most trusted servants; an inside job appeared impossible.[84]

While the CIA hoped for a better opportunity, Lumumba chose not to wait for his enemies to close in. On the night of November 27, in the midst of a raging thunderstorm, he managed to slip through the double cordon of troops. In a darkened car, he drove away toward Stanleyville, where he could count on support and perhaps safety.

He never reached Stanleyville. Under circumstances that remain unclear, Lumumba was arrested by Mobutu's soldiers and returned to Leopoldville. Though Lumumba was now in the hands of his enemies, the CIA still considered him a serious threat. Hedgman reported that the Congolese army seemed on the verge of mutiny[85] and that Lumumba had lost none of his persuasive abilities. On January 13, 1961, Hedgman wired a warning about Lumumba's "powers as demagogue [and] his able use of goon squads." Hedgman declared, "Refusal take drastic steps at this time will lead to defeat of [U.S.] policy in Congo."[86]

Four days later, the Congolese government decided to turn Lumumba over to others of his enemies and let them do the dirty work. Mobutu's men loaded Lumumba onto a plane and flew him to Elisabethville, where he was killed sometime during the next two weeks. Apparently, the CIA had little to do with the final deed, though it certainly approved of the result. Upon learning of Lumumba's arrival, the chief officer in Elisabethville cabled to Washington, "Thanks for Patrice. If we had known he was coming we would have baked a snake."[87]

"It is now clear that we are facing an implacable enemy whose avowed objective is world domination by whatever means and at whatever cost," General Doolittle had written to Eisenhower in 1954. In the report that supplemented his briefing to the president on the CIA, Doolittle continued:

There are no rules in such a game. Hitherto acceptable norms of human conduct do not apply. If the United States is to survive, long-standing American concepts of 'fair play' must be reconsidered. We must develop effective espionage and counter-espionage services and must learn to subvert, sabotage and destroy our enemies by more clever, more sophisticated, and more effective methods than those used against us. It may become necessary that the American people be made acquainted with, understand and support this fundamentally repugnant philosophy.[88]

Allen Dulles subscribed to both the premises and conclusions of Doolittle's report. Dulles believed that the United States was locked in mortal combat with the Soviet Union. But he recognized that the realities of the atomic age dictated an inversion of the maxim of Clausewitz: politics was now war by other means. The cold war, in Dulles' opinion, was essentially a war, and the rules of war applied. The security of the United States demanded that Americans learn to "subvert, sabotage and destroy" their enemies by means "more clever, more sophisticated, and more effective" than those used against the United States.

From this perspective, the assassination plots against Lumumba were completely justifiable, and there is little reason to believe that Dulles lost sleep over their morality. War was a nasty business; there was no use denying it. Dulles' job was to ensure, to the best of his ability, that the United States did not lose the war.

Like Dulles, Eisenhower also shared Doolittle's opinions. He accepted the Doolittle report without serious dissent; he consistently supported Dulles and the CIA through eight years in office. The president paid more attention than Dulles did to the political nuances of the struggle with communism, but he agreed that the United States must have the capacity to wage covert war against those who threatened American interests.

Since the mid-1970s, the question of Eisenhower's role in the CIA's assassination planning has sparked considerable debate. Eisenhower supporters have tended to claim that when the president spoke of the "elimination" of Lumumba, he meant the removal of the Congolese leader as a political factor, no more. Assassination, according to this version, was something Dulles understood was unauthorized but planned anyway, or, more likely, the result of an overzealous misreading by Dulles of Eisenhower's intentions. In either case, according to this line of argument, the president neither approved nor was aware of any assassination plans. Other observers, while unable to produce direct evidence of presidential complicity in assassination planning, have been convinced by circumstantial evidence that Eisenhower knew of the plots against Lumumba and approved them, or, if he did not know, lacked knowledge only because he chose to remain ignorant of details of which it was inadvisable for a president to learn.[89]

Considering Eisenhower's background and style of command, it seems more likely that he did not know specifically of the assassination plots than that he did. From World War II through the years of his presidency, Eisenhower focused his attention on broad matters of policy. Military commanders and presidents, he believed, were paid to make decisions; details were for subordinates. At Normandy in 1944, he decided the overall design of attack; staff officers implemented the plan. Regarding the Congo in 1960, it sufficed for Eisenhower to inform Dulles that he wanted Lumumba removed. It was up to Dulles to determine how. The CIA director had demonstrated in the past that he could do a job without detailed directions. Eisenhower assumed he could do so again.

In any event, too much emphasis on the narrow question of whether Eisenhower explicitly ordered Lumumba killed obscures a larger point. From the president to the director of the CIA and on down the chain of command, such moral self-assurance permeated the administration that American officials willingly countenanced activities that the Doolittle report accurately described as "fundamentally repugnant" to long-standing American ideals. Eisenhower may not have been responsible for the details of these activities, but he set the tone of his administration and he fostered the atmosphere in which they flourished.

Yet such responsibility apparently rested as lightly on Eisenhower's conscience as it did on Dulles'. The president was not given to introspection; he did not seem to worry that by adopting the tactics of America's enemies, the administration might subvert the values it aimed to preserve. Or if he did, his confidence in the ethical preeminence of the United States led him to conclude that the country could survive such divergence from standards attainable in a more peaceful world.

II
Lieutenants

4

Walter Bedell Smith and the Geneva Conference on Indochina

Beyond the inner circle of the Dulles brothers and Milton, Eisenhower relied most heavily on two men. Walter Bedell Smith and Robert Murphy functioned primarily as implementers of policy choices made at the top; but to characterize them simply as implementers would underestimate their role in the administration. In various critical situations, Smith and Murphy served as Eisenhower's men on the spot. Such crises demanded immediate decisions regarding the best methods of pursuing the administration's overall objectives; under such circumstances, the distinction between policy formulation and implementation blurred.

This said, though, it remains true that Eisenhower valued Smith and Murphy primarily as individuals who could get a job done. Eisenhower had developed close personal ties with each man during World War II; more important, he had developed great confidence in their ability to act quickly and responsibly—to act as he would have acted—under difficult conditions. When difficult conditions arose during his presidency, Eisenhower again called on their special skills.

"Diplomatic" was not normally the first word people used to describe Bedell Smith. To many of those who had worked for him, it might well have been the last. "He was brutal, brutal," said one CIA official, speaking of Smith's stint as a director of the intelligence agency. "Every staff meeting was a squash court, and you never knew who was going to get hit next.

He used to say that every officer had a right to one mistake—and you've just had yours."[1] Lyman Kirkpatrick, Smith's executive assistant at the CIA and no milquetoast himself, characterized his boss as a "formidable personality."[2] Even Eisenhower, one of the few people Smith really admired, had come in for an occasional tongue-lashing during the war when Smith's ulcers had acted up. Eisenhower once explained the secret of getting along with his chief of staff. "Remember, Beetle[3] is a Prussian and one must make allowances for it." Eisenhower later chuckled over the fact that Smith had been named ambassador to Moscow at a time when the Soviets were causing particular problems for the United States: "It served those bastards right."[4]

So it must have seemed ironic, or at least curious, that when the Geneva conference on Indochina began in May 1954, Smith headed the American delegation. Smith was then undersecretary of state, and many observers considered his presence, and the secretary of state's absence, a signal that the Eisenhower administration intended no serious negotiating. Yet even had this been the case, and had the task of the American delegation merely been to stay out of trouble, one would have thought that a certain diplomatic subtlety was called for. Few denied that Smith had his gifts, but many doubted that subtlety was among them.

When the first conference session began on May 8, 1954, Smith sat opposite the foreign ministers of America's chief allies and rivals: Anthony Eden of Britain, Georges Bidault of France, V. M. Molotov of the Soviet Union, and Zhou Enlai of China. John Foster Dulles had come to Geneva earlier for several sessions of the overlapping conference on Korea, but the secretary departed a few days before the discussions on Indochina began. In excusing himself, Dulles told Bidault that he thought he could do more in Washington for the success of the conference than he could in Geneva, referring vaguely to alternatives that could be offered if the communists did not make "honorable proposals."[5]

Dulles' argument was thin; in other cases he did not allow distance to interfere with the discharge of his duties. The real reason Dulles absented himself and left Smith in charge was that Dulles wanted to make sure that if the Indochina conference uncovered any diplomatic booby traps, they exploded in someone else's face. When Dulles left Geneva on May 3, France's future in Indochina looked bleak. Four days later the fortress at Dien Bien Phu fell to the Viet Minh, and it became nearly certain that any settlement achieved at Geneva would include the acknowledgment of communist control over a large part of northern Vietnam. At a time when Dulles hoped that the American people would forget his calls for the liberation of Eastern Europe, he had no desire to become involved in a surrender in Southeast Asia.

Throughout the Geneva conference, Dulles remained sensitive to indications of congressional and public dissatisfaction over the administration's Indochina policy. In mid-July, when Pierre Mendès-France, the new French prime minister, all but begged Dulles to return to Geneva for the conference's climactic sessions, Dulles declined, saying that memories of Yalta were still fresh in America. In explaining why the United States would probably not sign the final accords, Dulles revealed why he personally would have nothing to do with the conference. The United States government, Dulles said, could not be placed in a position of seeming to approve the "sale" of Indochina into "Communist captivity." Already, American participation in the conference had proved "a political liability" for the president and himself; the administration could not go further and become associated with a settlement that critics could portray as "a second Yalta."[6]

Had Eisenhower insisted that Dulles represent the United States in Geneva, the secretary, of course, would have stayed. The president, however, did not insist, partly out of respect for Dulles' judgment, but also because of his confidence in Smith.

Eisenhower's confidence derived from several factors. To begin with, there was Smith's sheer intellectual power. Nearly everyone who watched the man in action came away impressed with the force of his mind. Smith's education as a youth ended with high school, but he honed his natural gifts through wide reading and various army-sponsored courses. Lyman Kirkpatrick remarked on Smith's "photographic memory" and "encyclopaedic mind."[7] Kim Philby, the British-cum-Soviet intelligence agent, learned to respect Smith's "outstanding intellect" and "precision-tool brain" while working with and against the CIA. "Many times," Philby declared, "I saw him read a long memorandum, toss it aside and, without a pause for thought, paragraph by numbered paragraph, rip its guts out—real virtuoso stuff."[8] Allen Dulles described him as "extraordinarily good" at judging people. Said Dulles, "He could see through bunkum in people as quickly as anybody I ever saw."[9] Eisenhower, whose opinion counted most, described his wartime chief of staff as a "god-send—a master of detail with a clear comprehension of the main issues." Eisenhower wrote to a friend during the war, "I wish I had a dozen like him. If I did, I would simply buy a fishing rod and write home every week about my wonderful accomplishments winning the war."[10]

In the second place, for all his ulcer-driven temper, Smith was in fact a highly capable diplomat. Eisenhower recognized this quality in Smith; in 1946, upon hearing of Smith's selection as ambassador to the Soviet Union, he commented to his old friend, E. E. Hazlett, "I know of no one better qualified for the job."[11] Of particular significance was Smith's demonstrated skill at getting along with sensitive allies. When the Geneva conference began, it seemed clear that managing France and Britain would be at least as important as confronting the communists. Eisenhower respected Dulles as a student of foreign affairs, but he realized that Dulles' personality often offended others.[12] By contrast, Eisenhower trusted Smith's deft touch with the French and the British.

Eisenhower knew from his wartime experience that Smith got along well with Britain's leaders. In 1943, when Eisenhower was preparing to depart the Mediterranean theater for England, Winston Churchill had expressly requested that he leave Smith behind to advise the British commander in Algiers.[13] Anthony Eden also had learned to appreciate Smith during the war, and his admiration had grown in subsequent years. Eden wrote later of Smith, "He could feel strongly, yet was always understanding. He was forthright, but a friend."[14] On the other hand, neither Eden nor Churchill warmed at all to Dulles. Eden had taken the extraordinary step of suggesting to Eisenhower in 1952 that he choose someone other than Dulles as secretary of state;[15] Churchill expressed his feelings in a remark that Dulles was the only case he knew of "a bull who carries his china closet with him."[16]

Eisenhower was aware that the French had been no less impressed than the British by Smith. In 1954, the president reminisced that "a very great soldier of France"—probably Charles de Gaulle—had once assured him that his place in military history was secure, "since the only requisite for an enduring spot in the history of battles was wisdom in selecting a Chief of Staff." The French soldier had gone on to say that "no one in World War II was quite as wise, or at least as fortunate" as Eisenhower in this regard.[17] While this wartime experience with the French did not apply directly to the situation in 1954, due to changes in French leadership, it did give Eisenhower strong reason to believe that French sensibilities were in good hands with Smith.

Third, Eisenhower knew that Smith shared his basic philosophy of the cold war. Smith believed that communism posed a grave and uncompromising threat to the values that the United States represented, and he expected that the United States and the Soviet Union were in for an extended period of hostility. Smith once claimed that he had recognized the implacability of the Russian challenge as early as 1942.[18] But hostility did not necessarily mean war; under modern circumstances it must not mean war. The job of American leaders was to manage the cold war, not to try to win it at once. Victory would come in time. In 1947, Smith wrote to Eisenhower from Moscow, "If we remain calm, firm and strong; do our part to place in order the household of western democracy, and demonstrate that free enterprise can outstrip economic regimentation, we have little to fear."[19] To which Eisenhower replied, "Although we must never lose sight of the constant threat implicit in Soviet political, economic and military aggression, we must remember also that Russia has a healthy respect for the power this nation can generate." Eisenhower added, "It is a grievous error to forget for one second the might and power of this great republic."[20]

After Eisenhower became president, he appointed Smith undersecretary of state. The appointment culminated some subtle maneuvering within the new administration. Eisenhower had briefly considered Smith for his executive chief of staff, but he discarded the idea of a second general in the White House as smacking of a military takeover of the government. Meanwhile, Dulles wanted to ease Smith out of his position as director of the CIA, in favor of brother Allen. Foster Dulles believed, no doubt correctly, that he would find Allen more congenial and less threatening than Smith. Dulles, therefore, approached Eisenhower with the request that he select Smith for undersecretary, a post prestigious enough to attract Smith but also one that reported to the secretary rather than the president. Smith initially responded by saying that he wanted to retire. Since 1950, when he had most of his stomach removed, he had suffered poor health; a once robust individual of 185 pounds, he had shrunk to 135 by the end of 1952. But Eisenhower wanted him at the State Department, and as a good soldier he went where he was ordered. Dulles liked the result because he could watch over Smith; Eisenhower liked it because Smith could keep an eye on Dulles.[21]

Observers in the State Department commented on the special relationship between Smith and the president. Robert Murphy noted that Eisenhower and Smith habitually talked by telephone "maybe several times a day." According to Murphy, Smith would tell Eisenhower, "Ike, I think you ought to do this." Or, "I think that's a hell of a thing. Don't do that." By contrast, Murphy said, Dulles always remained on a "Mr. President" basis with Eisenhower.[22] Alexis Johnson, who served as the delegation coordinator at Geneva, remarked, "Bedell had a personal association with the President that Dulles didn't have." Where the Eisenhower-Dulles relationship often seemed formal and stiff, "Bedell Smith in his own inimitable way could call the President up, even though he was in his bath, and go over there and see him."[23]

While Smith enjoyed a close friendship with Eisenhower, he never got along with Dulles. Part of the problem was that he found life after the CIA confining. In early 1953 he told an acquaintance, "Now that I am out of the intelligence racket, I rather miss it. It did have one advantage—that of being complete czar of all the works with very few people to question one's decisions and lots of facilities for carrying them out."[24] Further, Smith held a low opinion of Dulles personally. At a 1947 diplomatic conference in Moscow, a group of Americans, including Dulles and Smith, gathered after hours, musing idly over what kinds of jobs their Russian counterparts might have if they lived in the United States. When the name of Andrei Vishinsky, the old Bolshevik noted for his dogmatic deviousness, came up, Smith did not hesitate. "Why, there's no doubt about it. He would have been senior partner at Sullivan and Cromwell."[25]

Smith's assessment of Dulles did not improve after the two joined the State Department. As undersecretary, Smith sought to rebuild the morale of the diplomatic corps, ravaged as it was by the trials of McCarthyism.[26] Dulles, with his demeaning demand for "positive loyalty" and his throwing of Davies and Vincent to the wolves of the right, only made the undersecretary's job more difficult. On a number of occasions, Smith became incensed at having his administrative judgment overruled; at least once he threatened to quit, telling an aide, "I'm not going to take that from Foster Dulles or anyone else."[27]

In fact, Smith did not take such treatment for long; he resigned after twenty months. That he remained at State as long as he did was primarily due to his loyalty to Eisenhower. Smith had entered the State Department as Eisenhower's man; as Eisenhower's man he went to Geneva.

An earlier chapter described how Eisenhower and Dulles decided, before the Geneva conference began, not to make any hasty moves toward intervention in Indochina. Despite the fact that the position of the French in northern Vietnam was rapidly crumbling—all the more rapidly following the surrender of the garrison at Dien Bien Phu on the eve of the first conference session—the administration continued to hold to its insistence on conditions that made American intervention unlikely.

However, the president and the secretary of state did not dismiss the possibility of intervention entirely. The French might still be persuaded to offer unfettered independence to the Associated States of Vietnam, Laos, and Cambodia, and they might come to accept the necessity of a pledge not to withdraw their troops after the arrival of American forces. The British might yet be convinced that Anglo-American solidarity required an agreement to support the United States in Southeast Asia. The probabilities of such developments were not great, but neither were they nonexistent. Besides, even had the administration decided not to intervene, the possibility of intervention offered one of the few bargaining chips the Americans could take to Geneva. Prudence dictated that it not be squandered.

While these considerations occupied the minds of American leaders, the Geneva conference began on May 8, 1954.[28] The idea of the conference was to gather all interested parties in one place to arrange a settlement of the eight-year-old Indochina war. However, the negotiating soon began to look less like a conference than like a floating collection of bilateral talks that happened to be located in the same city, with nearly as many dialogues as combinations of delegations. Smith engaged in several sets of discussions, the most significant being with the Russians, the British, and the French.

In some respects, Smith had less trouble with the Soviets than with the British or the French. From the beginning of the conference, it seemed likely that the communists would be able to achieve a settlement favorable to the Viet Minh without serious concessions at the negotiating table. Smith's cabled summary of a session ten days into the talks reflected this basic fact. "Meeting made no progress whatsoever. Communists showed no signs of any willingness compromise. . . . Communists appear confident and in no hurry get down to business."[29] The next day, Smith reiterated the message. "Communists have not given an inch and I do not believe they will make any concessions. They have a big fish on the hook and they intend to play it out."[30]

With the Russians content to await the results of the continuing Viet Minh offensive in northern Vietnam, Smith and Soviet Foreign Minister Molotov might have had little to talk about. In fact, however, the two men did a great deal of talking. Their discussions in official conference sessions tended toward predictable monologues, but in numerous private interviews they exchanged candid observations on the course of events in Indochina and in the world generally. In the records of these confidential meetings, Smith emerges as a tough but realistic diplomat, a practical soldier who recognized a military defeat when he saw it and did not try to duck the consequences. With a conspicuous lack of dramatic posturing— left to others in the administration—Smith sought to cut the losses of the United States, and he urged a retreat to defensible lines.

Smith had known Molotov from the days of his tour as ambassador to the Kremlin. Shortly after the conference began, the two men met privately to renew their old acquaintance. From the beginning, they spoke frankly about matters they could not discuss in public, but which each knew to be true. At their first meeting, Molotov commented on Secretary Dulles' abrupt departure from Geneva just as the Indochina conference commenced; he observed that it was "too bad" that Dulles had "to go home so early." The Soviet diplomat remarked that there had been "all sorts of rumors in the press" about why Dulles had left, but he added, "Of course, one shouldn't necessarily believe all such stories." Smith, feeling no obligation to hide the obvious, admitted that Dulles' departure owed to the political situation in the United States. The secretary, Smith said, had gone back to Washington to avoid giving critics an opportunity to disrupt the administration's foreign policy. Molotov noted approvingly the fact that Smith was "a military man," and he suggested that this ought to facilitate the business of the conference. He asked Smith what sort of final settlement he had in mind, but Smith declined to be drawn out.[31]

Smith's relationship with Molotov continued cordial and direct, even as it grew evident that the Russians intended no serious bargaining. At times, Smith wondered if the conference would ever make any progress. After a few weeks of Molotov's polite stubbornness, Smith told reporters that he was beginning to fear that the headquarters of the American delegation would become his permanent home; he said he could picture himself wandering the corridors of the Hotel du Rhone with a long, white beard.[32] In the meantime, though, Smith found his sessions with Molotov valuable for the insights they provided into the Soviet foreign minister's character and thinking.

On May 23, Smith dined with Molotov. A long conversation followed dinner; as Smith recorded afterward, the foreign minister was "completely relaxed, quite friendly, and objective." Smith remarked to Dulles on the great change that had come over Molotov's diplomatic style since Stalin's death the previous year. "He went further, was much more frank, made no charges, by implication or otherwise, no recriminations, and it was as though he were looking at the whole situation through a magnifying glass and analyzing its various aspects."[33] At one point in the conversation, Smith told Molotov that he thought the United States and the Soviet Union could work out their problems peacefully. Smith added, however, that he was not so sure about some of Russia's allies. "Molotov looked up immediately and said China," Smith reported. "I said yes, China. Well, he said, you must remember that China is still a very young country, and you must also remember that China is always going to be China, she is never going to be European." Molotov added, rather mysteriously, that someday the world would know that at times—he mentioned the Korean War specifically—the Soviet Union had acted as a restraining influence on China.[34]

Late in May, Molotov left Geneva for a few days to visit Moscow. On his return, Smith noticed a hardening in the official line of the Soviet delegation.[35] This shift appeared designed to give aid to the opponents in Paris of the government of Joseph Laniel, in the hope of undermining support for continued French resistance in Indochina.[36] Smith responded by telling Molotov that Communist obduracy might lead to serious trouble. Smith asserted that military intervention was "the last thing" the Eisenhower administration desired, but he added that the United States might feel forced to take action. The Viet Minh, said Smith, "were entitled to just consideration," but if "their appetites were too great and if they over-reached themselves a crisis could ensue which . . . might might well lead to U.S. armed intervention."[37]

Ten days later, on June 18, Smith again raised the issue of what the Viet Minh were fairly entitled to. By this time, the communist negotiators insisted that the Viet Minh be awarded most of northern Vietnam. Smith told Molotov that the Eisenhower administration recognized the strength of the Viet Minh, but he said that in holding out for all of the Red River delta, including the key cities of Hanoi and Haiphong, "they were demanding too much." Molotov countered by saying that French claims were extravagant. French demands for territory in both northern and southern Vietnam reminded him of an "old Russian proverb" about chasing two rabbits at once. The moral was that the chaser would probably catch neither rabbit. Smith turned the proverb around and said that the Viet Minh were the ones chasing two rabbits in wanting both Hanoi and Haiphong.[38]

In his commentary to the State Department following this exchange, Smith summarized his opinions regarding Soviet objectives. At the beginning of the conference, Smith said, the Russians had aimed chiefly at forestalling American intervention. The means to this end had been occasional hints by the Soviet delegation at an eventual compromise that would leave the French in control of part of Vietnam's northern province of Tonkin. As the possibility of American intervention diminished with each passing week, the communists had begun "raising the ante." By June 19, the date of Smith's summary, the Soviets considered American intervention improbable, though they kept a "sharp eye out" for a change of mind in Washington. Smith concluded:

In the whole area [Indochina] the determining factor for the Communists will continue to be their estimate of the likelihood of US or joint intervention and nothing short of a conviction on their part that this intervention will take place will stop them from going ahead with their plans for taking all of it eventually, through military conquest, French capitulation, or infiltration.[39]

Smith's talks with Molotov, while straightforward and sometimes enlightening, produced little of substance because the United States lacked leverage with the Soviets. Although everyone of influence in the Eisenhower administration believed that the Kremlin inspired, if not directed, the Viet Minh insurgency, there seemed little that the United States could do to get the Russians to call off the communist offensive in Indochina. Had massive retaliation been a genuine strategic policy, the administration might have threatened Moscow with a nuclear strike; of course no such action was ever contemplated.

The United States possessed more leverage with Britain. America's closest ally in two world wars was now sliding in the direction of becoming an American client—though American leaders could never utter such a thought. After a postwar loan, the Marshall Plan, and NATO, Americans tended to think of Britain as a country to which much had been given, and from which much might therefore be expected. In the case of Indochina, the Eisenhower administration sought a British commitment to support American policy, whether this involved military intervention to prevent a victory by the Viet Minh, or, after intervention fell by the wayside, a collective security treaty for Southeast Asia.

Whether the administration could put its influence with the British to use remained to be seen. By 1954, Britain had lost much of its empire, but its leaders had not lost the self-assurance that came from running other people's affairs for two centuries. The British had gained a healthy fear of what war in the modern age might mean; when Churchill had come to power in 1940, the English had been singing "There will always be an England," but after the introduction of atomic weapons, they could not be so sure. Accordingly, the British government did not intend to give a blank check for Southeast Asia to the Eisenhower administration. Smith soon learned that Churchill and Eden firmly opposed military intervention.[40] Such a course, they thought, if it did not lead to world war, would probably rend the Commonwealth, and it would certainly make life more difficult for the British in Malaya and Hong Kong. Besides, from Eden's perspective, there was no telling what intervention might do to the foreign minister's plans to succeed the already failing Churchill as prime minister.

Regarding a possible security pact for Southeast Asia, the British were less adamant. They held that a Southeast Asian analogue of NATO—inevitably dubbed "SEATO"—might be worth talking about, but only after negotiations at Geneva had been given a try.[41] The British believed that the communists, especially the Chinese, thought that the United States was looking for an excuse to attack China. Discussion of a collective security agreement, which might furnish the excuse, therefore diminished the possibility of a peaceful resolution of the Indochina war. On May 15, Eden wrote to Churchill, describing his reaction to recent "noises off," as he called them: "I myself fear that this new talk of intervention will have weakened what chances remain of agreement at this conference. The Chinese, and to a lesser extent the Russians, have all along suspected that the Americans intend to intervene in Indo-China whatever arrangements we arrive at here." Eden continued, "The Chinese also believe that the Americans plan hostilities against them. These reports help to convince them that they are right."[42]

Smith attempted at Geneva to change Eden's mind. Smith did not seriously expect to persuade the British to join a military expedition, but he did hope to gain agreement to a SEATO, and this before the conference ended. Only thus would the pact carry much weight in the negotiations.

Complicating Smith's task was a mutual distrust between Eden and certain high officials in the State Department and at Geneva. Walter Robertson, the assistant secretary for Far Eastern affairs and Smith's deputy at Geneva, habitually reported to Washington that the British appeared willing to accept a settlement in Indochina at any price.[43] Later Robertson would characterize Eden as "the most devious foreign minister among our allies of that period."[44] Eden, in return, thought little of Robertson. In a note to Churchill, Eden described Robertson as "so emotional as to be impervious to argument or indeed to facts."[45]

Relations between Eden and John Foster Dulles were notoriously bad. Eden considered the secretary of state generally unreasonable;[46] Dulles suspected his British counterpart, at various times during the conference, of proposing cease-fire arrangements that would lead to a communist takeover of all of Indochina. Dulles also feared that Eden, by trying to push the French into a hasty settlement, one that the Eisenhower administration could not accept, would leave the United States to bear responsibility for the failure of the conference.[47]

By contrast, Smith and Eden continued to get along well. Eden considered Smith a welcome relief from Dulles and from the rest of the American delegation; after a meeting with the Americans, Eden wrote to Churchill, "Only Mr. Bedell Smith seemed to have any real comprehension of the reasons which had led us to take our present position."[48] Smith sought to ensure that Eden maintained this favorable opinion. So careful, in fact, was Smith regarding Eden's opinions that some members of the American delegation began to worry. Walter Robertson considered Smith too trusting of Eden. Robertson warned darkly of Eden's influence over Smith; he went so far as to write a personal letter to Dulles complaining that Smith preferred Eden's counsel to that of his own staff at Geneva.[49]

Throughout the conference, Smith acted in a fashion calculated to minimize the problems created by the antipathy between the State Department and Eden. From the beginning, Smith asked Dulles for "as much latitude as possible" in dealing with Eden.[50] Dulles, for the most part, went along. Two weeks into the conference, Smith found occasion to exercise this latitude. On May 20, Dulles cabled Smith, expressing annoyance at what he considered British reneging on a pledge to begin exploratory talks that might ultimately lead to a SEATO. Dulles suggested that Smith raise the matter with the British.[51] Smith told Dulles that he was going to hold off on a protest, though he assured the secretary that he shared his indignation. "I agree these things are hard to swallow, but you know how pettish both Eden and Churchill can be at times."[52]

Through May and June, Smith worked assiduously to keep Anglo-American relations on a friendly, personal footing, and his efforts paid off. One of the noteworthy features of the otherwise forgettable and dreary official conference meetings was the close cooperation that obtained between the American and British delegations. During their private sessions, Smith and Eden admitted the divergence between the positions of their governments, but when they spoke for the public record they nearly always presented a united front.[53] Eden often shared confidential missives with Smith;[54] Smith responded by letting Eden read American messages. They cooperated so closely that Dulles, on occasion, felt obliged to state explicitly that certain information was to be kept from Eden.[55] Further, Eden acted as a liaison between the American delegation and that of the Chinese. Eden warned the Chinese that they would have only themselves to blame if their continued obstinacy and violent criticism of the United States led to American intervention. Eden cautioned Zhou Enlai not to push the United States too far. Americans, he said, were "slow starters," but once started they went "all the way." Eden added that Britain, in case of a confrontation, would stand with the United States.[56]

On the issue of greatest concern to the administration regarding Britain— the question of British backing for a SEATO—Smith reported substantial progress. Even before the conference began, Smith had considered the difference between the American and British positions on united action in Southeast Asia to be primarily a matter of timing.[57] This difference diminished as the conference wore on. By the first part of June, Eden and Churchill had moved almost all the way to where Smith and the administration wanted them to go. How much of the shift reflected Eden's belief that the negotiations were breaking down, and how much was due to Smith's personal diplomacy, is difficult to say. Certainly the latter factor was crucial, if only in the negative sense of preventing the animosity between Eden and Americans such as Dulles from derailing Britain's progress toward acceptance of a security pact. In any event, on June 9 Smith expressed to Dulles his belief that Eden was prepared "to move ahead quickly" on a coalition for Southeast Asia.[58] Smith's estimate proved accurate. In the last week of June, Eden and Churchill traveled to the United States; at the end of their visit, Churchill joined Eisenhower in a declaration of intent to "press forward with plans for collective defense" in Southeast Asia.[59]

Smith had a more difficult time dealing with the French than with either the Russians or the British. The Soviet Union was an admitted opponent of the United States; Britain was a firm and generally reliable friend. Where France fell between these poles, Americans could not always tell. The French were allies, to be sure, but their reliability often seemed open to question. In American relations with France, the annoyances of alliance politics were heightened by what appeared to American leaders to be an identity crisis of the French empire. Eisenhower offered his assessment of France in a letter to NATO commander Alfred Gruenther: "She wants still to be considered a world power, but she is entirely unready to make the sacrifices necessary to sustain such a position. She prefers to limit her sacrifices and so, finally, she is bound to be shown up, as in Indo-China, as incapable of doing anything important by herself."[60]

French imperial problems gave rise to political troubles for the Laniel government; together they made French diplomats hard to get along with. This did not surprise Smith, for he had found the French difficult even in better times. Smith had known Foreign Minister Georges Bidault for several years, and he had early acquired an impression that the French diplomat's good judgment was not entirely to be trusted. "I would not gamble too much on his discretion under certain circumstances," Smith wrote to George Kennan in 1948.[61] Smith thought French leaders generally irritable. "I don't have to tell you how extremely touchy and sensitive they are. They have nursed their bruises ever since the war, seeming rather to take pride in the black and blue spots than to make an effort to develop a thicker skin."[62] French irritability, Smith believed, resulted from a less than straightforward style of diplomacy. Smith summarized his opinion of the French, and contrasted it to his estimate of the British, in a report to George Marshall, then secretary of state. Describing the manner in which diplomats from the two countries reacted to the inevitable occasional failures of communication, Smith wrote, "While the British will, I believe, accept a subsequent frank explanation at its face value, the French will only swallow about 75% of it, and will always retain a lingering suspicion and doubt, bred from the fact that they usually have a bit of sharp practice on their official conscience."[63] Smith would not have taken issue with Eisenhower's comment regarding French reliability: "A typical French promise is only a basis for future discussion."[64]

At Geneva, Smith's earlier estimate of French judgment and trustworthiness gained confirmation before the conference was many days old. Following a private session with Molotov, Smith relayed to Bidault, in strictest confidence, some facts of the discussion he thought helpful to the French. Bidault proceeded—with "incredible stupidity," as Smith described the episode to Dulles—to transmit the information to the French delegation's press secretary, including a detail regarding one point in the conversation at which Smith had supplied a word Molotov had been searching for. The French press secretary—"who tells everything," Smith said—then reported the conversation to a French news correspondent, who published the story, complete with the denial-proof detail. Smith fumed as he wired, "This demonstrates practical impossibility of speaking to French with anything like real frankness."[65]

Even had the French been exemplary negotiating partners, their predicament in Indochina and the precariousness of the Laniel government's hold on power would have made Smith's relations with Bidault trying. Initially Smith attempted to persuade the French to accept the conditions that Eisenhower had placed on American intervention: complete independence for the Associated States and a guarantee that the French would not withdraw after the introduction of American forces. Before long, however,

Smith realized that he could realistically hope for no more than a stiffening of French resolve at the negotiating table.

In April, as the Viet Minh tightened the ring around Dien Bien Phu, Smith had predicted that if the fortress fell domestic political pressures would force the Laniel government to a settlement at almost any cost.[66] When the news of the garrison's surrender reached Geneva in early May, Smith had to deal with the consequences of an accurate prediction. Bidault, whom Smith had described as in a "bad mental condition" even before the siege ended, was in a worse state upon hearing of the outcome of the final assault. Smith reported that the French foreign minister was "dog-tired" and wanted "to cry on somebody's shoulder." Smith assured Bidault that this one battle did not decide the war. Dien Bien Phu, he admitted, was a tragedy for the individuals involved, but it was not the military disaster some people made it out to be. If handled properly, Smith said, it did not have to be a psychological disaster either.[67]

Smith made his final remark more for its firming effect on Bidault and the French government than out of belief in its accuracy. Smith feared that Dien Bien Phu would indeed prove to be a psychological disaster. Two weeks earlier, at a staff meeting in Washington, he had listened to a suggestion that a gallant last stand by the outnumbered French might act as a spur to Gallic pride. He rejected the idea. Speaking as a student of military history, he commented that a remember-the-Alamo reaction normally developed only early in a war. After eight years of French struggle in Indochina, Smith saw no possibility of such an effect.[68]

Whether from Smith's encouragement or from his own resilience, Bidault soon demonstrated that he was not ready to give up the struggle. Within a week, Smith might have felt that he had succeeded too well in restoring Bidault's confidence. The French foreign minister never flatly rejected Eisenhower's conditions for intervention, but Smith could see that Bidault was not about to agree to them either. What Bidault wanted was the *threat* of American intervention, which would yield intervention's bargaining advantage, without the unpleasantness of submitting to American demands. Bidault's design became apparent when he told Smith that their two countries should leak word of combined military planning. "Lightning should not strike" during the conference, Bidault said, but "rumbles of distant thunder" were useful, and the sooner the better.[69]

Bidault's attempt to keep alive the possibility of American intervention by not rejecting administration conditions, while preventing intervention by not accepting American terms, struck Smith as annoying but understandable. Bidault himself felt justified in stringing the Americans along because he believed that the Eisenhower administration was doing something similar to France. Bidault later complained that the Americans hedged their offers of help with unrealistic demands, and he asserted that they imposed these demands in an incremental fashion that fatally weakened the Laniel government. "Every hesitation by the Americans," Bidault wrote, "made the opposition in France worse, and each time the opposition got stronger in France, the Americans hesitated even more." He concluded bitterly, "We were left by our allies to struggle on alone."[70]

To Bidault, such hesitation may have appeared malicious, but in fact it merely reflected the Eisenhower administration's, and especially the president's, style of decision making. Eisenhower deliberately postponed difficult policy choices, waiting as long as possible before taking irretrievable steps. "I have so often been through these periods of strain," the president wrote during another tense period, "that I have become accustomed to the fact that most of the calamities that we anticipate never really occur."[71] Even when crises failed to work themselves out, extra time made clearer the nature of appropriate responses. In the case of Indochina, Eisenhower seriously considered intervention, but he did not intend to be rushed. If the administration intervened, it would do so on terms guaranteed to protect American, and administration, interests. When these terms proved impossible, intervention died a quiet death.

The administration's disenchantment with intervention paralleled Smith's—and partly resulted from Smith's. As director of the CIA Smith had actively pressed technical and other assistance on the French.[72] After his move to the State Department, he maintained a close interest in French problems with the Viet Minh; in January 1954 Eisenhower selected him to head an ad hoc advisory committee on Indochina. At that time, Smith contended that since Indochina was of such importance in the battle against communism, the administration ought to be prepared to intervene with naval and air forces.[73] Over the next few months, however, Smith became increasingly persuaded by arguments against unilateral American action. In late April, Smith told the National Security Council that air strikes and training assistance might bolster the French will to continue the struggle, but he noted that the American public would insist upon certain conditions.

Most important among these, he said, were the cooperation of American allies, proof that the Associated States genuinely desired American intervention, avoidance of identification with continuing colonialism, and a French pledge of complete independence for Indochina.[74]

Immediately after his arrival in Geneva, Smith continued to admit the possibility of air strikes, but as Dien Bien Phu surrendered and the French and British failed to provide the prerequisites for intervention, Smith shifted his emphasis to training assistance. He commended the French for the so-called Navarre Plan, designed to strengthen French Union forces through the dispatch of recruits from France and the training of local troops. However, he considered the plan's originator, General Henri Navarre, incompetent and said he ought to be fired. By the middle of June, Smith's recommendations for support of the French encompassed only organizational and training assistance; he no longer advocated the use of American force.[75]

As he backed away from intervention, Smith provided little help to Bidault in producing the rumbles of American thunder the French foreign minister wanted. Aside from this, however, Smith was solicitous of the health of the Laniel government. Perhaps more than the rest of the Eisenhower administration, Smith considered Laniel and Bidault preferable to the alternatives then available in Paris.[76] Furthermore, strengthening the political position of Laniel and Bidault in France tended to strengthen their government's diplomatic position in Geneva.

On a number of occasions, Smith recommended a more tolerant attitude toward the French than the State Department was inclined to take. At the end of May, for example, he urged Dulles to refrain for the moment from insisting on French guarantees of the right of the Associated States to withdraw from the French Union. Smith recognized that the guarantees would eventually be necessary, but he contended that to demand them at once would be counterproductive. Such pressure, Smith said, "would not produce sufficiently favorable effects in Vietnam to counterbalance undoubtedly adverse effects, including diminished support [in the] French Assembly and [by] public opinion for immediately required military measures in Indochina."[77]

In other instances, Smith decided that gentle treatment of Bidault and his aides ought to be supplemented by something more vigorous. Early in May, Smith told the French that their failure to advise the American delegation of certain of their armistice proposals led him to suspect that they were "holding out" on him. French officials quickly denied any such thing. Smith told Bidault's deputy that the Eisenhower administration would much prefer supporting French proposals at the conference to opposing them, but that the French would have to start making some difficult decisions.[78] Somewhat later, Smith declared bluntly to Bidault that France's problems in Indochina reflected a failure of political leadership rather than military blunders. Smith told Bidault that in view of French superiority in manpower and weapons, something was "obviously wrong" when the French suffered defeat after defeat. Any "second rate general," said Smith, ought to be able to win the war, given the proper political atmosphere.[79]

Smith's efforts in Geneva proved no match for the problems confronting the Laniel government. In mid-June, Laniel and Bidault fell from power, both succeeded by Pierre Mendès-France. In American eyes, the entree of Mendès-France did not augur well for Indochina; the new prime minister almost immediately pledged to achieve a cease-fire within a month or resign. Eisenhower's press secretary James Hagerty caught the mood in the administration when he labeled the promise "a major political and diplomatic mistake." Hagerty commented, "The Commies will never let the free world meet such a deadline and Mendès-France should have known that."[80]

Eisenhower himself, though he tended to believe that a change from Laniel would be a change for the worse,[81] had on occasion hoped for something better. In a letter to Alfred Gruenther at the end of April, Eisenhower commented on the French situation, "The only hope is to produce a new and inspirational leader." Lest Gruenther get the wrong idea, Eisenhower added quickly, "I do *not* mean one that is 6 feet 5 and who considers himself to be, by some miraculous biological and transmigrative process, the offspring of Clemenceau and Jeanne d'Arc."[82] Later, Eisenhower apparently began to think de Gaulle might not be so bad. In his memoirs he wrote, "During this period I often expressed a thought in conversation with Secretary Dulles. 'France ought to recall General de Gaulle,' I said."[83]

The change in governments in Paris required a reevaluation of the administration's strategy, and Eisenhower called Smith home. The situation looked grim, as Smith told a gathering of congressional leaders at the

White House in the last week of June. Smith predicted that the French would end up agreeing to a partition plan recognizing Viet Minh authority in most of northern Vietnam and leaving the communists in effective control of a large part of Laos as well. Smith added that he thought the British would accept such a settlement because they believed they had no other choice. At this point Senator William Knowland spoke up, attacking the Geneva conference and declaring that a Far Eastern Munich was at hand. Never one to suffer those he considered fools, Smith retorted that Geneva was no such thing. Munich involved a surrender without a fight; the communists would gain nothing at Geneva, he said, that they had not already acquired by force of arms. Eisenhower stated his agreement with Smith, perhaps forming the thought he would later commit to his diary regarding Knowland: "In his case there seems to be no final answer to the question 'How stupid can you get?' "[84]

The possibility of partition had worried the administration for some time. By the logic of the battlefield, such an outcome was almost inevitable, as Smith had recognized in May.[85] But partition would certainly embarrass an administration that had come into office promising to reverse the trend of communist expansion. Accordingly, Smith spent most of May and June trying to camouflage the partition he knew would come. At one point, he sought to persuade Bidault to work for a settlement that would separate the French Union and Viet Minh armies but avoid clean lines of demarcation between the resulting zones.[86] In another instance, he urged the French to offer a slice of southern Vietnam to the Viet Minh in exchange for a French enclave in the north.[87]

Following the elevation of Mendès-France to the premiership, undisguised partition came quickly. The French were determined to end their pain, even if this meant handing half of Vietnam over to the communists—which, in fact, they did.

With partition, the only question left for the administration involved whether to recognize the Geneva settlement. The weight of domestic politics made recognition almost impossible. Knowland might have been wrong in thinking Geneva another Munich, but many joined in his error. Others deemed Yalta a better analogy, but their point was the same; and the administration did not intend to add to their arsenal of criticism.

Dulles in particular must have shuddered to hear allegations from the floor of the Senate that "the dead hand of the Acheson regime" still guided American policy.[88] So worried, in fact, was Dulles over the fallout from Geneva that he opposed Smith's return to the conference for the final sessions. Eisenhower thought Dulles' concerns exaggerated, and the president decided to send Smith back.[89] However, Eisenhower recognized the dangers of what doubtless would be interpreted in certain quarters as appeasement, and he did not want to affront those who would have liked to make Geneva a major issue.

Smith understood the domestic worries of the administration, but still he argued against rejection of the conference accords. What seemed politically convenient at the moment, he contended, might prove diplomatically disastrous in the future. Smith made his case in a memorandum that bears quotation at some length for its prescience and for the light it casts on Smith's perceptions of the cold war. Writing while the details of partition remained unclear, Smith stated:

Whatever settlement comes out of the Conference, it will reflect the inability of our side, notably France, Viet Nam, and the U.S., to reach an acceptable basis for continuing the fight to hold the Tonkin Delta against a Communist advance. Do we guarantee that settlement, or do we disassociate ourselves from it?

If the settlement, an unpalatable reflection of unpalatable facts, is one which we would consider not only unsatisfactory but about which we would be prepared to do something practical and remedial, then we should not become associated with it. If it were possible for us, either in association with others or alone, to act quickly and effectively, we would wish to avoid any restriction on our freedom of action.

But if, as now appears probable, we will have no choice other than reluctantly to accept, whether by association or otherwise, the general results of the military defeat which is the dominant theme of the present phase of the Conference, then it may be that it should be our endeavor, at least from a long-term foreign policy point of view, not only to obtain through united diplomatic action as good a settlement as possible, but also to see to it, by participation in the guaranteeing of the settlement, that the other side is not tempted by the weakness and disunity of the opposition to violate the settlement reached. There will remain, after this Conference, important military and political assets in all three countries of Indochina which it will be to our interest actively to preserve.

I realize fully the considerations which make our association with the current weakness of the Franco-Viet Namese [sic] military and political position undesirable. However, I cannot escape the feeling that for us to disassociate ourselves from the harsh reality to which our friends are bowing would accelerate Communist momentum in Southeast Asia, decrease the prestige of the U.S. as a realistic, responsible and reliable ally in the long period of struggle ahead, and thus possibly discredit or weaken our capacity to conduct U.S. foreign policy.[90]

In a narrow sense, Smith's arguments proved futile. On July 21, hours after the Geneva conference adjourned, Eisenhower announced that the United States was "not prepared to join in the Conference declaration." Officially, the administration would have nothing to do with the partition of Vietnam. But Smith's line of reasoning was not without effect. The president agreed with much of Smith's argument for the necessity of accepting an arrangement the administration could not prudently change, and in his statement of July 21, Eisenhower declared that the United States would not "use force to disturb the settlement."[91]

In essence, Eisenhower straddled the issue. He implemented Smith's recommendation in a manner designed to create as little domestic controversy as possible. By saying that the United States would not overturn the Geneva settlement, and by adding that his administration would consider its violation by others a grave matter,[92] Eisenhower came close to guaranteeing the partition of Vietnam. But by not making a formal declaration of such a guarantee, he avoided giving hostages, in the form of millions of Vietnamese, to his conservative critics. It was a shrewd maneuver, and it worked. The anticommunist front in Southeast Asia stabilized for the remainder of Eisenhower's term in office; so, for the most part, did the anti–anticommunist front in the United States.

5

Robert Murphy and the Middle East Crisis of 1958

When Smith retired in the fall of 1954, Eisenhower still had a close personal contact in the State Department. The president had known Robert Murphy, the number-three man at State and the highest of the permanent officials, almost as long as he had known Smith; indeed, Eisenhower, Smith, and Murphy had spent much of World War II in each other's company. Though the bond between Murphy and Eisenhower never quite matched that between the two soldiers, the president greatly respected Murphy's abilities as a diplomat, and especially as a diplomatic troubleshooter.

On several occasions, Eisenhower sent Murphy, often with minimal instructions, to deal with crises abroad. He dispatched Murphy to Seoul in 1953 to persuade South Korean President Syngman Rhee to agree to a truce in the Korean War.[1] He directed Murphy to Belgrade in 1954 to get Tito to come to terms with the Italians regarding Trieste.[2] In 1956, at the beginning of the Suez crisis, Eisenhower threw Murphy into the rapidly opening breach between Washington and London. In the spring of 1958, he had Murphy shuttle between Paris and Tunis as a mediator in the Franco-Tunisian dispute of that year.[3] In 1960, he called Murphy from retirement to assess the uncertain situation in the Congo.

Murphy's most important mission for Eisenhower, though, occurred in the summer of 1958. A bloody coup in Iraq installed a potentially anti-Western regime there and signaled a probable deterioration of American influence throughout the Middle East. The government of Lebanon, the firmest of American allies in the region, felt especially endangered and requested protection. To secure Lebanon and the interests of the United States, Eisenhower sent fourteen thousand American troops to Beirut. To ensure that the troops achieved their goal, Eisenhower sent Murphy.

Murphy's assignment in the Middle East in 1958 paralleled in several ways his first action with Eisenhower: the North African invasion of 1942. In both instances, activities centered in Arab countries where French influence overlay the traditional culture. In each case, American forces entered a situation in which the degree of resistance they would encounter was unknown. Each time, political factors mattered as much as military ones in determining the success of the operation. In 1958, as in 1942, the United States worked closely with the British. Finally, in both Lebanon and North Africa, Murphy acted with an authority and an independence rarely granted to career officials in the State Department.

In the summer of 1940, following the signing of an armistice between Germany and the Vichy government of France, Franklin Roosevelt had summoned Murphy to the White House. Despite the Franco-German truce, Roosevelt hoped that France might be brought back into the war against Germany. To the Democratic president, North Africa seemed a likely place for the resistance to resume, especially after the appointment of General Maxime Weygand as commander of French forces in Africa. Weygand had been prominent in the defeat of the Germans in World War I, and Roosevelt did not believe he would continue to acquiesce in German domination of France.

In this White House meeting, Murphy soon discovered that Roosevelt had singled him out for the job he had in mind. A member of the Foreign Service since 1917, Murphy had drawn postings in Germany in the 1920s and France in the 1930s. Consequently, he knew the languages, politics, and national characteristics of the two antagonists. Furthermore, Murphy was a Roman Catholic, a circumstance Roosevelt thought useful for dealings with Murphy's coreligionists among the French. The president suggested, only half in jest, "You might even go to church with Weygand!" Roosevelt instructed Murphy to visit French North Africa and determine the likelihood of inducing the French there to return to the fighting, or at the least, to remain neutral. As the meeting ended, Roosevelt characteristically added, "If you learn anything in Africa of special interest, send it to me. Don't bother going through State Department channels."[4]

Murphy arrived in Algiers in December 1940, and he spent the next month traveling across the vast reaches of France's North African empire. He became convinced of the importance of the region's resources, and he was pleased to meet French soldiers thoroughly antipathetic to the Nazis. On this trip, he negotiated with Weygand a preliminary economic agreement, made final the following February, designed to provide American aid to French forces in North Africa that might someday be useful in fighting the Germans.[5] It was delicate business, made possible only by the facts that the United States remained legally a nonbelligerent, that the Nazis did not care to dispense with the facade of Vichy autonomy, and that Hitler had more pressing matters to worry about—most notably the impending invasion of Russia. Murphy sent Roosevelt his assessment of the situation confronting the United States in Africa, along with suggestions for improving the position of potentially pro-Allied French forces. Roosevelt studied the report, as he noted in the margin, "with great interest."[6]

Until the American entry into the war, and for several months thereafter, Murphy continued to organize fifth-column activities in North Africa, gaining a knowledge of affairs and personalities that made him Roosevelt's expert on the region. When the president decided in mid-1942 on North Africa for the first major American landing of the war, he naturally turned to Murphy. The tall, distinctive-looking Irishman disguised himself as "Lieutenant Colonel MacGowan," on George Marshall's advice that "Nobody ever pays attention to a lieutenant colonel," and he left for General Eisenhower's headquarters in London. Marshall sent along a strong endorsement; he told Eisenhower, regarding Murphy: "He has impressed me very favorably and can be of great assistance in developing the situation from both the political and civil administrative angles."[7] Eisenhower agreed with Marshall about Murphy. Following an intensive two-day briefing, Eisenhower replied, "I have the utmost confidence in his judgment and discretion and I know that I will be able to work with him in perfect harmony."[8]

Among other topics at this meeting, Eisenhower and Murphy discussed the problem of arranging with the French in North Africa not to oppose an Allied landing. While most of the French officers had nothing but bitterness and hatred for the Germans, many of them took quite seriously their oath of allegiance to Vichy leader Marshal Petain. In November 1941,

Weygand had been recalled to France, requiring Murphy to cultivate other French officials. Beginning in the late spring of 1942, Murphy established contact, through Admiral Raymond Fenard, with the French commander in chief, Admiral Jean Darlan. Discreetly, Darlan indicated that under certain conditions he would consider joint Franco-American military operations against the Germans. During the latter half of 1942, Murphy maintained close touch with Fenard, who later said of this period and the eighteen months that followed: "Mr. Murphy dined at my house on an average, I believe, of once a month for two years. I am sure you don't think we talked about moonlight."[9]

From the beginning, Murphy informed Roosevelt of Darlan's overtures, but the president committed himself to nothing. Only as the date of the landing approached and alternatives to Darlan became increasingly infeasible did Murphy receive permission to strike a deal. On October 17, 1942, Roosevelt authorized Murphy to initiate any agreement with Darlan that would, in Murphy's opinion, assist the military operations. Discussions continued for three weeks more, as Darlan hesitated and American officials continued to search for an acceptable alternative. The night of the invasion itself found Murphy in Algiers in the company of Darlan; only as American troops fought their way into the city did Darlan give the order to French forces to cease fire. In the course of the next few days, Eisenhower's deputy Mark Clark, and then Eisenhower himself, flew to Algiers to meet with the French admiral and close the Darlan deal.[10]

Though the bargain with Darlan would bring a storm of criticism down on Eisenhower, the Allied commander considered Murphy's role in the affair exemplary. On November 14, 1942, Eisenhower wrote to the combined American and British chiefs of staff that Murphy had done "a grand job."[11] The glowing reports reached Roosevelt, and a few weeks later FDR promoted Murphy, naming him his "personal representative in North Africa with the rank of Minister."[12] The arrangement suited Eisenhower; he wrote to Murphy, "It will be a pleasure to have you on this job as you are so familiar with the situation in the theater of operations."[13]

Murphy remained with Eisenhower through the campaign in North Africa and through as much of the fighting in the Mediterranean as Eisenhower directed. With Eisenhower, Murphy attended the 1943 Casablanca meeting of Roosevelt, Churchill, and the contending French generals

Charles de Gaulle and Henri Giraud. He continued as Eisenhower's political attache during the invasion of Italy, up to the moment when Eisenhower left for London to plan the assault on France. In parting, Eisenhower congratulated Murphy on a job well done. Referring specifically to Murphy's activities prior to the landings in North Africa, Eisenhower wrote, "All of the accomplishments of this Allied Force might easily have been impossible without the preliminary work that you carried on during the many months preceding November 8th of last year."[14]

Three months after D-Day, Murphy and Eisenhower met again, when Roosevelt selected Murphy to be Eisenhower's political adviser on German affairs. Though Murphy's posting to Germany occasioned criticism from individuals who thought he had been too easy on the Germans during his tour in Vichy France in 1940,[15] the president continued to be pleased with what he termed Murphy's "outstanding services."[16]

If some of Murphy's critics were unhappy to see him leave the Mediterranean for Germany, so were some of his friends. In Africa, Murphy had formed an amicable and effective working relationship with his British counterpart, Harold Macmillan. The friendship that developed between the two men might have seemed surprising, since by temperament and background they could hardly have been more different. The aristocratic Macmillan came to North Africa by way of Eton, Oxford, and the British War Cabinet. Murphy's roots lay in working-class Milwaukee, and his higher education consisted of business college and night law school. His first position in the Foreign Service had been as clerk in the American legation in Bern during World War I, where he had served with Allen Dulles; his assignment to North Africa marked the high point of a hitherto undistinguished career.

Macmillan required some time to warm up to Murphy. In July 1943, he wrote in his diary, "I really feel now that I have got Murphy pretty well in hand. I try to give him all the credit, and he is delighted with a two-column article in the *Express;* very laudatory about him."[17] For another half-year, Macmillan remained unimpressed. Upon hearing a rumor that Murphy was leaving for Washington, to become a liaison between the White House and the State Department, Macmillan commented condescendingly, "I can imagine no worse choice. He is a pleasant enough creature and amenable to kind and firm treatment. But he has neither principles nor judgement."[18]

Gradually, though, Macmillan's assessment of Murphy improved. At the end of June 1944, Macmillan noted, "He really is an excellent colleague."[19] By the time the news arrived that Murphy was definitely being transferred, Macmillan expressed genuine disappointment. "It is very sad that he will be leaving us. By and large he has been an excellent colleague and a cheerful and genial friend. His Irish characteristics have made him sometimes a little difficult to deal with, but he has been to me personally I think loyal and helpful."[20] Macmillan's opinion of Murphy continued to rise after the war, for as long as he knew him. In his memoirs, Macmillan wrote, "He was open and forthcoming. He was generous perhaps to the point of indulgence. He was fair-minded, ready to see both sides of a question."[21]

Murphy's assignment in Germany lasted through the end of the war in Europe. He attended the Potsdam conference in the summer of 1945; as the only member of the American military government in Germany present, he served as observer and spokesman for Eisenhower. Following Eisenhower's return to the United States, Murphy stayed in Germany as adviser to Lucius Clay, the military governor of the American occupied zone. Murphy was closely involved in the Berlin airlift of 1948, although his belief that the Soviet blockade should be challenged more forcefully nearly caused him to resign.[22]

From Germany, Murphy was shifted to Belgium in late 1949. He renewed his acquaintance with Eisenhower, then stationed in Paris as commander of NATO. The two shared war stories and indulged a common passion for golf.[23] In 1952, Murphy became the first postwar ambassador to Japan, a position he held until Eisenhower's inauguration as president.

When John Foster Dulles assigned the Tokyo embassy to John Allison, a Far Eastern specialist, he recalled Murphy to Washington. Murphy's first job in the State Department was as assistant secretary for United Nations affairs; added responsibilities brought a promotion to undersecretary for political affairs. Beyond this, Murphy could not reasonably expect to rise, since the only two higher posts at State commonly went to presidential appointees.[24]

As the top permanent official in the State Department, Murphy met frequently with decision makers at the highest levels of the Pentagon and the CIA, as well as the FBI and other arms of the executive branch. Murphy handled himself competently in the day-to-day administration of the department and in the ordinary course of policy formulation, but these activities fully engaged neither his strengths nor his particular interests. Dulles, for one, did not consider Murphy primarily a policy man; rather, the secretary most valued Murphy's skills as a diplomatic fixer. Roderic O'Connor, Dulles' administrative assistant, later commented that Dulles saw Murphy as "a man who could handle lots of fires."[25]

Eisenhower concurred in this judgment, and when fires broke out in various parts of the world during the president's two terms in office, he repeatedly turned to Murphy to douse or contain them. Before 1958, the most important of Murphy's assignments took him to London in the immediate aftermath of the Egyptian seizure of the Suez canal.

President Gamal Abdel Nasser announced his decision to nationalize the Suez company on July 26, 1956. The next day, Eisenhower received a cable from Prime Minister Anthony Eden, denouncing Nasser's action and declaring, "My colleagues and I are convinced that we must be ready, in the last resort, to use force to bring Nasser to his senses. For our part, we are prepared to do so. I have this morning instructed our Chiefs of Staff to prepare a military plan accordingly."[26] Eisenhower, while sympathizing with Eden, was alarmed that the British were thinking of using force against Nasser before attempting to talk the matter out. In response to Eden's message, Eisenhower replied, "Your cable just received. To meet immediate situation we are sending Robert Murphy to London."[27]

As often in emergencies like this, Eisenhower dispatched Murphy with little notice and less formal instruction. The president summoned Murphy to the White House, where he told him to fly to London "to see what it's all about." Eisenhower had no specific recommendations. "Just go over and hold the fort."[28]

Murphy arrived in London late on a Saturday night. Perhaps by design, Eden had left town, leaving Murphy in the hands of his old colleague and friend, Harold Macmillan, now chancellor of the exchequer. Macmillan invited Murphy to dinner, where he attempted to impress on him the seriousness of British purpose. If his government did not take strong action to meet Nasser's challenge, Macmillan said, "Britain would become another Netherlands." A second wartime acquaintance, Field-Marshal Lord Alexander, joined the two. Alexander predicted that an operation to return the Suez canal to international control "would not take much," only one or two divisions, and he said that it would all be over in ten days.[29]

Macmillan later remarked of this and subsequent meetings with Murphy, "We certainly did our best to frighten him, or at least to leave him in no doubt of our determination." To his diary he confided, "It seems that we have succeeded in thoroughly alarming Murphy. He must have reported in the sense we wanted."[30] Macmillan overestimated the alarm Murphy felt, but he correctly guessed that Murphy relayed to Eisenhower the degree of British determination. Earlier in the day, Murphy had met with French officials, who had their own reasons for wishing Nasser ill, and when he returned to the American embassy from his session with Macmillan he filed a report to the White House describing the depth of hostility toward Nasser among the governments of the two countries. This report convinced Eisenhower of the extreme gravity of the situation; the president decided that Foster Dulles ought to join Murphy in London.

Until Dulles arrived, Murphy continued to "hold the fort." He conspicuously failed to offer encouragement to the British and French in their aggressive designs, and by his failure he helped deter military action. After Dulles' arrival, Murphy naturally receded to a secondary role, but Eisenhower appreciated the job he had done. The president wrote later, "Murphy had been successful, for the time, in inducing both British and French leaders to relegate the idea of immediate use of force to the background, pending the outcome of a conference of affected nations."[31]

Eighteen months after the Suez affair, violence once more threatened the Middle East. The storm this time centered in Lebanon, but American observers again detected the influence of Nasser.

In April 1958, the State Department's Office of Intelligence Research and Analysis produced an assessment of what it labeled the "Political Crisis in Lebanon." The analysts at State began their report: "Serious threats have arisen to Lebanon's carefully contrived governmental stability, long based on a bargain among the dozen religious sects of the country distributing major political and administrative offices on a confessional basis." The immediate problem, according to the report's authors, arose from the possibility that Lebanese President Camille Chamoun, a Maronite Christian, would attempt to modify the country's constitution to allow himself a second consecutive term in office. "President Sham'un [Chamoun] is convinced of his own indispensability to the maintenance of the government's pro-Western policies and the preservation of the political predominance of Lebanon's Christian community." If Chamoun succeeded in getting his amendment, the results might be disastrous. "This maneuver could pull the keystone completely out of the delicate structure which has enabled Lebanon's Christians and Moslems to live peacefully together."[32]

Chamoun's reluctance to leave office was the proximate cause of trouble in Lebanon, but the underlying source of difficulty was the fact that Lebanon's Moslems did not share the president's Western orientation. The State Department report continued, "The country's Moslems, constituting at least half of the population, are increasingly restive under Sham'un's openly pro-Western policies and are strongly attracted to the new and larger currents of Moslem Arab nationalism as crystallized in the United Arab Republic." In State Department thinking, the U.A.R., a recent marriage of Egypt and Syria, represented the latest manifestation of Nasser's desire to create an Arab political force strong enough to challenge the status quo in the Middle East. The threat of Nasser was what prompted Chamoun to contemplate an action that would itself tend to destabilize Lebanon and the Christian position there. "Sham'un is convinced that only under his guidance can Christian predominance in Lebanon be maintained and that this predominance can be assured only by joining hands with the West in opposing President Gamal Abd-al Nasir's [Nasser's] pan-Arab expansionism."[33]

The State Department paper noted that not all of Chamoun's fellow Christians supported the president; it described a growing split within the Christian community between supporters of Chamoun and those of the commander of the Lebanese army, Fuad Chehab. The latter, also a Maronite, had refused to assure Chamoun of the army's support if the president's political designs led to an insurrection, as seemed likely. Chamoun wanted to fire Chehab, but he judged such a move potentially dangerous. "Sham'un . . . reportedly has been considering the dismissal of Shihab [Chehab], but . . . Shihab's popularity among all Lebanese is so great that such a move could spark the crisis."[34]

The crisis seemed nearer in the wake of a visit by Nasser to Damascus, which had attracted what the State Department described as a "pilgrim-age" of sixty-five thousand Lebanese Moslems. Reports of Syrian arms shipments to Lebanon added to American concerns, as did alleged Syrian involvement in terrorist attacks against the Chamoun regime. American officials believed that a direct announcement of Chamoun's candidacy for another term might well set off "a new and more serious wave of UAR-directed terrorism."[35]

Such was the assessment of the State Department in mid-April. During the next two months, the situation in Lebanon deteriorated. On May 10, the American ambassador, Robert McClintock, reported street fighting in the northern city of Tripoli;[36] a few days later the revolt spread to Beirut, and Chamoun began to explore the reaction of the Eisenhower administration to a request for military intervention. Chamoun had reason to expect a favorable response; by the so-called Eisenhower Doctrine of 1957, the president had declared his intention to support friendly governments in the Middle East, with troops if necessary. Eisenhower told Chamoun that he would indeed consider intervention, but not to secure another term for him and only with the concurrence of at least one other Arab state.[37]

Before Chamoun made a formal request, however, the conflict died down. A stalemate ensued, with the country divided between regions held by Moslem insurgents and other territory under the control of the govern-ment. Through the middle of June, fighting remained sporadic. The appar-ently senseless character of some of the violence amazed Ambassador McClintock. On June 20, he described the shooting of an unarmed worker near his car by a Christian militiaman. The soldier explained that the worker might have been carrying a bomb. McClintock was no stranger to turbulent situations; his previous assignments included experience of wars and revolu-tions on four continents. But on this gratuitous killing, McClintock could only comment, "Result: No bomb, one dead laborer."[38]

McClintock did note some cause for optimism in late June. An Ameri-can reporter, after an interview with Chamoun, told the ambassador that the Lebanese president had said that he "never had any plans to seek to amend the constitution to stay in office six more years."[39] Shortly thereaf-ter, Chamoun declared publicly that he did not intend to serve beyond the end of his term in September. On July 12, McClintock reported to Wash-ington that General Chehab would probably succeed Chamoun.[40] The worst of the crisis appeared over.[41]

But in fact it had yet to begin. Two days later, on the morning of July 14, 1958, reports reached Washington of a coup in Baghdad, in which Iraq's pro-Western King Faisal and Premier Nuri as-Said were overthrown—later it was learned that they had been brutally killed—and a military junta thought to favor Nasser seized power. In Lebanon, radio broadcasts from Cairo and Damascus called on opponents of the Chamoun regime to rise in similar fashion against the reactionary anti-Nasser forces in Beirut.[42]

The Baghdad coup shook Chamoun and his colleagues. The Lebanese foreign minister, Charles Malik, later declared unequivocally, "Lebanon's life was at stake."[43] Chamoun himself immediately summoned McClintock and demanded American intervention. "Well, you see what's happening? Lebanon is in real danger. It was in real danger, but you couldn't see it as clearly as you can see it now. Now I want your assistance. . . . I want an answer within twenty-four hours. Not by words—but by action."[44]

The Eisenhower administration required a good deal less than twenty-four hours to decide on strong measures. Shortly after news of the Iraqi revolt arrived in Washington, a small group of top officials from the State Department, the Defense Department, and the CIA met to assess the impact of events in Baghdad on the American position in the Middle East. The two Dulles brothers, Robert Murphy, and Nathan Twining, chairman of the Joint Chiefs of Staff, agreed that the administration had to act swiftly. If not, they believed, Nasser would take over the whole area. American bases in the Middle East would be placed in jeopardy, and the United States would generally lose influence in the region. Around the world, American dependability would be called into question.[45]

A short time later, Eisenhower convened a session in the Oval Office. As the president later described his thoughts:

This was one meeting in which my mind was practically made up regarding the general line of action we should take, even before we met. The time was rapidly approaching, I believed, when we had to move into the Middle East, and specifically into Lebanon, to stop the trend toward chaos.[46]

Eisenhower listened to Allen Dulles' intelligence report and to Foster Dulles' political assessment to make sure that nothing had been overlooked; then he turned to Nathan Twining and asked, "How soon can you start, Nate?" To Twining's reply that preparations could begin immediately, Eisenhower responded, "Well, what are we waiting for?"[47]

When Eisenhower spokes of "chaos" in the Middle East, he meant something specific. During World War II, he had personally experienced the dependence of modern armies on oil; he never forgot the lesson. Throughout his presidency he remained sensitive to the possibility that the West might lose access to Middle Eastern oil. "We have come to the crossroads," Eisenhower told Richard Nixon in the wake of the Baghdad coup. "Since 1945 we have been trying to maintain the opportunity to reach vitally needed petroleum supplies peaceably, without hindrance on the part of any one." The president suspected that Nasser was fomenting trouble in the Middle East in order "to get control of these supplies—to get the income and the power to destroy the Western world."[48]

Others in the administration shared Eisenhower's suspicions about Nasser. Shortly after the White House meeting, the president, Allen Dulles, and John Foster Dulles met with a score of congressional leaders to explain the situation confronting the United States and to sound out legislative opinion regarding intervention. Allen Dulles, in describing the possibility of a military coup in Beirut to remove Chamoun, left no question as to the source of unrest in Lebanon. "The hand of Nasir has been clearly apparent." The secretary of state concurred in this assessment, stressing the propaganda that Nasser had been directing against Chamoun. "In Lebanon," he said, "Cairo has been whipping up sentiment and calling for violence by radio."[49]

At this meeting, the secretary went on to weigh the options open to the administration. First he explained the costs of intervention. "If we go in," Dulles said, "our action is likely to accentuate the anti-Western feeling of the Arab masses." This would be true despite the fact that "the governments of many of the neighboring states would probably like us to intervene. However, their leaders do not dare to say so." Dulles continued, "Our intervention would not therefore be likely to be a quick and easy solution. . . . While we will probably be able through the presence of our forces to hold Lebanon's independence, we would be drawn into the area and it is not clear how we could withdraw." Dulles did not think, however, that intervention would create much danger of confrontation with the Soviet Union. If the United States moved "quickly and decisively," he said, he doubted that "the Soviets would risk general war." "Their long-range missiles are not ready, and they are far inferior in long-range air-craft." Certainly, Dulles said, the Kremlin's "violent propaganda" against the United States would continue, but he expected nothing more threaten-ing from Moscow.

Dulles then turned to the probable results of not intervening. "The first consequence of not going in," he asserted, "would certainly be that the non-Nasser governments in the Middle East and adjoining areas would be quickly overthrown." This included Lebanon. "It does not appear that we can hold Lebanon free if we do not go in." Perhaps the most serious result of failing to intervene would be the effect of such a failure on American allies throughout the world. "Elsewhere, the impact of our not going in—from Morocco to Indochina—would be very harmful to us. Turkey, Iran and Pakistan would feel—if we do not act—that our action is because we are afraid of the Soviet Union. They will therefore lose confidence and tend toward neutralism."

Dulles concluded that the administration had little choice but to inter-vene. "If we do not act," he said, "we will have to take losses greater than if we do. We would soon be faced with a stronger Soviet Union, with a worsened and weakened situation on our side."[50]

Following the meeting with the legislative leaders, Eisenhower made the final decision to send in the marines. The president gave the order to Twining on the afternoon of July 14, and within a matter of hours the first wave of troops hit the beaches of Beirut.[51]

Robert Murphy was involved primarily as an observer in the decision to send troops to Lebanon. He had been following the situation in the Middle East with concern, and he shared the general attitude of the administration regarding the meaning of events there. A few years after the fact, Murphy told an interviewer:

I firmly believe that the Russians were doing their utmost to use Nasser for the purpose of the extension of their power and influence in this area, and that they were also trying to—and did—insert the Iraqi Communist party in that disorderly situation with the idea of gaining political capital and increasing their power and influence—fishing in troubled water.[52]

Until July 16, however, Murphy had no special responsibility for the Middle East. Indeed, during the first two weeks in July, his attention focused on a more mundane matter: pending legislation regarding passports. Murphy was testifying on the subject before the Senate Foreign Relations Committee when he received a telephone call from Dulles. The secretary of state directed Murphy to excuse himself; the president wanted him to prepare immediately to leave for Lebanon.[53]

To various individuals in the administration, Murphy seemed the prime candidate for the Lebanon mission. Nixon had called Dulles to suggest Murphy; the vice president told the secretary that Murphy would put "a peaceful touch" on the intervention.[54] Dulles, in turn, had recommended Murphy to Eisenhower.[55] As Dulles candidly told Murphy, he considered him "the best fellow we've got" for the job.[56] From the president's perspective also, Murphy was the obvious choice. Perhaps Eisenhower noted the parallels between the landing in Lebanon and the invasion of North Africa in 1942; perhaps not. In any event, Eisenhower understood that Murphy was just the person to make certain that American troops achieved their objective with as few casualties as possible. The political situation in Lebanon was confused, but hardly more confused than affairs had been in North Africa at the time of the Torch operation. The key to the landing in Lebanon, as in North Africa, was to persuade the locals not to resist.

Furthermore, Eisenhower wanted someone on good terms with the British. Chamoun had requested help from Britain as well as from the United States; meanwhile, Jordan's King Hussein, threatened by the same Nasser-inspired radicalism that had toppled his cousin Faisal in Iraq, began looking to London and Washington for assistance. Harold Macmillan, now prime minister, favored a joint Anglo-American operation in support of Chamoun and Hussein. Eisenhower demurred. The president did not wish to widen the American intervention, and he wanted to minimize the likeness of the Lebanese landing to the British invasion of Egypt eighteen months earlier. British leaders, of course, caught the parallel. In response to Eisenhower's rejection of a common effort, Macmillan remarked wryly, "You are doing a Suez on me."[57]

Eisenhower's refusal of military collaboration resulted in a division of labor: American marines went to Beirut, British paratroopers to Amman. The division of labor, however, extended only to deployment. Over the next several weeks, Washington and London cooperated closely in mutual diplomatic and logistical support. As matters turned out, relations between the United States and Britain remained friendly throughout the double intervention; Murphy's friendship with Macmillan proved to be unredeemed insurance. Such Anglo-American cooperation in the Middle East was hardly inevitable, though, as the events of 1956 had demonstrated, and Eisenhower wanted to make sure that he was covered.

Having decided to send Murphy to the Middle East, the president summoned the veteran diplomat to the White House. Murphy was probably not surprised when Eisenhower offered no specific guidelines. Murphy later recalled, "My oral instructions from the President were conveniently vague, the substance being that I was to promote the best interests of the United States incident to the arrival of our forces in Lebanon."[58]

By the time Murphy reached Beirut, American forces there included nearly seven thousand troops, with tanks, armored amphibious vehicles, and howitzers with atomic capability. An initial confrontation between American troops and Lebanese forces, largely due to the suddenness of the invasion,[59] had been prevented from developing into open combat by the quick action of Ambassador McClintock, who persuaded General Chehab to interpose himself between his own men and the advancing American column.[60] With the military situation apparently under control, Murphy argued against expanding American activities to other parts of Lebanon, and he turned his attention to the political aspects of the occupation.[61]

For his first task, Murphy chose to visit the leaders of the various factions in Lebanon in an effort to reassure them regarding American motives. Because the Eisenhower administration had sent troops at Chamoun's request, the Lebanese opposition naturally suspected the United States of intervening in Lebanese affairs for the purpose of maintaining Chamoun in office. Murphy sought to dispel this belief through talks with rebel leaders, in spite of the obvious annoyance that such talks provoked in Chamoun. The Lebanese president grew uncomfortable when Murphy began meeting with the opposition; Chamoun later remarked of Murphy's discussions with the insurgents, "It didn't help our relationship."[62]

Murphy's initial contact with the rebels took place in an old section of Beirut that was a stronghold of Moslem irregulars. Murphy attempted to procure an escort from General Chehab, but the latter was reluctant to send any of his troops into the neighborhood. Fortunately, Murphy ran into a friend from the North African days, more recently a consultant to the Arabian-American Oil Company. William Eddy, an American naval attache in Tangier when Murphy was laying the groundwork for the Torch invasion, was fluent in Arabic and had contacts among the rebels. After Eddy arranged a meeting, Murphy explained to the insurgents the peaceful intentions of the United States. He insisted that the Eisenhower administration was not interested in the personal fortunes of Chamoun, but only in the independence and security of Lebanon. As evidence of the friendly nature of the American intervention, Murphy cited the fact that not a single person had been killed in the landing of troops. By way of emphasis, he alluded to the atomic weapons at the disposal of the American commander, pointing out that if the U.S. forces chose to be unfriendly, they could level Beirut within a matter of minutes.[63]

During the next several days, Murphy met with Druze leaders and with representatives from the Moslem forces in the north. He repeated his statement that the Eisenhower administration did not aim to extend Chamoun's tenure; the United States sought only peace. Again the American military presence underlined his remarks. When the marines first landed, McClintock had reported, "Opposition forces seemed stunned."[64] Murphy concurred, saying later, "The shock of American intervention was very great for them. I think the impact of American force, the way it was used, on the Arab mind was one of the best things that we possibly could have done."[65]

From a substantive standpoint, an important part of Murphy's job involved ensuring that Chamoun did not change his mind about another term. In conversations with Murphy, the Lebanese president disparaged the loyalty and competence of Chehab, his likely successor. Chamoun declared the Lebanese army infested with elements "bought by Nasser," and he doubted the will and ability of Chehab to control these subversives.[66] Ultimately, however, Chamoun became convinced that the Americans really did not intend to keep him in office, and he moderated his stance. When he threw his support to Chehab, Murphy believed that a peaceful resolution of the crisis would quickly follow. Murphy never quite understood Chamoun's motives; he later commented, "I felt that he was the victim of his own political excesses and that he had overreached himself in the brambles of Lebanese politics." Still, when Chamoun announced his decision to step down, Murphy did not ask his reasoning; he diplomatically congratulated the Lebanese president on an honorable choice.[67]

While Murphy calmed affairs in Lebanon, the Eisenhower administration worried about the situation elsewhere in the region. In certain respects, Lebanon was the least of the administration's problems. It remains very much open to doubt whether military intervention was required to prevent a civil war in Lebanon and to preserve that country's independence. As noted above, Chamoun had announced before the American landings that he would not succeed himself. Indeed, one immediate and unintended result of the American intervention was to cause rebel leaders to conclude that Chamoun, with American encouragement, might be going back on his word. As soon as Murphy explained that the United States did not favor a second term for Chamoun, much of the impetus immediately behind the insurrection dissolved. As Murphy said later, "Once they became convinced of that and the Lebanese were able to find a compromise candidate in the person of General Chehab, who was acceptable to both sides, we had the answer to the problem."[68]

Undoubtedly the Eisenhower administration could have indicated its decision not to support Chamoun, and to back Chehab, without landing fourteen thousand troops in Lebanon and sending the seventy ships and forty thousand men of the Sixth Fleet to patrol the country's coastline. In fact, the primary purpose behind the show of force was symbolic: to impress leaders of the region and of the world with the administration's determination to protect Western interests in the Middle East. Consequently, Murphy's assignment did not end when he left Beirut at the end of July. From Lebanon he traveled to several other countries, amplifying and interpreting the message of the intervention.

His first stop was Jordan. In the wake of the Iraqi coup, the CIA had described the position of King Hussein as extremely precarious. Hussein had uncovered an antigovernment plot, designed by pro-Nasser officers in the Jordanian army; he had arrested forty of the conspirators. Still Allen Dulles said, "The position of King Hussein hangs in the balance."[69] In

Amman, Murphy arrived at a similar conclusion. As he later described Hussein's predicament:

His little kingdom was surrounded by revolutionaries in Iraq, rival Arabs in Syria, Jews in Israel, none of whom Hussein could trust. There were twenty-five hundred British soldiers camped outside the capital city; Jordan had only a slender supply line running through difficult terrain to the Gulf of Aqaba; half a million Palestinian refugees were superimposed on the country's own population; there was practically no money in the till.

Murphy found Hussein's courage in the face of these daunting odds impressive. "King Hussein surely had a stacked deck against him, but he would not abdicate." Murphy offered moral support to Hussein, but not as much diplomatic backing as the Jordanian king desired. Hussein told Murphy that he hoped that the United States would not officially recognize the new government of Iraq. For Hussein, recognition was a personal matter, as the Kassim regime had been responsible for the murder of Hussein's cousin. Murphy took note of Hussein's request, but he could do no more. He had already been informed that the Eisenhower administration, seeking to encourage Baghdad toward the West, would announce its decision to recognize Kassim the following day.[70]

Murphy next visited Israel, where he found Prime Minister David Ben-Gurion intensely suspicious of Nasser. On the day of the Iraqi coup, the CIA had predicted that Israel might occupy the West Bank to deepen its defenses.[71] During Murphy's visit to Tel Aviv, Ben-Gurion declared that if Nasser's forces threatened to capture Jordan, by subversion or other means, Israel would feel obliged to seize the West Bank regardless of international consequences. Knowing that Murphy was on his way to Cairo, Ben-Gurion pointedly remarked that he hoped Nasser had no illusions about Israel's intentions or its ability to put them into practice.[72]

Before he went to Egypt, Murphy flew to Baghdad to assess the situation in Iraq and to ensure that the country's new rulers did not misread the American presence in Lebanon. The trip proved worthwhile; Murphy found Kassim convinced that the Lebanon intervention portended an invasion of Iraq. Murphy sought to disarm Kassim's distrust by pointing out that his flight to Baghdad had taken him across hundreds of miles of Iraqi desert. He reminded Kassim that the American president was a soldier himself, and he asked good-naturedly why Eisenhower would want to send troops to invade the "Godforsaken stretches of Iraq." Kassim smiled. Murphy then voiced certain worries of his own. He commented on the large number of Russian soldiers in Baghdad who seemed to be working closely with the Iraqi Communist party. Kassim responded by assuring Murphy that he and his fellow officers had not risked their lives making a revolution just to become puppets of Moscow. To Murphy's expression of concern that Nasser might have an undue influence in Iraqi affairs, Kassim replied that his country was not about to become dependent on Egypt either. Murphy found Kassim's declarations persuasive; he later commented that when the general spoke of Nasser his voice took on a "quiet ferocity."[73]

From the beginning of the crisis, as noted above, the matter of oil had been central to administration thinking. Foster Dulles had feared that American intervention in Lebanon might prompt the destruction of oil pipelines from the Persian Gulf to the Mediterranean.[74] At a White House meeting on July 20, Middle East expert George Allen had suggested that in order to keep the oil flowing, the United States would have "to learn to live with" the various Arab nationalists. Eisenhower had replied that the issue was clear: "We must win them to us or adjust to them."[75] This concern over Iraqi oil had been an important factor behind the swift recognition of the Kassim government.

Therefore Murphy listened with great interest as Kassim said that he had told Nasser that there must be no interference with the oil pipelines across Iraq. Murphy was even more pleased when Kassim announced that his government intended to increase oil shipments to the West by at least fifty percent. On the whole, Murphy thought that the United States could live amicably with the new regime. When he left Baghdad, Murphy took away the conviction that Kassim was "grimly determined" to maintain Iraq's independence.[76]

Murphy had not initially intended to stop in Cairo, but while in Beirut he had received a request from Nasser for a meeting. Following the landing of American troops in Lebanon, the Egyptian leader had made a quick trip to Moscow, presumably to determine the Kremlin's reaction to this new development. When a forceful Russian response failed to appear, Nasser apparently decided that he should consider working toward better relations with the United States.

Such, at least, was the interpretation Murphy placed on his invitation to Cairo, and a five-hour conversation with the Egyptian president did not dispel it. Murphy found Nasser to be at once a realist and sentimentalist. As expected, Nasser considered American policy in the Middle East distorted in favor of Israel. He recognized, however, that little could be done about the situation, and when Murphy brought up the subject he merely shrugged his shoulders and passed to another topic. But when the conversation turned to Britain and past foreign control of Egypt, he became extremely sensitive. "It seemed to me that Nasser enjoyed indulging in national self-pity," Murphy said, "He made emotional references to the three centuries of Turkish rule and the seventy-five years of British domination over downtrodden Egyptians."

Murphy explained the position of the Eisenhower administration regarding the intervention in Lebanon. Nasser seemed to accept Murphy's statement that the administration had no plans to send troops beyond that country, and he declared his friendly intentions toward the Chehab government.[77] In the course of the conversation, Murphy discovered no reason to question Nasser's motives and devotion to the Arab cause, and he believed that Nasser had the best interests of the Egyptian people in mind. Murphy suspected, however, that Nasser had unleashed forces in the Middle East he could not control. "I left," Murphy said, "with a feeling of uneasiness about the pressures on Nasser which could lead to methods not conducive to peace."

From Cairo, Murphy returned to the United States by way of Addis Ababa, where he delivered Eisenhower's good wishes and reassurances to Ethiopian Emperor Haile Selassie, and England, where he compared notes with Britain's Middle East hands. Murphy landed at New York, arriving in time to brief Eisenhower for a UN speech defending American actions in preserving peace in Lebanon and the surrounding area.[78]

Murphy's 1958 journey to the Middle East was his last major journey for Eisenhower. Seventeen years after his first mission with the Allied commander in North Africa, Murphy decided in 1959 to retire.

Eisenhower, however, did not want to let him go. Planning a good-will tour of Asia and Africa for the end of 1959, the president told Murphy that he needed a political adviser. Murphy offered little resistance; he agreed to stay on for the extra months the trip required.[79]

Even this turned out not to be the president's final call on Murphy's services. In the summer of 1960, Eisenhower summoned Murphy from retirement for a mission to the Congo. Officially, Eisenhower charged Murphy with conveying America's congratulations to the newly independent nation. Unofficially, he directed Murphy to assess the personalities and prospects of the leading contenders for power there, especially Patrice Lumumba. In light of Murphy's experience as a behind-the-scenes operator, and considering what the administration was planning for Lumumba, the assignment made a fitting end to Murphy's career.[80]

III
Agitators and Agents

6

C. D. Jackson: Psychological
Warriors Never Die

The individuals sketched thus far all occupied positions in the main chan-
nel of the adminisration's foreign policy process. Smith and Murpy stood
downstream from the Dulleses and Milton, but they too had a major
impact on administration policy. In a different, more marginal, category
were C. D. Jackson, Harold Stassen, and Henry Cabot Lodge. Relegated
to the periphery of the policy process, they served two purposes: to bring
new ideas and fresh approaches to administration diplomacy, and to act as
agents of influence with groups the administration sought to cultivate.

By temperament and experience, C. D. Jackson was ideally suited to his
role as bureaucratic provocateur. An inveterate optimist, Jackson made
friends easily and lost them rarely. His activities as Eisenhower's special
assistant for psychological warfare required him to intrude into the spheres
of some of the most territorial individuals in the administration, but he
almost never bruised egos or raised hackles. He possessed one of Washington's lowest batting averages, in terms of ideas accepted and put into
practice, but he seldom let failure discourage him from swinging away his
next time up.

Jackson had seen his first action in psychological warfare, and had first
worked with Eisenhower, in 1943 in North Africa. Following a successful
mission to Turkey for the Bureau of Economic Warfare, during which he
had managed to persuade the Turks to modify a strategic metals agreement

with Germany, Jackson was appointed deputy director of psychological warfare for Allied forces in the Mediterranean. His primary qualification for the job, aside from a knowledge of Europe and its languages acquired during travels as a young man, was an inventive self-confidence developed as a protege of Henry Luce of the *Time-Life-Fortune* chain. Jackson brought to his task a mind that spawned ideas—the stock in trade of a psychological warrior—at an astonishing rate, and a personal self-confidence that refused to waver in the face of rejection or failure of his plans.[1]

Jackson reveled in his work in North Africa. He later described his tour of duty there as "an absolutely fascinating assignment."[2] Jackson savored the excitement of the war and the challenge of matching wits with the Nazis. For a psychological warrior—especially for a novice like Jackson— these were heady days. Psychological warfare, which defied close definition but included anything that might create an atmosphere favorable to the conduct of war or diplomacy, was an immature art and one that afforded great opportunities for a newcomer with Jackson's ingenuity and drive. More important, the psychological warriors enjoyed a great deal of freedom in practicing their tricks. In the context of total war, there were few restrictions, beyond considerations of effectiveness, on what they might attempt.

Jackson soon convinced Eisenhower of the value of psychological warfare; when the general left the Mediterranean for England, he took Jackson along. The eighteen months that followed constituted the most satisfying period of Jackson's career as a psychological warrior. His job involved softening the will of German forces to oppose the Normandy invasion and providing aid and comfort to the French resistance. He succeeded sufficiently to win the Legion of Honor from the government of liberated France.

With the war's end, Jackson, like many a mustered-out soldier, found life after victory to be rather tame. He rejoined Luce at *Time*, but he kept his eyes open for opportunities to maintain his psychological warfare skills, especially as it became clear that the end of the war did not mean the advent of peace. Appointed by Luce to the job of establishing international editions of *Time* and *Life*, Jackson became involved in psychological warfare against the communists on a small scale: he promoted capitalism and its bourgeois values by disseminating as many copies of his magazines as possible into countries like Czechoslovakia before the Iron Curtain slammed down.[3]

As the cold war deepened, Jackson saw life growing more interesting again. The communist coup in Czechoslovakia in 1948 prompted him to say, "We seem to be right in the thick of it again, only this time I feel that the issues are somewhat clearer to the U.S. than they were in 1939/40."[4] An increasing conviction of Moscow's malign intentions reinforced Jackson's activist inclinations. As the crisis in Eastern Europe intensified, his hopes of action against the Russians heightened. In May 1948, Jackson wrote with undisguised satisfaction: "Maybe it's Spring, maybe it's the Marshall Plan, maybe it's the Italian elections—but whatever it is, the U.S. is flexing its muscles, and not too stupidly at that."[5]

Jackson's hopes for a forceful American response did not last long. The Truman administration took less-decisive action than he thought necessary against what he considered unmistakable evidence of the Soviet Union's aggressive designs. Jackson's impatience mounted through the Berlin blockade and the communist victory in China. In late April of 1950, he vented his frustration in a letter to a wartime friend:

The sinful ignorance of great sections of the American people of what the Russian implications are is utterly incredible. I am furious at the simpering crowds of fuzzy-headed, self-styled Liberals fascinated by this Russian mystery, totally oblivious of the fact that they will be the first ones stood up against a wall and shot if Communism were ever to take over in this country. And this despite the fact that the only honest thing about the Russian has been his repeated dress rehearsals, open to the public, of exactly what will be done, and how it will be done, when he takes over. It was the same thing with Hitler, who even went to the trouble of writing a book about it, and we still didn't believe.[6]

Out of boredom and exasperation, Jackson decided to take on "the hammer and sickle boys"[7] personally. Receiving a leave of absence from *Time* in 1951, he assumed leadership of the National Committee for a Free Europe (NCFE), an ostensibly independent, in fact CIA-funded, organization responsible for operating Radio Free Europe. For a year, Jackson worked closely with the CIA, then headed by Walter Bedell Smith, and with various Eastern European refugees, directing the broadcast of counter-communist propaganda to countries of the Soviet bloc.[8]

Eisenhower's election in 1952, which Jackson abetted as a speech writer, raised the possibility that he might once again practice psychological warfare on an official basis. Jackson had been paying close attention to American efforts in his specialty; he held no higher opinion of Truman's efforts here than he did of Democratic diplomacy generally. In 1951, Truman had established the Psychological Strategy Board. From the beginning, bureaucratic backstabbing had plagued the PSB;[9] as Jackson explained the situation to Eisenhower in December 1952, psychological warfare fell into the domains of four separate agencies or departments in addition to the PSB: the CIA, the State Department, the army, and the air force. "These organizations are highly competitive—in fact to the point of sabotage." A lack of leadership from the White House encouraged the saboteurs. "The real reason for this fratricidal warfare is not so much mutual dislike or empire-building ambitions as it is the realization that the Government of the U.S. has neither policy nor plan for conducting the cold war."[10]

A month later, Jackson offered his remedy for the situation. By this time Eisenhower had accepted the idea of improving coordination among the various offices engaged in psychological warfare. By this time, too, he had decided that Jackson would play a central role in the coordinating. The president's confidence in Jackson's abilities had not lessened since the war; if anything, Jackson's activities with Radio Free Europe and on the Eisenhower campaign team had increased his respect. Jackson therefore enjoyed a certain freedom to define his position in the new administration; in a letter to White House chief of staff Sherman Adams, Jackson outlined what he would require:

As you have had a chance to observe during the campaign, I don't generally need or ask for titles or trappings in order to get a job done. However, the Washington jungle is a more devious place to operate than the corridors of the Commodore [Eisenhower's campaign headquarters], and therefore whatever prestige can be bestowed would be of great practical value in the way of giving me the necessary leverage. . . . To elaborate on this idea a little more, the source of all real influence is, of course, the White House. Therefore, I feel that White House identification . . . is absolutely essential in order to initiate action.[11]

Jackson got his White House identification, and within weeks of Eisenhower's inauguration, he took up his post as the president's special assistant for psychological warfare. The problem of institutional reorganization remained, however, and Eisenhower turned this task over to a special commission headed by William Jackson, an intelligence veteran who had assisted Allen Dulles in critiquing the CIA in 1948. C. D. Jackson sat on the (William) Jackson Commission; officially he represented the State Department—an early indication of his skill at getting along with John

Foster Dulles—while informally he represented the president. In the meantime, he managed such psychological warfare operations as could not wait until the Jackson Commission submitted its report. In late February 1953, Jackson described his activities to an associate:

I figure that I wear three hats.

(1) Membership on the Jackson Commission as the designee of Secretary Dulles—a gay Tyrolean number to be tossed away in May or June when the Commission winds up its affairs.

(2) Hat number two is a somewhat more formal affair—grey snap brim—which has to do with the day-to-day emergencies and even the longer-term plans which simply cannot wait until May or June for the Jackson Commission findings. In other words, the show must go on while we are attempting to convert the operation to something new and different and more dynamic. A part of this activity is simply to be available as guide, counselor, or needler as the case may be.

(3) Hat number three is a really serious affair—midnight blue homburg—and this consists in constantly informing and persuading the members of the Government as to their cold war responsibilities. This is a really tricky one, because if badly handled it simply results in my attempting to push my betters around, which would have negative instead of positive results. I have to be forceful, and yet I must not use my elbows or give the impression that I am too big for my britches.[12]

By midsummer of 1953, Jackson managed to doff hats one and two. Following the Jackson Commission's recommendation, the PSB disbanded, replaced by the Operations Coordinating Board. Comprising representatives from the State Department, the CIA, the Department of Defense, the Foreign Operations Administration (which handled foreign aid), and the White House, the OCB assumed the task of coordinating psychological warfare operations.[13] Jackson, in midnight blue homburg, represented the White House.

Jackson discerned the first big chance to put his psychological warfare ideas into practice while the Jackson Commission remained at work. On March 4, 1953, he listened with excitement to reports that Stalin lay dying. For Jackson, the news had a double edge. "This morning's developments, both in Moscow and in Washington, point up both a great need and a great opportunity," he wrote to Robert Cutler, Eisenhower's assistant for national security affairs. "As to the need, it is hardly an exaggeration to say that no Agency of this Government had in its files anything resembling a plan, or even a sense-making guidance, to cover the circumstances arising out of the fatal illness or death of Stalin."[14]

After describing, with annoyance tempered by the knowledge that more competent hands now held the controls, what the different offices should have done in advance of such an eventuality, Jackson went on to analyze the nature of the opportunity. "During the present moment of confusion, the chances of the Soviets launching World War III are reduced virtually to zero, and will remain in the low numbers so long as the confusion continues to exist." That being the case, Jackson asked, "Shouldn't we do everything possible to overload the enemy at the precise moment when he is least capable of bearing his normal load?" He added hopefully, "It is not inconceivable that out of such a program might come further opportunities which, skillfully exploited, might advance the real disintegration of the Soviet Empire."[15]

Jackson had been striving for the "disintegration of the Soviet Empire"— liberation, in other words—since he had decided half a decade earlier that Russia was the new Germany and Stalin the new Hitler. Now, scarcely six weeks in office, the opportunity arose "to win World War III without having to fight it," as he liked to say in describing the goal of psychological warfare.[16] Small wonder he felt excited.

Jackson mentioned to Cutler some specific steps to put pressure on the communists. He suggested hardening the American negotiating position in Korea. He recommended more forceful action against the Arbenz government in Guatemala—what he described as "tipping the wink to Trujillo and El Salvador and the Guatemalan exiles that we won't interfere in case some trouble should start spontaneously." He said he had already described "a nasty idea or two" to his friends at Radio Free Europe. Finally, as a more comprehensive approach to the situation, Jackson advocated the establishment of a National Security Council task group to survey the administration's options and "to report not with theories, but with an all-embracing plan."[17] When the task group came together, Jackson and the other members produced some additions to his original list—among them, the broadcast of reports to the Soviet Union and China highlighting strains between the two leading communist states, and an offer of one hundred thousand dollars to the first Soviet MiG pilot who would defect, with airplane, to the West.[18]

Not everyone in the administration shared Jackson's gung-ho spirit.

The CIA agreed that Stalin's death made the Soviet Union especially vulnerable to psychological warfare,[19] and the Department of Defense approved several of Jackson's proposals,[20] but the State Department objected that the aggressive pursuit of a psychological warfare campaign would likely backfire. "Indeed," wrote Walter Bedell Smith, "the adoption of such a course at this time would probably tend to assist the new regime to consolidate its position and might thus prevent the later emergence of opportunities which could be exploited."[21]

Although Smith transmitted the message that State wanted nothing to do with Jackson's psychological warfare offensive, the message itself originated with John Foster Dulles. The secretary of state was backing away from the campaign promises of liberation; he recognized that a serious attempt to detach satellite states from the Soviet orbit entailed a risk of general war, and he refused to take the chance. Moreover, Dulles had basic reservations about the practice of psychological warfare generally. His cautious instincts told him to move slowly and carefully, and only over ground well surveyed in advance. Psychological warfare was by nature opportunistic; when conducted by enthusiasts like Jackson, it was the antithesis of the style that Dulles had discovered to be effective in his four decades of diplomatic experience.

Dulles' resistance coincided with a belief on Eisenhower's part that the moment called for reducing tensions, not cranking them up. Already Stalin's successors talked of peaceful resolution of disputes, and world opinion was responding positively. The United States, the president felt, could not afford to appear less interested in peace than the Russians.

Admitting failure, Jackson quickly retreated to Eisenhower's side. He silently buried his provocative suggestions, and he devoted the next month to helping the president and speech writer Emmet Hughes produce what many judged the most effective oratorical exercise of Eisenhower's career: the "Chance for Peace" address of April 16, 1953.[22]

For Jackson, setbacks merely heightened the challenge of the game. He responded by getting on to the next round. And there always was another round, for Jackson constantly had new approaches and novel plans to try out. Even had his own brain lacked fertility—which it never did—the contacts he had developed through his travels, through *Time*, through the

NCFE, and through the expansiveness of his personality would have kept him well supplied with psychological warfare suggestions.

In the late spring of 1953, riots broke out in East Germany. Walt Rostow, whom Jackson had met the previous year through NCFE and who was then at the Center for International Studies, a CIA-funded think tank at the Massachusetts Institute of Technology,[23] wrote Jackson that the German situation afforded a psychological warfare opening. "The East German revolt means that the chances of unifying Germany without major war have vastly increased," Rostow declared. He reasoned that the Soviets now had to consider East Germany militarily insecure, perhaps disposing them to relinquish control over the country. Rostow suggested that the United States propose a demilitarization of Germany. Though he doubted that the Kremlin would accept, he thought the idea would be valuable from a propaganda perspective. "The main point is this: the Russians may, of course, refuse our evacuation proposals; but I think we should try them first to give us a sound moral and political basis for moving on to the encouragement of full scale revolt."[24]

Jackson did not want to go quite so far as that. Pressuring the Soviets was one thing, but urging a full-scale revolt was something else, especially after the chilly response his ideas for exploiting Stalin's death had received. Rostow might be willing to risk war with the Soviet Union over East Germany, but Jackson was not, if only because he had learned that Eisenhower was not. A month later, he explained the predicament in which he and the rest of the administration found themselves:

The big problem we face when we call for action behind the Iron Curtain is the extent to which we are willing to back that action if serious trouble develops. It would be both immoral and inefficient to provoke massacres, which would not only kill off the best men, but would also destroy our position in the minds of the people behind the Iron Curtain.[25]

The problem Jackson described defined the limits of psychological warfare in peacetime, and it should have ended his hopes for liberation. The basic issue was how far psychological warfare could go before it became real warfare. During World War II, when Jackson had won his spurs, the problem did not exist. Total war meant that nothing was off limits. But the cold war, to the extent that it was a war at all, was a limited war. Psychological warriors like Jackson had as much trouble adjusting to this fact as did regular soldiers like General Douglas MacArthur. They might say the right words, as Jackson did in the above passage, but often the words did not sink in. For Jackson, the failure to draw the correct conclusions from the premises he admitted to be true would lead to increasing frustration.

But that was later. In the meantime, there was much to be done. As he concluded the above letter: "I do not want you to think that we are being overwhelmed by the negative aspects. Quite the contrary."[26]

Since psychological warfare comprised such a nebulous field of activities, Jackson often took liberties in domains tenuously related to foreign affairs. As if Attorney General Herbert Brownell did not have enough to worry about regarding the convicted atomic spies Julius and Ethel Rosenberg, Jackson suggested making "one more try to crack" them. Jackson worried about the bad press the United States was receiving overseas. An acquaintance in France reported the feeling there: "Real democracies do not execute spies in peacetime." Jackson's contact added that the United States was heading for its "greatest psychological loss since the end of the war."[27] Hoping to gain incontrovertible proof of the Rosenbergs' guilt as well as information about their Soviet contacts, Jackson offered a plan "to get some really skillful Jewish psychiatrist . . . to insinuate himself into their confidence during these next thirty days, and if they did show signs of coming along, a stay of execution for another thirty or sixty days could be arranged while the work progressed." Jackson assured Brownell, who apparently felt he did not need any more advice on the subject:[28] "I am sure you understand that my interest is not in saving the Rosenbergs. They deserve to fry a hundred times for what they have done to this country."[29]

Wandering into another bailiwick, Jackson suggested at the time of the East German riots that the secretary of labor issue a statement challenging Soviet allegations that American instigation lay behind the German unrest and asserting instead that the violence resulted inevitably from communist-imposed slavery. Timed to coincide with the release of a report by the International Labor Organization on forced labor around the world, the statement would say something on the order of: "Slaves will always eventually rise. It is the Communist system which has within itself the seed of its own destruction—forced labor, slavery." Among the same lines, Jackson proposed for Western Europe a "Slavery Week," or "*La Semaine de l'Esclavage*," or "*La Settimana delle Schiave*," or whatever was appropriate in the languages Jackson did not speak. The idea behind each recommendation, and a principle basic to the conduct of psychological warfare, was to keep the enemy off balance and on the defensive.[30]

Sometimes, however, the people thrown off balance fought on Jackson's own side of the cold war. The State Department, especially, eyed Jackson warily. Jackson tried to disarm the suspicions of Foggy Bottom critics who considered him a dilettante by admitting that their apprehensions were only natural: "I can fully appreciate the instinctive irritation of a large number of intelligent, conscientious, seven-days-a-week, fifty-two-weeks-a-year professionals at what may appear to them to be a one-shot, off-the-top-of-the-head effort by some ad hoc enthusiasts."[31] Jackson's candor did little to calm the misgivings at State, especially on the part of Dulles. It did have some effect, though; at the personal level, Jackson and Dulles got along well.[32]

Jackson added to his troubles with the professional diplomats by proposals that sometimes bordered on the hare-brained. Late in 1953, for example, he recommended that the administration offer to establish official diplomatic relations with the Soviet Ukraine, in an attempt to call the Kremlin's bluff regarding repeated assertions that the various republics in the Soviet Union were autonomous and sovereign.

With gusto, State Department analysts drew and quartered Jackson's scheme. Such a plan, they said, would antagonize the ethnic Russians and give the impression that the United States was following a separatist policy toward the Soviet Union. It would reinforce Moscow's claim that the various Soviet republics actually did govern themselves. It would lend support to the Soviet assertion that the republics had the right to enter into relations with other states. Finally, it would run afoul of the American Congress, which was not about to recognize another communist country. To all of this, Jackson could only reply, "Okay, you win."[33]

Proposals like the above fostered a belief among some State Department veterans that Jackson listened too much to Eastern European exiles whose political agenda had little in common with the interests of the United States. George Kennan offered Jackson some fatherly advice on emigres. Kennan warned, for instance, that a number of persons who passed themselves off as Ukrainian patriots were not Ukrainians at all, but Poles and Ruthenians whose backgrounds included collaboration with the Nazis in the 1930s. "I feel sorry for these people, and understand the reason for their restlessness," Kennan wrote, "but honesty compels me to face the fact that they are probably selling the U.S. Government a dangerous bill of goods."[34]

Jackson, of course, knew that many of the exiles with whom he dealt were something less than they tried to appear. In a letter to Henry Cabot Lodge at the United Nations, Jackson related a questionable proposition recently outlined to him by a group of Rumanians. "This is typical," he said, "of the kind of 'end run' they are always trying to pull." Jackson divided emigres into two categories: the "nice, honest, but slightly gaga," and the "conniving."[35] The fact remained, however, that Jackson thought the exiles might be useful. To a much greater degree than did the State Department, Jackson believed that the United States and the exiles might usefully make common cause.

For all the friction and difficulties of his first eight months in the White House, Jackson refused to be disappointed. In September 1953, he summarized his view of the world situation and the outlook for psychological warfare. In a memorandum to Eisenhower, Jackson described "several important victories in the cold war," including the truce in Korea, the overthrow of the Mossadeq government in Iran, and the electoral victory of Konrad Adenauer in West Germany. All this added up to "a tremendously significant change in the world atmosphere—a change in our favor," which outweighed some minor reverses. Looking to the future, Jackson declared to the president:

If we are willing to view these developments as something more than the routine ups and downs of foreign affairs; if we can see them as a coherent whole instead of as disconnected victories and defeats; if we are willing to see the present position as one from which a series of favorable chain reactions might be started, I believe that great progress can be made rather faster than we might suspect, or than will be possible if we fail to grasp this moment as one during which the fly-wheel of history has slowly begun to turn in our favor.

Jackson asserted further, "We stand at a moment of greater opportunity than we could realistically appraise since 1946." He added, however, with a note of urgency that would become his trademark, "These moments do not last forever."[36]

Jackson's moment at the White House did not last forever, either. In the early spring of 1954, he returned to New York to *Time*, as he had planned when he took the White House job. Had his psychological warfare recommendations elicited a more positive response from the president and the State Department, perhaps he would have delayed his return to a more remunerative private life. As it was, Jackson hardly considered his role as advocate of psychological warfare at an end.

Leaving Washington on friendly terms with Eisenhower—as indeed with everyone with whom he had worked—Jackson remained in close contact with the administration. The president would recall him several times during the next six years to work on speeches and give advice at critical moments. Always Jackson would press for a more vigorous psychological warfare campaign against the Soviets. Almost always he directed his recommendations to Eisenhower, for he believed that only the president could make psychological warfare successful. He expressed his views in a letter to Eisenhower shortly after his departure: "No individual, or committee, or agency engaged in this work, can get anywhere unless they are constantly aware of the fact that *you* are setting the climate, and *you* want something done."[37]

Jackson did not leave the White House without some achievements to his credit. In addition to his efforts on the "Chance for Peace" address, he played a central role in coordinating the delivery of the diplomatic initiative that centered on the president's "Atoms for Peace" speech at the United Nations in December 1953. The idea of an address on the nature of war and peace in the atomic age had been bouncing around the administration for most of a year. Following an article in *Foreign Affairs* by the former head of the Manhattan Project, J. Robert Oppenheimer, calling for candor on the part of the American government regarding the threat that modern weapons posed to humanity, Eisenhower handed Jackson the assignment of writing a speech in reply. Eisenhower and Jackson hoped that the American people, once apprised of and presumably sobered by the stakes in the nuclear game, would support an administration arms control initiative.

Jackson worked up several drafts, trying to achieve just the right combination of grim facts and hopeful possibilities. Neither came easily, especially when the Pentagon and the Atomic Energy Commission opposed revealing the size of the American nuclear arsenal and Foster Dulles resisted the basic idea of disarmament. Still, Jackson pressed on, with the president's support. Through the autumn of 1953, he led a series of break-fast meetings—which gave rise to the code name "Wheaties" for the project—that resulted ultimately in Eisenhower's offer to contribute fissionable material to an international atomic stockpile.[38]

In the development of the offer, Jackson served primarily as a mediator between the White House and the various departments and agencies concerned with national security and atomic energy. As the date of Eisenhower's UN address approached, Jackson augmented this role by adding the duties of chief propagandist, and he set to work orchestrating the accompaniment to the president's featured performance in New York. A week before the speech, Jackson headed a working group that put together a twenty-six-point checklist for ensuring that the address achieved maximum psychological impact. Jackson and his associates assigned individuals and offices the task of providing background interviews for domestic and foreign news correspondents, with special attention given to selected columnists and commentators. They drafted instructions for American missions overseas regarding communications with presidents, premiers, and foreign ministers. They furnished scripts to American-sponsored radio networks, acknowledged and otherwise. They briefed cabinet officers and lesser administration officials on appropriate responses to anticipated questions. They laid plans for planting favorable articles in journals like *Foreign Affairs* and for letter-writing campaigns from foreign-born Americans. They organized a campaign to have the "Atoms for Peace" speech chosen "Story of the Year" by the Associated Press, and they promoted Eisenhower for the Nobel Peace Prize.[39]

Not all of the ideas came to fruition, of course. Jackson did not expect that they would. Still, he found the results of the operation gratifying. Several months later, after a follow-up announcement specifying details of the proposed American atomic donation, Jackson expressed his satisfaction to a friend:

The Soviets have never been over a more formidable barrel, for what they are now faced with is a really black and white situation, the kind they hate. Either they have got to pony up some fissionable material, which they don't want to do (and maybe they haven't got so much of it), or they have got to stand revealed before the whole world as an enemy of mankind—and on the absolutely unassailable issue of Atoms-for-Peace.[40]

Jackson's pleasure at the success of the "Atoms for Peace" initiative was offset during most of 1954 by a fear that the United States was suffering losses in another theater of the psychological war with the Russians. The economic offensive mounted by the post-Stalin Kremlin worried many persons close to Eisenhower, but none more than Jackson. By April 1954, Jackson felt that the Soviet edge in economic aid had reached a critical stage, creating a perception of a vacuum in Washington. "The realization of this particular vacuum in our leadership has suddenly begun to gain momentum abroad," Jackson wrote to Dulles, "and if the realization is allowed to progress for many more months, we will be making the temptation of Russian economic and trade blandishments almost irresistible not only many of our precariously balanced friends, but even to some of our very good friends."[41]

The problem of Soviet seduction in aid, Jackson believed, followed from a more fundamental liability inhibiting American psychological warfare operations. Because the United States, he thought, had been slow to recognize the nature of the communist threat in the late 1940s, by the time the American response came, it had to be, for the most part, a military response. The war in Korea, the formation of NATO, and American support for the rearming of Germany afforded examples. Meanwhile, the Soviet Union, which in reality engaged in indirect aggression and war by proxy, spoke in soothing tones about its great desire for peace. The result was an inversion of reality in the eyes of the world. "While the Soviets were capitalizing on the repetition of the symbols of peace while actually waging war," Jackson stated, "we were forced to capitalize on the symbols of war while actually trying to preserve the peace." Recent news that American hydrogen bomb tests had created clouds of deadly radioactivity worsened the predicament. "The curse was almost off the A-bomb—which was just about to be accepted as the newest conventional weapon—when the H-bomb went off, and people said to themselves, 'This one we cannot live with; there must be some other way.' "[42]

What Jackson was leading up to was his other way: a program of economic aid inspired by the Marshall Plan, which Jackson considered a brilliant, if insufficiently exploited, piece of psychological warfare. Working from analyses and projections devised by Walt Rostow and Max Millikan at MIT's Center for International Studies, and others, Jackson promoted what he called a World Economic Plan. From the standpoint of economics, WEP consisted primarily of a program of directed investment in underdeveloped areas, costing the United States something in the vicinity of ten billion dollars in loans over five years.[43] From the perspective of psychological warfare, WEP represented an effort to wrest the peace initiative back from the Soviets by proving, in Jackson's phrase, "that the Free West offers more than the Communist East."[44]

Jackson tended toward single-mindedness. He once told friends, "I always seem to be a monomaniac on something."[45] Between 1954 and 1956, WEP became his *idée fixe*, supplanting even liberation, which he had shelved temporarily for lack of support. Furthermore, he suffered from chronic impatience; every moment, he thought, was the moment of truth. In the autumn of 1955, Jackson wrote of the continuing Soviet economic offensive in Asia: "The pistol is at our heads in India, Burma, Japan, and portions of Southeast Asia." He related in detail various Soviet advances in winning clients, noting, among other things, that Burma's U Nu was "making economic goo goo (gu gu) eyes at Moscow." With the characteristic flair that ensured an audience for his memos, if not always support for his schemes—and with an interpretation slightly at odds with his earlier analysis to Dulles—Jackson continued:

The moment of decision is on us in a great big way on world economic policy. So long as the Soviets had a monopoly on covert subversion and threats of military aggression, and we had a monopoly on Santa Claus, some kind of seesaw game could be played. But now the Soviets are muscling in on Santa Claus as well, which puts us in a terribly dangerous position.[46]

Jackson's crisis-mongering, in this case, produced results in the White House. Other voices joined his in favor of a more liberal foreign aid policy, and by the beginning of Eisenhower's second term, the president had begun seeking larger appropriations from Congress. The requests were not all that Jackson desired, and Congress balked at granting them.[47] By that time, however, Jackson's attention had turned elsewhere, back to the notion closest to his heart.

From 1954 to late 1956, while he had been playing the liberation theme only softly, Jackson never lost touch with his contacts in Eastern Europe. In November 1954, Jackson wrote a letter to CIA director Allen Dulles reporting unrest in Hungary. Some of Jackson's exile friends had told him that communist leaders in Budapest felt so threatened that they were publicly minimizing the communist aspect of their rule and emphasizing its nationalist character. They no longer flew the red flag; they replaced the "Internationale" with the Hungarian anthem. Behind these changes stirred a widespread popular campaign of sabotage and passive resistance to communist rule. "We know how to do these things," Jackson quoted his Hungarian source. "We used to do it all the time to the Hapsburgs."[48]

Unrest in Hungary persisted until October 1956, when it became open revolt. Precipitating the Hungarian revolt was a concurrent challenge to Soviet control in Poland. To Jackson, the simultaneous rising of two satellite states seemed to offer the possibility of a renewed psychological warfare offensive, even after the Soviet army suppressed resistance in both countries. "Aggressive, imperial Communism received a terrible blow in the one-two punches of Poland and Hungary," Jackson wrote, in a letter to the White House. "Their close to two-million-man military and paramilitary organizations in the satellites were conclusively revealed as unreliable for the purposes of their Soviet masters. The international mystique and omnipotence of Communism was sorely cracked if not shattered."[49]

But Jackson believed that for the United States to capitalize on the opportunity required dramatic action. He recognized that the administration could not intervene militarily in Hungary,[50] and he was sensitive to the charges of trigger-happiness sometimes leveled at psychological warriors. Earlier, while offering recommendations for encouraging unrest in East Berlin, Jackson wrote, "May I add that I am not suggesting an airlift of 75mm. recoilless rifles, which is what I have been accused of."[51] But in the Hungarian crisis, Jackson was dismayed that Eisenhower seemed willing only to scold the Kremlin. In a telegram to the White House at the height of the crisis, Jackson said, "Regret to say there is absolutely no popular sex appeal in writing letters to Bulganin." Contending that Eisenhower alone of Western leaders could credibly challenge the Soviets on Hungary, Jackson argued that the "ghastly situation" in Hungary would not be resolved unless the president stood "toe to toe against the Kremlin gang." As a minimum response, Jackson urged an appearance by Eisenhower at the United Nations to call for censure of the Soviet Union; more appropriate would be the breaking of diplomatic relations with Moscow.

"I recognize this has disadvantages," Jackson commented, "but don't let anybody tell you it means war."[52]

Jackson could not ignore the complications caused by the concurrent crisis in the Middle East. A "Devil-sent diversion," he called it. He objected, however, to Eisenhower's evident desire to deal with the Suez troubles first. "The Middle East is our weak flank; Eastern Europe is the Soviet weak flank; and if we concentrate all our efforts on our own weak flank and do not exert any simultaneous pressure on theirs, we have in effect been sucked in to playing their game on their field in accordance with their timing."[53]

Jackson's arguments did not convince Eisenhower, though the president was moved by the obvious depth of Jackson's feelings. "I know that your whole being cries out for 'action' on the Hungarian problem," Eisenhower replied. "But to annihilate Hungary, should it become the scene of a bitter conflict, is in no way to help her."[54]

For one of the relatively few times in his career, an unsatisfactory turn of events managed to appreciably diminish Jackson's natural ebullience. "As one psychological warrior to another," wrote Jackson to an old associate, "I will admit to a certain sense of frustration these days. The tragedy of Hungary haunts America, and yet so far we have limited ourselves for all practical purposes to arm-waving at the Russians." Still, Jackson did not despair. Eastern Europe had again proved insecure for the Soviets. "The Kremlin," he declared, "has been rocked to its foundations."[55]

For the next two years, Jackson continued to urge the administration to take strong action on Hungary. By early 1957, the tactic he had adopted was to advocate the expulsion of the pro-Moscow Kadar government of Hungary from the United Nations. Jackson apparently thought this the strongest move Eisenhower might countenance. In arguing for expulsion, Jackson described to Allen Dulles an unease he claimed Americans felt at inaction regarding Hungary.

American has a definite sense of malaise about Hungary, ranging all the way from embarrassed self-consciousness to a real guilt complex. American wants *action* in the case of Hungary, and feels frustrated because it realizes how pitifully few are the possible, reasonable, feasible, courses of action. The denial of credentials to the Kadar representatives at the UN would be the kind of action that America craves, and would receive national and virtually unanimous enthusiastic applause.[56]

Despite Jackson's arguments, Eisenhower refused to support expulsion. The president contended that consistency would require an attempt to expel the Soviets, since the Budapest regime was no less representative than the government in Moscow.[57]

Jackson was upset and disheartened. His counsel unheeded at the White House, he again confided in Allen Dulles. "As you know to your sorrow," Jackson wrote, "every now and then I build up a sufficient head of steam on something or other to blow in the form of a letter to you. Here we go again."[58] Turning to Allen Dulles came naturally to Jackson. Their professional spheres overlapped; the CIA's covert operations followed logically from Jackson's psychological warfare activities, in much the way that overt military operations had traditionally extended diplomacy. The psychological warrior and the spy chief both relished the intrigue and conspiratorial atmosphere surrounding clandestine activities; each considered his work part of an absorbing, if deadly serious, game. In certain respects, Jackson and Dulles saw the cold war as an opportunity to recapture the excitement of what had been in many ways the high point of their lives: World War II. For Dulles, this meant a resumption of espionage work; for Jackson, it involved a return to psychological warfare under Eisenhower.[59]

Jackson, therefore, could expect a sympathetic hearing from Dulles when he wrote, as he often did during 1958 and 1959, of the desirability of "hotting up" Eastern Europe and resurrecting liberation. During the Berlin crisis of that period, for example, Jackson wrote to Dulles:

We have just about run out of acts by which to give the Soviets pause. Even getting a third or a half of SAC [Strategic Air Command] in the air no longer has the bite it once had. But there is one thing that still haunts the Kremlin, and that is a general uprising in the Eastern European satellite belt. Were we really smart in abandoning the policy of liberation and carefully never mentioning the word again? But smart or not, shouldn't the word and the concept be very skillfully revived now? I know that we suffered a terrible setback in Hungary. But now our own backs are considerably closer to the wall. . . . It seems to me that the re-infiltration behind the Iron Curtain of the concept of liberation would be the most powerful deterrent that we could exert short of World War III.[60]

Dulles could commiserate, but he could do little to alter the fact that the administration had buried liberation long before. Eisenhower had made it plain on several occasions, most emphatically in 1956, that he wanted nothing to do with the idea. When Jackson spoke of resurrecting liberation, therefore, no one listened.

But Eisenhower never shunned Jackson personally, though he ignored most of Jackson's advice. Jackson was easy to like, and the president liked him. Eisenhower was not one to cut off old friends, especially those he had known from the war. Besides, Jackson wrote good speeches; to the end of his presidency, Eisenhower valued Jackson's skill at turning phrases. And Jackson had important contacts among right-wingers who distrusted the administration's internationalist and Eurocentric tendencies. Of this group, Jackson's boss at *Time*, Henry Luce, probably possessed the greatest potential for causing trouble, through his conservative views and the wide audience his magazines reached. Jackson served as an agent in hostile territory; to have alienated Jackson would have gained nothing and risked much.

Even more important, Eisenhower valued Jackson's advice. Though he usually chose not to act on it, the president thought it had salutary effects. By challenging the ideas of the State Department and the Pentagon, Jackson provoked discussion and sharpened administration policy. Eisenhower especially counted on Jackson to present views at odds with the more cautious approach of John Foster Dulles; Jackson's presence kept Dulles on his toes. At one point early in 1958, Eisenhower went so far as to offer Jackson a job in the State Department as a replacement for disarmament adviser Harold Stassen. But when Dulles, recognizing Eisenhower's game, opposed the plan, the president let the matter drop.[61]

Despite Jackson's access to the president, the administration continued to reject his ideas. He grew increasingly impatient at Eisenhower's failure to reconsider liberation. In the middle of 1959, Jackson wrote a long letter to Eisenhower, describing his frustration at administration policy and asking whether the president still believed in psychological warfare. Perhaps because he had had so little luck recently in promoting psychological warfare, Jackson used the alternative and slightly narrower term "political warfare."

The following has been boiling up in my mind over quite a number of months. Possibly you wish that I would sit on the lid and forget about it. . . . My concern has to do with the attitude of the Administration toward this thing we call "political warfare." Over the last eighteen months I have become increasingly aware of either a lack of interest, lack of understanding, or even positive dislike of the practice of political warfare.

Jackson thought it ironic that he should be writing such a letter to Eisenhower.

After all, it was you, first in North Africa and later in SHAEF, who almost alone among our top military characters understood that psychological warfare was a positive weapon to be used along with the other weapons in your arsenal. . . . It was you who . . . set up the so-called Jackson Committee . . . to explore the problems and possibilities of political warfare. . . . It was you who . . . created the post of Special Assistant to the President with a portfolio in political warfare.

To this personal appeal, Jackson appended his familiar refrain: "I feel as I have never felt before that the 'moment of truth' has come in political warfare."[62]

Unfortunately for Jackson, the "moment of truth" had come, and gone, several years before. Jackson's basic problem was that he and Eisenhower had fundamentally different conceptions of the usefulness of psychological warfare in peacetime. In 1953, the president had remarked, "Psychological warfare can be anything from the singing of a beautiful hymn up to the most extraordinary kind of physical sabotage."[63] Although Eisenhower as Allied commander in Europe in World War II had allowed his psychological warriors to demonstrate the full range of their virtuosity, Eisenhower as president insisted on keeping them closer to the hymn-singing end of the spectrum. Eisenhower did not object to strong action in achieving American goals; his approval of CIA-directed coups in Iran and Guatemala, for example, indicated that where the benefits of intervention promised to outweigh the costs, he supported a vigorous approach. But in the Soviet sphere of Eastern Europe—the focus of Jackson's attention and designs— the president realized that any similar intervention was out of the question.

And intervention was what Jackson's calls for liberation were all about, though Jackson refused to admit it. Despite his disclaimers that he was not suggesting air drops of recoilless rifles, if liberation meant anything at all it included the willingness to back agitation with force. Once the Soviet tanks started rolling, as Hungary demonstrated they would, the United

States would face the choice of intervening or watching the destruction of those whose revolt it had encouraged.

Jackson's frustration with Eisenhower's cautious policy followed from his failure to think through to the consequences of his calls for "hotting up" the satellite states. Jackson was an intelligent and generally perceptive individual; the failure of his analysis in this case is not easy to explain. Probably it resulted from a combination of an action-oriented temperament and a desire to relive the days when psychological warriors knew few restraints. In addition, through his work with exiles from the Soviet bloc at Radio Free Europe and elsewhere, Jackson had become personally involved in their troubles; to a large degree he took their cause as his own. In doing so, he lost his sense of proportion and most of his influence with the president.

7

Harold Stassen and the
Perils of Disarmament

From his own experiences in World War II, Dwight Eisenhower knew well the horrors of modern war. Largely because of this, he believed that one of his major responsibilities as president was to work to ensure that another such war—or, in the atomic age, a war far worse—not occur. Three months after his inauguration, Eisenhower delivered the "Chance for Peace" address, which outlined an alternative to a continuing arms race. He followed this at the end of 1953 with "Atoms for Peace," a call for nuclear cooperation rather than confrontation. Eisenhower offered these initiatives and others like them—the Open Skies proposal of 1955, for example—in part for their propaganda value, of course. But their function as propaganda, domestic and foreign, should not obscure the fact that they embodied some of Eisenhower's deepest convictions. The president sincerely hoped that superpower relations might reach a point where arms control, and even disarmament, would become possible.

But the possibility of a reduction of arsenals repeatedly foundered on Eisenhower's belief in a moral imbalance between the United States and the Soviet Union. "We must consider the factor," Eisenhower wrote C. D. Jackson, "that atomic weapons strongly favor the side that attacks aggressively and by surprise."[1] While the United States would never strike first, the Soviets might; thus the United States could not let down its guard. Responding to an individual who expressed disappointment at the lack of progress toward disarmament, Eisenhower wrote:

Do you not ignore completely in your discussion the central fact of an almost religious commitment in the Soviet Russian mind to the eventual extinction of our political system and way of life, to be achieved by military means if other methods fail? This country has repeatedly offered a sensible proposal which would lead to complete and total disarmament. Every time such an offer has been made, the Russians have flatly refused cooperation.[2]

Events never convinced Eisenhower that he could achieve a reasonable disarmament agreement with the Soviet Union. But neither did they persuade him to stop trying. Halfway through his first term, as international pressure mounted for an end to nuclear testing, which threatened the world with radiation-induced maladies of undetermined severity, Eisenhower decided to give arms control top priority.[3] He created the position of special assistant to the president for disarmament, whose occupant would have official access to the president through cabinet rank, and physical access via an office in the White House. For this position, Eisenhower selected Harold Stassen.

Bringing to his new job a record as a solid administrator, Stassen also brought a reputation for self-promotion. In the late 1930s and early 1940s, Stassen had been a young, bright star in an aging and generally dim Republican firmament. Barely past thirty, he had been elected the youngest governor in Minnesota's history; by 1944 he was considered a possibility for the Republican presidential nomination. Four years later he made a spirited but unsuccessful run against Thomas Dewey. By 1952, some of the luster had rubbed off; his chances for the top spot on the GOP ticket seemed slim as the convention approached. There remained, however, a possibility that a deadlocked convention, unable to choose between front-runners Eisenhower and Robert Taft, would turn to the still-appealing ex-*wunderkind*. The deadlock never occurred, partly because Stassen—as he repeatedly reminded Eisenhower later—threw his support and that of the Minnesota delegation behind Eisenhower's candidacy at the decisive moment.[4] Later Stassen claimed that he had considered himself a stand-in for Eisenhower during the early phases of the 1952 campaign; he said he had intended to "hold the ramparts" while the reluctant candidate made up his mind.[5]

Following Eisenhower's nomination, Stassen had not ingratiated himself with certain elements of the Republican party by his prompt advice that Richard Nixon resign when reports emerged of irregularities in the vice-presidential candidate's financial past. Stassen shared good company on this issue, though, and after Nixon survived the affair Stassen's standing with the president-to-be remained firm. Stassen was capable—Nixon himself conceded that[6]—and he had a large following among young party moderates. Eisenhower, always looking for able administrators and for ways to rejuvenate the party, thought Stassen a promising person to bring into the new administration.[7]

Eisenhower first placed Stassen in charge of the Mutual Security Agency; later the president shifted him to the Foreign Operations Administration. Each office held purse strings for foreign aid. Stassen acquitted himself well in these positions, which required the ability to elicit cooperation from the many departments and offices involved in economic diplomacy, although his style proved longer on energy and imperviousness to criticism than on charm. He made some enemies,[8] but strong-minded people usually do. When Eisenhower chose to phase out the FOA and transfer its responsibilities to the State and Defense departments, he gladly sought another job for Stassen.

The elimination of the FOA coincided with Eisenhower's decision to renew the administration's focus on arms control. The president wanted a person who could gather assorted ideas relating to disarmament into a unified and presentable program. Eisenhower described what he had in mind in a letter to Stassen in March 1955. "You are aware of my conviction that some individual, on behalf of the President and the State Department, must develop within the Administration and the nation and also before the world a firm and single basic policy toward the question of disarmament." The director of such an effort would have to combine bureaucratic toughness with a polished public presence. "I feel that such an individual must not only be a coordinator and spokesman within the Administration, but must also spearhead efforts to inform and instruct the American people in the basic factors affecting this vital subject."[9]

Stassen replied with the usual professions that he would of course be honored to serve the president in any capacity. In fact, he did not think much of the idea, for he was not ready to consign the FOA to the bureaucratic boneyard. A few months before, as the FOA's rivals in the State and

Defense Departments began to close in, Stassen had kept them at bay by resurrecting an old proposal for an Asian Marshall Plan. In the aftermath of the French defeat in Indochina, the notion stirred considerable interest within the administration and thus offered the possibility of a reprieve for the FOA. At the time he received the telegram from Eisenhower inviting him to become special assistant for disarmament, Stassen was stumping Pakistan publicizing the new Asian aid fund.[10]

But Stassen's hopes for keeping the FOA alive proved vain. Some in the State Department accused him of grandstanding with talk of a Marshall Plan for Asia, which naturally conjured images of billions of dollars in American grants. State had no such sweeping plans, and department officials knew that neither did the Treasury or Congress. By his loose talk, Stassen raised expectations and guaranteed that whatever aid finally did emerge from the appropriations process would seem miserly.[11]

As time ran out for the FOA, anti-Stassenites at State hoped that they had seen the last of him. They interpreted Eisenhower's offer of a position in disarmament as a polite way of easing Stassen out. Robert Murphy later recalled, "When he was offered the job, I don't believe anybody expected that he would accept it." Murphy thought Eisenhower intended for Stassen to turn the job down. But the critics midjudged their man. Murphy continued, "To everyone's surprise he accepted it."[12]

Stassen assumed his new duties on March 19, 1955, and he lost no time in setting to work. Stassen's opponents admitted his dynamism; they took it as evidence of overweening ambition. "He grabbed the ball and ran very hard with it," Murphy said. "He was determined that he was going to get a disarmament agreement to which the name of Harold Stassen would be attached."[13] Not surprisingly, Murphy and his colleagues at the State Department looked with little favor on Stassen's enthusiasm. As he charged forward, they dug in their heels.

Stassen's principal antagonist was John Foster Dulles. For three years the two contested for the direction of America's disarmament program, clashing over matters of bureaucratic turf and diplomatic philosophy. In important respects, Stassen and Dulles represented the two strains in Eisenhower's thinking on arms control: hopefulness and suspicion. This accounts, at least in part, for Stassen's relative longevity. While Eisenhower remained undecided about disarmament, he sought to ensure that he heard both sides of the issue.

On bureaucratic grounds alone, Dulles would have found Stassen's presence threatening. Dulles recoiled at the thought of a new competitor in the foreign policy field. Walter Bedell Smith and C. D. Jackson had challenged Dulles' hold on the president's attention, but they had been persuaded to leave. Now the secretary had to put up with someone else. Dulles especially distrusted Stassen's self-advertising tendencies, and he cringed at the thought of a politician, even one who had demonstrated his skill as an administrator,[14] dabbling in a field as sensitive and fraught with hazard as disarmament. Nuclear strategy was a perilous game; the brink was no place for amateurs.

Philosophically, Dulles thought disarmament an idea whose time had not come. Three months after Stassen began his new job, and a few weeks before the Geneva summit conference, the chief public promoter of massive retaliation recorded in a personal memorandum his reasons for considering disarmament ill-advised. In the first place, Dulles noted, such credibility as massive retaliation possessed depended on the perceived ability of the United States to respond to Soviet provocation with overwhelming force; any agreement that diminished America's retaliatory power diminished that credibility.[15]

Second, Dulles had in mind other uses than deterrence for the American nuclear arsenal. He believed that the United States could translate strategic superiority into diplomatic advantage. Dulles reckoned that in any arms race the Soviet Union would be no match for America; the United States could spend the Russians into submission:

Our economic base, almost equal to that of all the rest of the world together, can support indefinitely the high cost of modern weapons. . . . The Soviet bloc economy cannot indefinitely sustain the effort to match our military output, particularly in terms of high-priced modern weapons. Already there is evidence that the Soviet economy is feeling the strain of their present effort and that their leaders are seeking relief.

The United States ought to make clear how the Russians might achieve relief: by engaging in "better international conduct." The Kremlin's post-Stalin peace offensive and its "vast propaganda effort to bring about the abolition of atomic weapons" demonstrated that Moscow felt the pressure;

the Soviets were seeking to make a political virtue of the economic necessity of cutting back on arms. Dulles argued that the United States should not ease up at this crucial moment. Rather, the administration should "continue the pressure."[16]

Dulles did not overlook the fact that many people in the United States and in allied countries found the concept of massive retaliation repellent. "The frightful destructiveness of modern weapons creates an instinctive abhorrence to them and a certain repulsion against the strategy of 'massive retaliatory power.' " This feeling, when added to an uncomfortable sense in Western Europe of dependence on the United States, helped create a nearly irresistible sentiment for motion toward arms control. Dulles acknowledged the mood, and he prepared to deal with it. He recommended that the administration declare itself in favor of supervised limitations on weapons—not because he wanted an agreement, but because he wanted to placate the administration's critics. He advocated strictures on negotiations with the Soviet Union so narrow as to preclude any meaningful pact:

Since . . . the present and likely future position [of the United States] . . . gives greater protection than any plan that rested upon agreement and supervision, we should not seek quickly or radically to alter the present situation. We should proceed cautiously so long as the present situation gives us important bargaining power.

Specifically, Dulles countenanced nothing beyond a plan "to test out in the most simple way possible the possibilities of limited mutual inspection" and a concurrent effort "to resolve some of the major political issues [with the Soviet Union] such as the armament of Communist China, the Soviet control of the satellites, the promotion of international Communism and the unification of Germany." Further than this—toward a comprehensive pact for arms limitation or an agreement without political conditions—Dulles refused to go.[17]

More precisely, Dulles refused to go beyond this position willingly. At times he had little choice. In July 1955, at Geneva, Eisenhower decided that the administration had to do something dramatic to wrest the peace initiative from the Soviets. A few months earlier, the Kremlin had made what appeared to much of the world to be an important concession by agreeing to the establishment of observation stations in the Soviet Union—

and in the United States, of course. The Russian proposal had the announced purpose of preventing secret mobilization of armed forces and thus diminishing the possibility of surprise attack. The unstated aim, which mattered more since the Eisenhower administration had declared a similar inspection scheme in Korea grossly deficient, was to gain for Moscow the mantle of chief advocate of peace.

Consequently, Eisenhower called Stassen to Geneva in late July to discuss ways of recapturing the momentum on arms control. In a meeting with the president and many of his top advisers, Stassen described an inspection plan that outdid the Russians and avoided the problems inherent in fixed observation posts.[18] The heart of Stassen's proposal was a program of aerial surveillance by the United States and the Soviet Union of each other's territory. What the press would call "Open Skies" did not originate with Stassen; the administration had discussed the idea for some time.[19] But Stassen's suggestion at just this moment struck a responsive note in several individuals at the meeting. The two top military men present, Arthur Radford of the Joint Chiefs of Staff (JCS), and NATO commander Alfred Gruenther, thought the plan a good one. Gruenther in particular said that the proposal had "a great deal to recommend it." Most important, the president backed the plan with enthusiasm, as just the stroke needed to give new life to the administration's disarmament efforts.[20]

Dulles, facing solid support for Stassen's proposal, fell into line. Though Open Skies covered more ground, literally and figuratively, than the secretary would have liked, and though it demanded none of the concessions on outstanding political issues between the United States and the Soviet Union he thought desirable, he conceded that the idea seemed "very promising."[21]

With Eisenhower's acceptance of Open Skies, Stassen had reason to believe that he was making progress in his position as disarmament adviser. The Soviets rejected the plan, of course,[22] but that rejection counted for less at the moment than the fact that Stassen appeared to be winning his contest with Dulles over the shaping of arms control policy. The press had taken to calling Stassen the administration's "secretary of peace," an appellation that aroused public feelings quite different from those elicited by the brooding demeanor of the secretary of state. As for Eisenhower, the Geneva summit seemed to indicate that the president was moving closer to Stassen, who deemed disarmament desirable and possible, and further from Dulles, who considered arms control misguided.

Stassen believed that the specific nature of an agreement between the United States and the Soviet Union carried less weight than the simple fact of agreement. He argued that the United States possessed a sufficient lead in weapons that the administration could afford to be bold.[23] Disarmament, he held, would thrive on success and starve on failure. The important thing was to get started. Time and again, Stassen generated new ideas and repackaged old ones, hoping to find something that would appeal to both the Russians and the president. Considering the suspicions on both sides, the task was nearly impossible. But Stassen ignored the odds, and despite repeated rebuffs he persisted.

Stassen's hopefulness became especially evident in the autumn of 1955; and it led him into trouble. Buoyed by Eisenhower's support at Geneva, and prompted to try a new approach by the Kremlin's lack of interest in Open Skies, Stassen developed an inspection program that took as its point of departure the Russian offer to allow outside observers into the Soviet Union. He worked at his usual furious pace through the autumn of 1955, and in December he presented to the National Security Council an extremely ambitious proposal. The centerpiece, and most controversial part, of Stassen's plan was a provision calling for the stationing of twenty to thirty thousand foreign inspectors inside the Soviet Union.

Stassen usually held his own in conference; he enjoyed a reputation as an effective presenter. But this time he failed completely. The magnitude of his scheme took Eisenhower aback. The president said he was "quite sure the Soviets had never given any thought to any inspection plan" that involved such a large number of inspectors. Dulles ripped into Stassen's recommendations. The secretary characterized Stassen's approach as "completely unrealistic," and he declared that the administration could be "absolutely sure" that the Kremlin would never agree to twenty or thirty thousand non-Russians snooping about the country. Dulles warned that if the administration aired such a plan the United States would become "a laughing stock."[24]

Such rough treatment certainly stung; but Stassen probably worried more about some further comments by Eisenhower indicating that the president was beginning to agree with Dulles that political concessions by the Soviets would have to accompany arms control. Eisenhower spoke of developing "two parallel programs, one to contain a series of political settlements and the other to contain progressive steps toward disarmament." The president declared that the United States "could make no progress in one program without concurrent progress in the other."[25]

Stassen must have wondered at the change that had come over Eisenhower since Geneva. The proposal Eisenhower had accepted then, though less sweeping than Stassen's later plan, still spanned a wide field with its call for an exchange of blueprints of every military installation in the United States and the Soviet Union and the establishment by each country of air bases in the other for launching surveillance missions. Furthermore, the president had attached no political preconditions to Open Skies. Now, less than half a year later, Eisenhower seemed to be advocating a cautious, limited approach to arms control, and he appeared to be holding disarmament hostage to intrinsically unrelated progress elsewhere on the diplomatic front.

Two factors, in all likelihood, accounted for the apparent change in Eisenhower's attitude. First, Dulles had softened his own antidisarmament approach. At and after Geneva, the secretary had been increasingly impressed by the strength in many quarters, at home and abroad, of support for arms control. Dulles believed that the administration needed something to show for its disarmament talk. Further, he had come to the opinion that minor reductions in conventional weapons and forces might ease pressure for arms control without giving up America's strategic advantage. In February 1956, Dulles told Dillon Anderson, Eisenhower's special assistant for national security affairs, that he could accept the idea of mutual troop reductions.[26]

Dulles, however, never judged support for arms control to be more than a diplomatic and political expedient. In June 1955, he had described his opinion on disarmament in the form of a syllogism:

The major premise in any United States plan should be that, under present conditions, we cannot afford to take, and need not take, substantial risks. The minor premise is that Soviet creed and conduct, as they now are, when applied to modern conditions, do inherently import grave risks into any formal plan. The conclusion is that present steps to stabilize or curtail armament should be tentative and exploratory only[,] until good faith and good will are demonstrated by the Soviet Union.[27]

Dulles never witnessed what he considered Soviet "good faith and good will"; indeed, until his death in 1959 he believed communists incapable of such. This said, it seems evident that whatever concessions Dulles made to disarmament had the principal purpose of preserving American credibility, and his own. Dulles did not intend to drop his public guard against the communists, nor against conservatives in America, but he realized that intransigence had its limits. He recognized that the United States could not afford to be seen as always opposing arms control—and that neither, within administration councils, could he. Geneva had demonstrated that Eisenhower wanted to explore the possibilities of disarmament. If Dulles wished to maintain his influence with the president and to avoid losing ground to Stassen, he would have to adopt a more flexible approach to disarmament. This the secretary did.

The second circumstance that accounted for the apparent shift in Eisenhower's attitudes on disarmament, and the one that made possible the success of Dulles' tactical maneuvering, was the fact that Eisenhower still had not made up his mind on the subject. As in other areas of policymaking, the president preferred to procrastinate, keeping his options open as long as possible. At Geneva he had tossed the arms control ball to the Russians; until they threw it back he could afford the luxury of indecision. As he listened to the competing arguments of his advisers, his position remained fluid. In the autumn of 1955, the president was moving in the direction of Dulles on the matter of political preconditions to disarmament, but he had acquired little momentum in that direction, or any other. If Stassen were resourceful, he might yet regain Eisenhower's confidence and once more seize the initiative on disarmament.

As 1956 began, Stassen set to work on a plan designed to meet what seemed to be Eisenhower's new requirements. Moving with his accustomed dispatch, Stassen managed by the first week in February to lay on the president's desk a package of proposals, complete with a draft letter to Soviet Chairman Nikolai Bulganin and draft messages to Congress and the American people. Eisenhower knew by this time that Stassen abjured half-measures; still he must have found Stassen's seven-point program surprising.

The plan represented a compromise between the bold comprehensiveness that naturally attracted Stassen and the cautious incrementalism that had dominated the discussion at Stassen's disastrous appearance before the NSC in December. This ambivalence, if not confusion, was evident in the language Stassen used to characterize the package in his suggested message to Congress; in a single sentence, he described the proposal as both "far-reaching" and "limited." Three points of the program were familiar or otherwise unexceptional: Stassen reiterated the Open Skies offer to the Soviet Union, he extended it to other countries, and he invited the Russians to join with the United States in reaffirming their pledges not to use nuclear or other weapons for aggression.

The other four points deserved more notice. Stassen advocated that the Soviet Union and the United States agree to significant cuts in the size of their conventional forces, to 2.5 million men on each side, with corresponding reductions in armament and budgets; he urged a bilateral freeze on the production of nuclear weapons, with future developments in the atomic field to be dedicated to peaceful uses; he suggested that Open Skies be enforced, if an international police force established for the purpose so chose, by tactical nuclear weapons donated from the stockpiles of the United States and the Soviet Union; and finally he suggested that after an initial trial period the continuation of the program be accompanied by negotiation of unresolved political differences between the great powers.[28]

The first reaction to the proposal came from Dulles, though the secretary did not direct his response to Stassen. While Stassen's paper circulated among Eisenhower's chief advisers, Dulles discussed with Arthur Radford, who shared the secretary's basic antipathy toward disarmament, what they both considered Stassen's latest dim ideas. Like Dulles, Radford worried that something might actually come of the plan. Dulles, referring sneeringly to Stassen's "magnum opus," acknowledged that the proposal created "plenty" of problems for Radford and the military, but he reminded the JCS chairman that the package created even more difficulties for the State Department. Dulles went on to assure Radford that he would monitor the progress of the new scheme closely.[29]

Dulles' watchfulness paid off—from the secretary's point of view. At an

NSC meeting two weeks later, the council rejected Stassen's proposal. The minutes of this meeting remain classified, and so the particular grounds for setting aside the program are not entirely clear. Probably the president and others believed Stassen had tackled too much at once; the council advised Stassen to concentrate on ways of testing the feasibility of his ideas on a limited scale.[30]

The record of a meeting at the White House several days afterward sheds some light on the positions of the participants at the earlier session. In this conference, discussion centered on one aspect of Stassen's plan: his proposal for cuts in troop strengths. Representatives from the Pentagon objected to the idea of numerical limits on military manpower. Deputy Secretary of Defense Reuben Robertson stated that a reliable inspection system should be in operation before the administration agreed to specific numbers. Robertson held that a ceiling would bind the United States, whose manpower figures were public knowledge, but would be unenforceable against the Soviets without inspection.

Radford seconded Robertson's argument. The admiral conceded that a troop limit might attract a favorable public response and that it might help keep the allies in line. But he claimed that by proper management of public relations and reminders of the great reductions in American troop strength since World War II, the administration could sufficiently demonstrate its peaceful intentions. With respect to the allies, especially Britain and France, Radford asked why the United States always had to "dance to their tune." He worried that the troop reduction formula represented an attempt by the supporters of disarmament to get a foot in the Pentagon door; he asked whether, if this were accepted, there would be demands for further cuts.[31]

Dulles hesitated to differ with Radford, but he ended up doing so. He said he had "great sympathy" for the point of view of the military, and he admitted the danger of committing the United States to a manpower figure and then being unable to hold the Soviets to their side of the bargain. The secretary, however, placed more weight on maintaining good relations with the British and the French, and he reminded those present that the proposed limits involved a forty percent troop cut for the Soviets, against only ten to fifteen percent for the United States. On balance, Dulles concluded, the administration ought to support the reductions.[32]

Dulles no doubt gained confidence from the fact that he spoke after

Eisenhower had already expressed approval of the troop limitations. The president opened the session by taking exception to a Defense Department letter stating that the administration ought not to agree to any troop reductions, even if an inspection system were in place, until diplomatic problems between the superpowers had been resolved. Eisenhower did not deny the significance of linkage between disarmament and other political issues, but he observed that the establishment of a reliable inspection system would "bring about the greatest and broadest possible resolution of world problems." The president also stressed the importance of establishing America's good faith in the disarmament sphere; what the administration required was something specific and concrete "to carry the disarmament struggle along." "We need it . . . ," he said, "to hold our allies." Otherwise, "we may find France and even the United Kingdom aligned with the Russians against us."[33]

Stassen, who sat silent through this meeting, could not have been discouraged by the discussion. And despite his failure to gain approval for his latest plan, he must not have been overly disheartened by the events of the previous month. In the cover letter to Eisenhower that accompanied his proposal, Stassen had emphasized the importance of creating a positive image for the administration on the topic of disarmament—"mobilizing favorable public and governmental world opinion" was how he phrased it.[34] Although the president had not accepted Stassen's package, Eisenhower's remarks indicated that on the important matter of strengthening American credibility on the arms control issue, he and Stassen were thinking along similar lines.

Early in March, Stassen departed Washington for London to attend the third springtime session of the United Nations Subcommittee on Disarmament. Since 1954, the subcommittee had made little progress in narrowing the gap between United States and the Soviet Union on arms control,[35] but Stassen hoped for better luck this time around. In the second week of April, he reported good news on the matter that had most worried Eisenhower. "We have made headway in moving the Western Four governments closer together," he wrote. Stassen included press clippings documenting his claim, and he added that following several of his off-the-record talks to influential groups in England, the British in particular were coming around.

"Recognition of the logic of your policies is gradually growing." Regarding the Soviets, Stassen said it was too early to tell whether they were interested in serious negotiation or only in propaganda.[36]

As matters turned out, propaganda was what the Russians had in mind. They called for troop reductions like those Stassen had proposed, but they balked at the inspection and verification procedures the Eisenhower administration had made clear it would require. Consequently, Stassen and the American delegation opposed the Soviet plan, seeming to much of the world to be blocking disarmament.[37]

Stassen's stay in London did not lead to any breakthroughs, but he found the spring and early summer of 1956 a personally encouraging period nonetheless. Stassen appeared to have the backing of the president, to such a degree that he began pushing once again for some of the items of the package he had presented early in the year. He revived, for example, the concept of a United Nations atomic police force. In a conference with Eisenhower at Gettysburg in July, Stassen pointed out the symbolic value of supplying the UN with a nuclear arsenal: it would strengthen the hand of the international organization, and it would "take some of the edge off" resentment at the great powers' monopoly of nuclear weapons. The president neither approved nor rejected this idea, but on the whole he reacted positively to Stassen's approach, and he noted with satisfaction Stassen's efforts to generate momentum on disarmament.[38]

Relations between Stassen and Dulles were a good deal rockier during this period. Communication lapses between Washington and London led to conflicting statements; when the press picked these up and made an issue out of the differences between the secretary and the disarmament adviser, Dulles telephoned Stassen to tell him that he had been "embarrassed" by the situation. Dulles indicated in no uncertain terms that he did not want such embarrassment to recur.[39] On a more substantive level, Dulles attacked Stassen's plan for an international nuclear force. He predicted that the idea would meet little favor in the UN; he said that most countries would resent even the suggestion that atomic weapons be used in a police action.[40]

Stassen weakened his position in the administration in the summer of 1956 by a serious political miscalculation. In late July, he informed Eisenhower that private surveys indicated a large amount of public dissatisfaction with Vice President Nixon, and he suggested that Eisenhower replace

Nixon on the ticket for the upcoming election. A few days later, with Eisenhower out of the country visiting Panama, Stassen announced a plan to nominate Massachusetts Governor Christian Herter for the number-two position. Then the roof fell in. The anti-Nixon groundswell that Stassen hoped for failed to develop, Herter declined the proffered post, and Eisenhower dumped Stassen—temporarily—instead of Nixon, suspending Stassen from his job in the administration. The denouement proved especially humiliating: Herter nominated Nixon for the vice presidency at the Republican convention; a chastened Stassen seconded the choice.[41]

Though Stassen's penance eventually regained for him his disarmament post, the fiasco marked the beginning of a long slide downhill. His credibility with Republican regulars had vanished, as Senate Minority Leader William Knowland told Dulles in a September conversation. And the problem extended beyond the Republican party. Knowland said that he "did not see how Congress could have confidence in the judgment of anyone who had been as ill-advised as Stassen had been"; he added that he "doubted that Congress would have confidence in his continuing conduct of disarmament matters."[42]

Dulles had been looking for an opportunity to get rid of Stassen. Now he began to move. Dulles found an ally in Sherman Adams, who considered Stassen a distinct liability for the administration. With the November election only weeks away, however, the secretary and the White House chief of staff moved carefully. In a telephone conversation in mid-September, Adams cautioned against any action that might give even the appearance of administration indifference to arms control. Adlai Stevenson, Eisenhower's Democratic opponent, had already charged the Republicans with backwardness of the disarmament issue, and Adams did not want to provide Stevenson with any more ammunition. Dulles said that something would have to be done about Stassen, but he agreed that any steps would have to be taken "moderately and slowly."[43]

His antagonists at bay for the moment, Stassen managed to hold onto his position until the embarrassment of his blunder paled in the glow of Eisenhower's sweeping reelection. During the campaign, Stassen maintained a low profile, but his unsinkable nature became evident again as soon as the votes were counted. And more trouble followed.

The day after the election, Stassen laid on the president's desk a lengthy memorandum that included advice for dealing with problems far beyond those in Stassen's disarmanent portfolio. The recommendations in this memo were breathtaking in their scope and audacity, and they could not but have cast doubt again on the sound judgment of their author. Stassen described a plan for a UN-enforced peace in the Middle East, to include provisions for a treaty between Israel and the Arab states; he called for readjustment of borders along the Jordan River and the resettlement of Palestinian refugees; he suggested American funding for Egypt's Aswan dam and the renovation of the Suez canal. Turning to Eastern Europe, he urged the president to request negotiations leading to the departure of Soviet troops from Hungary and their replacement by UN forces sent to supervise free elections. Stassen missed few stops on his *tour d'horizon*. He said that the administration ought to pressure the French to pull out of Algeria; he articulated the need for regional trading arrangements in the third world; he advocated opening negotiations with China for the unification of Korea. Almost as an afterthought, he remarked that disarmament ought to be part of this world policy.[44]

Eisenhower shunted Stassen's proposal off to the lower levels of the State Department; with Suez and Hungary still boiling, he had more important things to do than listen to unsolicited and ill-considered advice. By this point, certainly, and probably from the time of the Stassen-Nixon dispute the previous summer, Eisenhower realized that in Stassen he had a loose cannon on the administration's desks. In mid-December, when the world's concurrent crises eased a little, the president took Stassen aside and told him that there would have to be some changes. The conversation was, in Eisenhower's words, "brutally frank." Not long afterward, Eisenhower suggested to Dulles that the best solution of the Stassen problem would be to transfer Stassen out of the White House and into the State Department, where his subordinate status to the secretary would be unmistakable.[45]

That the president did not come right out and fire Stassen must have surprised some observers within and outside the administration. Eisenhower's reluctance to take this final step probably had several causes. From a political standpoint, Stassen still seemed to have significant appeal for young moderates within the Republican party, whom Eisenhower continued to hope to attract.[46] Bureaucratically, Eisenhower understood the advantages of having Stassen around as a counterbalance and spur to Dulles. At the personal level, Eisenhower liked Stassen. Sometimes the president could not understand Stassen's need for personal recognition,[47] but on the whole he thought Stassen's motives honorable. To a friend, Eisenhower wrote of Stassen, "He has been a very controversial figure; many people admire him while many dislike him intensely. Of course he is not either what his ardent friends or his ardent enemies picture him, but he is an assiduous worker and he is devoted to the whole purpose of disarmament."[48]

Eisenhower's belief that Stassen was devoted to arms control tipped the scales, at this point, in Stassen's favor. At the beginning of 1957, Eisenhower had not given up hope that some progress could be made toward disarmament. Stassen's energy was unmatched; he was invaluable in bulldozing through the organizational underbrush of the administration. Even if some of his ideas seemed startlingly misguided, at least he kept the ideas coming. As long as he did, he might be useful.

Dulles had a mixed reaction to the possibility that Stassen would report to him rather than to Eisenhower. The secretary preferred to see Stassen dismissed altogether, or at least shifted to some out-of-the-way position. For several months, Dulles had discussed Stassen's future with Sherman Adams. Precisely what passed between the two is impossible to say; many of the pertinent documents remain closed to researchers. No record was kept of certain conversations, as in the instance of a December 17, 1956, telephone call between Dulles and Adams, at the beginning of which Dulles took the unusual step, for him, of telling his secretary not to listen in.[49]

Whatever Dulles might have hoped to achieve with Adams, in late December 1956 he broached the issue of Stassen's future with Eisenhower. Dulles told the president that Stassen's activities had shaken public confidence in his reliability; he suggested that Stassen be relieved of his disarmament duties and assigned to an embassy in Scandinavia or the Netherlands.[50] Eisenhower demurred. Pursuing his earlier comments, the president decided to shift Stassen to the State Department.[51]

Unable to rid himself of Stassen, Dulles did his best to neutralize his rival by making plain who would be running the arms control show. In a conversation with Stassen in early February, Dulles told Stassen that the latter's transfer was not one that he had sought, and he declared, a bit disingenuously, that he was not trying to "enhance" his authority. But he went on to say that it was his understanding that Stassen would no longer regularly attend cabinet and NSC meetings. Following Stassen's rejoinder that he thought the president would want him at these meetings to express the "liberal" viewpoint, Dulles reminded Stassen that he, Dulles, "would expect complete loyalty to State Department policies whether or not Stassen agreed." Dulles, perhaps anticipating a flanking maneuver through the news media, added specifically that this principle applied to Stassen's communications with the press.[52]

Despite his demotion, Stassen retained his enthusiasm and drive. Following his reprimand by Eisenhower in December, he ceased to offer grandiose plans for solving the world's problems at a single blow, but his penchant for broad thinking on arms control and related issues did not diminish. Stassen suggested a presidential appearance at the UN in support of the international nuclear police force he had previously recommended; he called for a two-year suspension of atomic testing; and he raised again the idea of a freeze on the production of nuclear weapons.[53]

When Stassen presented his ideas at a meeting of the NSC, however, Dulles quickly cut him down. By this time—March 1957—Stassen had completed his move to the State Department, but Dulles had not yet managed to keep Stassen out of high-level policy sessions. The secretary did his best, though, to make Stassen feel unwelcome. Stassen's presentation consisted of arguments for his recent proposals, with special emphasis on formulating strategy for upcoming disarmament talks in London. After letting Stassen state his case, Dulles commented that while the American delegation in London surely needed a clear idea of administration aims, Stassen's proposals did not provide much realistic guidance. The minutes of the meeting describe Dulles' response:

There was certainly no reason [the secretary said] to think that the Soviets would accept the general plans that Governor Stassen had described. . . . So, while Governor Stassen's plan was interesting and useful, it was not at all likely to eventuate in the near future as a reality.[54]

Dulles went on to stress that Stassen must adhere to established administration policy when he went to London. The secretary noted that much of what Stassen had presented had not been officially approved by the NSC and the president, and that these ideas must not be used without "prior consultation back in Washington." A few minutes later, Dulles softened this proscription slightly by admitting that Stassen might discuss with the allies certain matters not yet formally adopted by the administration, but only if he did so "with great caution." Eisenhower expanded this remark by saying that if Stassen deviated from official policy he must present his ideas "on a purely personal basis."[55]

After this meeting, Stassen left for London. Within a short time, the suspicions of his critics regarding his willingness to follow instructions began to seem justified. A proposal that the United States and the Soviet Union agree to a twenty-five percent reduction in conventional forces appeared to observers in the State Department to indicate that Stassen again was wandering off on his own. At this point, Eisenhower was prepared to defend such exploring as legitimate in the search for a basis for agreement,[56] but a few weeks later, Stassen made an error Eisenhower could not dismiss.

Through the middle of April 1957, Stassen had not been hopeful that anything important would come of the London conference. He had written Eisenhower, "The obstacles are, of course, very great and the odds continue to be adverse."[57] Shortly after this, however, Stassen returned to Washington for a White House briefing during which the president decided to try out one of Stassen's earlier recommendations: a temporary ban on nuclear testing. Eisenhower sent Stassen back to England to present the plan to the British, the French, and the West Germans, and after discussions with them to raise the subject with the Soviets. The president authorized Stassen to take a "talking paper" that described the proposal.[58]

Encouraged by this turn of events, Stassen flew to London and promptly told the British and French about the change in administration position. Almost as promptly, before the allies had a chance to comment, he described the shift to the head of the Soviet delegation, Valerian Zorin. This excessive haste would have caused trouble enough, but, to compound the problem, Stassen gave Zorin a copy of the paper containing the proposal.

Within hours, irate reactions from the allies arrived in Washington. Eisenhower received a letter from an angry Harold Macmillan complaining at being put in a politically uncomfortable spot. Eisenhower admitted that he could not blame Macmillan for being upset. The French also registered forceful disapproval, and Dulles expected a similar response from the Germans, who were certain to feel "double-crossed." Dulles told Eisenhower that Stassen had "not acted in good faith"—the first occasion, apparently, on which Dulles made such a claim to the president. With Eisenhower's approval, the secretary ordered Stassen to tell Zorin that the administration disavowed his action and to request the return of the memorandum.[59]

This misstep dissolved what remained of Stassen's effectiveness within the administration. At the State Department, the cause of Stassen's difficulties seemed clear enough. "This was a case of being overeager to achieve results, I think," Robert Murphy commented. "It's quite normal and human to do—'If you just make one more little concession, you'll have it.' And boy! The Russians play that to the hilt."[60] Dulles told Adams that Stassen was so intent on reaching an agreement "on almost any terms" that he would, if necessary, sell the allies "down the river." Adams agreed. "You can't control him," Adams said. "You don't know what he will do next."[61] Most significantly, Eisenhower was forced to the conclusion that Stassen was unreliable. The president admitted to Dulles that for the first time his faith in Stassen was "seriously shaken."[62]

Still, Eisenhower did not want to fire Stassen, for he doubted that such an action could be adequately defended in public.[63] To many people in the United States and abroad, Stassen represented the administration's commitment to arms control. Stassen's faux pas, while inexcusable to professionals in government and diplomacy, did not seem sufficiently blatant to cause widespread indignation among the general public. Eisenhower hesitated to take a step that might be construed as dismissing the possibility of disarmament, and that might even scuttle the talks in London.

The solution Eisenhower chose was to allow Stassen to continue as chief negotiator for disarmament, but to make it painfully obvious to him that no more mistakes would be tolerated. To emphasize his displeasure and to remind Stassen of his subordination to the secretary of state, Eisenhower left the implementation of this decision to Dulles. The secretary recalled Stassen to Washington for a personal reprimand, and he selected a watchdog from the State Department to accompany Stassen back to London and report any hints of free-lancing. Eisenhower concurred in the appointment, though he thought Dulles heavy-handed in letting Stassen know that he was being observed. Commenting on one particularly blunt paragraph of a letter from Dulles to Stassen explaining the role of Stassen's new assistant, Eisenhower said that the passage was "unnecessary and almost humiliating." The president declared that if he had a job and received such a message from his boss, he would quit. But Dulles had already shown the letter to Stassen, who had acquiesced in its language, and Eisenhower let the matter drop.[64]

By this means, Dulles managed to isolate Stassen. Isolation, however, did not bring silence. Although Stassen confined himself to approved proposals in London and maintained an unexceptionably discreet public profile, he continued to speak his mind within the confines of the administration.

Early in the summer of 1957, Eisenhower met with some of America's foremost nuclear scientists, who argued against a ban on weapons testing. The scientists, led by Edward Teller, claimed that they needed to test in order to produce a "clean," virtually fallout-free hydrogen bomb.[65] Upon hearing of the meeting, Stassen objected strenuously to Teller's argument. He said that he had no desire to stop progress toward an explosive device that might have peaceful applications, but he asserted that there was more to the issue of "clean" and dirty" bombs than the scientists indicated. He declared that the Defense Department had resisted replacing old, dirty weapons with cleaner ones already available, and he reported that the Pentagon was working not only on ways to make explosives cleaner, but also on methods "to make bombs more poisonous, more radioactive, more dirty."[66]

Stassen's remarks made little apparent impression on the president, and his position in the administration continued to deteriorate. Through the late summer and fall of 1957, Stassen persisted in trying to move the administration toward a more flexible position on disarmament, but he met ever-diminishing success. If Stassen did not already realize it, a September exchange with Dulles ought to have convinced him that he had reached the end of his usefulness.

On September 23, Stassen presented to the secretary another arms control proposal, one that included nothing radically different from what he had advocated earlier. The plan called for the establishment of eight to ten monitoring stations in the Soviet Union and a like number in the United States, with other stations elsewhere around the world. The inspection stations would supervise a two-year suspension of nuclear testing, to begin in August 1958. During the two years of the ban, Washington and Moscow could conduct negotiations for the purpose of passing from a mere halt in testing to real disarmament. In addition, Stassen recommended a modified version of Open Skies as protection against surprise attack.

In support of his ideas, Stassen pointed out that the proposed test ban would take effect after a series of American blasts scheduled for the first part of 1958, when the United States would be in "a favorable position on tests." He also noted that if restrictions were not put in place soon, other countries, especially France, would begin developing nuclear weapons. Stassen predicted grimly, "The nuclear weapons situation will then be beyond control." He defended the reciprocal inspection plan as supplying useful intelligence data to the United States, and also on the grounds that it "would increase the chance of a favorable evolution of the people of the USSR toward freedom without war." Finally, Stassen claimed that his recommendations had a reasonable chance of acceptance, especially if the administration approached the Soviets alone, and not in conjunction with the NATO allies. "Informal quiet bilateral exploration of the USSR position, while keeping our Western partners informed, is the key for results."[67]

In his reply to this memorandum, Dulles let hardly a single Stassen assertion go unchallenged. The secretary began by declaring that the administration's present position on disarmament, established a few weeks earlier, had been achieved only after "months of the most thorough and difficult negotiations within and between the NATO countries." The American-NATO recommendations, which Eisenhower and the secretary had labeled "historic proposals of great significance," had been branded by the Soviets as a "sham." "If we now basically and precipitously alter them," Dulles wrote, "that in itself will certainly be judged in the eyes of world opinion as substantiating the Soviet characterization of them and we shall be put in a humiliating public position."[68]

After adding that Stassen's proposals would give the Soviet Union "immediate and immense political successes," the secretary launched into a personal attack on Stassen. Dulles said that the reasons Stassen gave for changing the administration position were "merely that these changes would make our position more acceptable to the Russians." Dulles flatly rejected the idea of private talks with Moscow. "This procedure would almost surely trouble, if not break, our NATO alliance. It was your bilateral talk in London that precipitated the grave crisis with the UK and Germany last June." The secretary charged Stassen with allowing international worries to compel appeasement. "The total impact of your proposals seems to me to reinforce the fear held by many both here and abroad that you feel some agreement between the United States and the Russians is so sought by world opinion that we should if necessary make such an agreement on Russia's terms."[69]

Not content with this abusive reply to Stassen's proposals, Dulles solicited the views of other persons he knew to be hostile to Stassen's ideas, and he passed them on to Eisenhower. Lewis Strauss of the Atomic Energy Commission, Nathan Twining of the Joint Chiefs of Staff, and Donald Quarles of the Department of Defense seconded Dulles' opinions on the complete inadvisability of Stassen's recommendations.[70] Dulles himself wrote to the president:

I have come reluctantly to the conclusion that Harold feels that we should seek some sort of an agreement with the Russians on almost any terms—their terms, if necessary. And indeed his memorandum means, in essence, that we accept their terms. My feeling is that this is a dangerous attitude; that the very process of seeking this agreement, by bilateral talks, will dangerously breach our relations with our Western Allies and after that is accomplished we may get no agreement at all, or at best an agreement which will have nothing in it worthwhile either in substance, or in means of verification of promises.[71]

Dulles told Sherman Adams that the Stassen affair was "shaping up for a showdown"; he wanted to sack Stassen immediately.[72] Eisenhower agreed that Stassen had to go, but he preferred to avoid an abrupt and complete break. After a conversation with the president, Adams suggested to Dulles that the secretary pack Stassen off as ambassador to Greece or somewhere similarly remote.[73]

Stassen continued to struggle until the end. In the second week of October, he made an impassioned argument to Eisenhower and Dulles for an immediate end to nuclear testing.[74] Ten days later, when Dulles offered him the embassy in Athens, Stassen declined, saying that this was a "historic moment" for disarmament. Stassen declared that he felt "very strongly" that the interests of peace required the United States to make "at least a partial agreement with the Russians." Even if he left the administration, he said, he intended to work within the Republican party for the acceptance of "sound doctrines" on disarmament. Dulles took this as a threat, inferring that Stassen aimed to instigate a revolt against administration policy. In a parenthetical comment concluding his record of the meeting, Dulles wrote, "I got the impression that Stassen plans to get out and to lead a so-called 'liberal' effort to get the U.S. to be more disposed to deal directly with the Russians and to make some sort of an agreement with them dealing at least with suspension of nuclear testing."[75]

By late 1957, support for an end to testing was widespread in America and around the world, and neither Dulles nor Eisenhower cared to see Stassen leap to the front of the test ban movement. This reluctance granted Stassen a brief reprieve, and even when the final break came in February 1958, Eisenhower told Adams that he hoped for a "treaty" with Stassen, by which Stassen would "say something nice" about administration policy when he departed.[76]

Stassen left the administration about as quietly as could be expected of one with his strong opinions. Forsaking national politics for the time being, Stassen decided to enter the 1958 race for the governorship of Pennsylvania.

At the time of his departure, Stassen was commonly counted a casualty of the disarmament struggle within the Eisenhower administration. Crossing swords with Dulles, according to conventional wisdom, was a perilous game; Stassen and his ideas on disarmament were the latest additions to the ranks of the vanquished. This judgment is correct in certain respects, and misleading in others.

Despite Stassen's terrific political and diplomatic errors, especially the 1956 challenge to Nixon and the 1957 London mistake that convinced the president that he was a net liability, Stassen managed to impress upon Eisenhower the need for some sort of action on disarmament. Stassen lost his battle with Dulles, but in three years of fighting he managed to move the battlefield, and the administration, closer to his desired goals. Whether his underlying intentions were those ascribed to him by critics like Robert Murphy, who considered Stassen essentially an expert at self-promotion,[77] or those Stassen claimed for himself when he said he worked principally for "the future well-being of humanity,"[78] Stassen helped push the president to the verge of an important decision on the nuclear question.[79]

Eisenhower still shared Dulles' suspicions about the basic premises of arms control; to that degree the secretary had indeed bested Stassen. But during the first half of 1958, Eisenhower began to feel that the United States could not afford to continue to resist demands to reduce the dangers of nuclear testing. In August of that year, the president announced his intention to suspend American testing for twelve months. Following a favorable response from the Soviet Union, this unilateral moratorium became unofficially bilateral, and it continued through the remainder of Eisenhower's tenure.[80]

Stassen by this time had failed in his effort to regain the magic of his earlier career, and he was heading for the political limbo with which he later became identified. While he had no one but himself to blame for many of the difficulties he had encountered in his job as disarmament adviser, he might have been excused for taking a certain ironic pleasure in reflecting that the moratorium the administration finally accepted was little more than a grudging version of the test ban proposal he had several times offered and seen several times spurned.

8

The Discovery of the Third World: Henry Cabot Lodge at the United Nations

He has an amazingly quick, clear mind, a capacity for comprehension of human situations. He is a natural debater. He always takes the offensive and tries to put the other man on the defensive. He can carry on a tremendous bluff—like a poker player. . . . He has a chip-on-the-shoulder, want-to-be-a-member-of-the-club side to his personality. . . . He can be very charming; he has very good manners and must have been well brought up by his mother. He can be very warm and I believe he can also be very ruthless, but I think he considers that he is leading a good life and doing the right thing by his own lights. . . . He holds in a mystical manner to this crazy Communist religion with its fatuous so-called "science of history." To talk with him about it would be like talking to a man about his religion and should not be done. He seems to have some Tartar in him. He is a despot. While very up-to-date in his understanding of modern economics, he is as medieval as King Saud in other respects. . . . He has an open mind on some things. When he is on an intimate basis with you he is honest and frank, but if in debate with you or fencing with you, or if he thinks you are trying to score on him he will quibble and split hairs.[1]

That Henry Cabot Lodge could write such an objective, even sympathetic, portrait of the world's most powerful communist, Nikita Khrushchev, in 1959 would probably have surprised many people in the United States had the portrayal been made public. Perhaps it would have surprised Lodge himself, when he was appointed American representative at the United Nations, to know that he would be writing about the leader of the Soviet Union in such detached terms before his time in office was up.

In 1953, Eisenhower chose Lodge for the UN post because of Lodge's ability to denounce the Kremlin and all its works. Lodge was, in some respects, the administration's answer to Joseph McCarthy, with the principal difference that Lodge went after real communists. Overnight, Lodge became a hero to the millions of Americans who felt that the United States needed someone to refute the scurrilous charges of communist spokesmen at the UN. Though Lodge's rhetoric, like that of the administration generally, exaggerated his philosophy—Lodge had been in politics too long not to know the political value of a verbal right hook to the jaw of a taunting and unpopular opponent—beneath his oratory lay a solid core of unquestioning anticommunism. Between democracy and slavery, he believed, between West and East, there was no middle ground and no compromise.

The years that followed Lodge's appointment, however, witnessed a remarkable transformation in his thinking. On the surface, the change had little to do with Lodge's beliefs regarding communism. Rather, it amounted primarily to a growing appreciation of the importance of the dozens of new states admitted to the United Nations in the mid-1950s. Simple parliamentary arithmetic told Lodge that if the UN were to remain as useful to the United States in the future as it had been in the past, the administration would have to pay attention to the needs and opinions of these countries that allied neither with America nor with the Soviet Union—the nations that consituted what was beginning to be called the "third world."

Yet one thing led to another, and in encouraging members of the administration to put themselves in the shoes of representatives of the nonaligned nations, the better to woo those countries toward the United States, Lodge discovered that the shoes did not fit American feet all that badly. Without becoming an ideological agnostic or losing his conviction of American ethical superiority, Lodge did absorb some of the neutrals' ability to look at the American-Soviet conflict from the outside, and he began to think that the communist threat might not be as imminent as it once had seemed. There was, he came to recognize, a middle ground between the spheres of the United States and the Soviet Union, and it grew bigger all the time.

Lodge began life a long way from the United Nations. Born in the house of his grandfather, Henry Cabot Lodge, he spent much of his youth under the tutelage of that venerable senator, since his father died when he was seven years old. Young Cabot turned eighteen the year the elder Lodge blocked the entry of the United States into the League of Nations, and just as he inherited his grandfather's Republicanism, he also acquired the old man's distrust of the reliability of other countries. In 1936, Lodge won election to the Senate, one of the hardy few of his party who survived the Democratic whirlwind of that year, and within a short time he became prominent among advocates of an armed isolation in response to threatening events in Europe and Asia—a Fortress America.[2]

After Pearl Harbor, however, Lodge reassessed his position. Through visits to the battlefront he became a reporter to Franklin Roosevelt and a supporter of the Democratic president's policies.[3] He later gained Roosevelt's admiration and envy by resigning his Senate seat to take a commission in the army.[4] Like many others of his generation, Lodge became convinced by the war that isolationism was an obsolete and dangerous philosophy. As the cold war set in, he could be found in the front ranks of supporters of the Truman Doctrine, the Marshall Plan, and NATO. By the beginning of the 1950s, he occupied a leading position in the internationalist wing of the Republican party.[5]

As a neointerventionist, Lodge spearheaded a drive to rescue the party from Robert Taft, the most formidable figure among the party's isolationists. The strategy centered on a plan to draft Dwight Eisenhower for the 1952 presidential nomination. Lodge and Eisenhower had known each other since the war; they had not become close personal friends, but Lodge had impressed Eisenhower enough that the general offered him a position on his staff at NATO.[6] And Lodge had grown convinced that only Eisenhower possessed the popularity and stature to stop Taft and prevent the Republicans from being cast into permanent exile in opposition, with evil consequences for party and country.[7]

Eisenhower rebuffed Lodge's initial attempts to persuade the general to announce for the 1952 nomination, but Lodge, and others, persisted.[8] Lodge took the liberty of entering Eisenhower in the New Hampshire primary, with the assistance of New Hampshire Governor Sherman Adams. Even before the candidate became a candidate, Lodge became his manager. Following victories in primaries, the convention, and the November election, Lodge stood to receive a top position in the new administration, especially since his Senate reelection bid had failed before the challenge of a young congressman with the charm and luck of the Irish, and money besides—John Kennedy.[9]

The question was where to put Lodge. Eisenhower considered him for White House chief of staff, but when John Foster Dulles suggested that Lodge replace the aging Warren Austin at the United Nations, Eisenhower quickly gave the nod. "Cabot's qualitites seemed almost unique," Eisenhower wrote later.[10] Lodge's three terms in the Senate had demonstrated his adeptness at parliamentary maneuvering; his success in guiding the Eisenhower campaign had shown his capacity for organization and detail. But above all, Lodge's flair for combative oratory attracted the president's attention. Eisenhower had been dismayed for some time at the way the Soviet representative at the UN, Andrei Vishinsky, had berated the United States, drawing an American response slowly if at all. The "poor, sick" Austin, as Eisenhower described him, "who when Vishinsky let loose announced he would reply to the Russian a week from Thursday," had to go.[11] Lodge seemed just the man for the job.

The appointment was not without difficulties. Lodge was a forceful and persuasive individual, and Dulles, who may have suggested the UN to keep Lodge out of Washington, soon discovered that he did not take instructions like an ordinary ambassador. Eisenhower exacerbated Dulles' distress by elevating Lodge to cabinet rank. A State Department veteran described the result. "There was a great tendency on Ambassador Lodge's part to act independently, we'll say, of the Secretary of State on the theory that he reported directly to the President. Organizationally, this was a little awkward at times and had to be handled with some tact."[12] But Dulles found the tact, and after a few initial embarrassments the two men worked out a modus vivendi.

Lodge immediately lived up to Eisenhower's expectations regarding his potential as a Bolshevik-basher. He was tall and handsome—great assets as television began to supplant print and radio as the common person's prime source of information. And he was never at a loss for words—a natural gift he had sharpened in earlier days as a journalist in the company of the master of withering riposte, H. L. Mencken. Cast opposite Vishinsky, who relished his role as America's favorite villain,[13] Lodge soon became the administration's best-known vindicator of democracy.

In a letter to Eisenhower, Lodge described his strategy. His goal, he said, was to end "the exasperation of American opinion caused by the Soviet Union's using the United Nations to promote its own propaganda while the United States apparently did nothing." Applying his experience as a reporter, he aimed "to answer every Communist attack *immediately* so as to break up their headlines, interfere with their news stories, and, actually, take the news away from them."[14] Lodge elaborated on the public reaction to his vigorous style. "Whenever I make a good hard rejoinder, I am flooded with letters and invitations to speak. People who recognize me on television in such unlikely places as Akron, Ohio, say: 'Good work! Hit them in the nose!' . . . It is a marvelously popular issue."[15]

Lodge's zest for trading verbal blows with communists did not diminish during his term in office, nor did he ever change his mind about the importance of fast footwork and quick counterpunching. In mid-1957, Lodge told his former Senate colleague, Lyndon Johnson, "The most desirable thing is to answer communist attacks at the very moment they are made so that the position of the United States gets out on the wires and is printed in the *same* news story or is heard on the *same* radio broadcast, or is in the *same* television show as that in which the original distortion appears."[16]

But as Lodge grew into his position, he increasingly came to realize that refuting propaganda, though necessary, could constitute only a small part of a policy for dealing with the communists. A number of factors influenced his opinion on the matter. The death of Stalin in 1953 seemed to offer the opportunity to chart a less hostile course toward the Soviet Union. The fall of McCarthy in 1954 allowed a certain relaxation on the administration's right flank. The Geneva summit of 1955 enhanced the image of the president as a man of peace. Most important, the birth of new nations filled the UN with members to whom the old terms of the American-Soviet debate were largely irrelevant.

When Lodge took office in 1953, the UN comprised fifty-six states. Three years later the number hit seventy-three, and it kept growing through the end of the decade. Most of the new members were Asian and African states that had recently gained their independence from the liquidating British and French empires. Though not equal in all respects to the permanent members of the Security Council, the new nations represented a significant collection of votes in the General Assembly, which Lodge considered the vital forum for shaping world opinion. At the halfway mark of his tenure, Lodge tallied the figures. The West could normally count on the cooperation of twenty-one American republics—though Lodge realized that the administration must not take Latin America for granted—and nineteen European and Commonwealth states. Against this total of forty were usually arrayed Russia and eight satellites, and often eleven Arab countries that objected to American backing for Israel. In the uncommitted category, Lodge found fifteen Afro-Asian swing votes, which number continued to increase. Since most substantive measures considered by the General Assembly required a two-thirds majority for passage, it seemed clear to Lodge that an important part of his job would involve hunting support among the uncommitted nations.[17]

Lodge was not the first to recognize the significance of the nonaligned states. In fact, Lodge's attention and that of the Eisenhower administration generally had been drawn in this direction by the activities of the Soviet Union in Asia and Africa. As Stalin's successors worked out a new hierarchy in the Kremlin, they pushed peace in Europe and stepped up assistance to the third world. Lodge expressed concern over Moscow's diplomatic initiatives in a letter to Eisenhower. "Stalin's death eliminated the violent sounds which helped to keep our allies together. In its place has now come the most effective campaign to date to break up NATO and to penetrate Africa and the Near East." Regarding the latter prong of the Russian offensive, Lodge cited examples of economic aid he had encountered on a recent trip. "I have just seen this in Libya (Soviet offers of road building material, hospitals, doctors, etc.) and Sudan (Czech tractors for cotton)." Lodge added that he had received similar reports from Saudi Arabia.[18]

Lodge believed that in its attempts to counter the new Soviet tactics, the United States operated at a disadvantage due to its alliance with colonialist Britain and France. The young nations of the world—and the young people of the world, who, Lodge thought, often identified with newly independent and nearly independent nations—looked askance at American claims of support for self-determination and international equality. "In countries as far apart as France and Japan there is evidence that the young people think that we are supporting the outgoing regimes, the Colonel Blimps." The situation was grave and deteriorating—Lodge noted "recent rather spectacular Soviet strides in the Near East"—and he suggested a radical reorientation of American priorities.[19]

Lodge's recommendation had three parts. The first would provoke little objection: the president ought to announce his support for independence or self-government for the remaining dependent possessions of the United States. In this, Lodge merely suggested an extension of existing administration policy. Earlier, Lodge had characterized an Eisenhower declaration of support for Puerto Rican independence, conditional upon an affirmative vote in Puerto Rico's legislature, as "a ten-strike" in terms of its impact on opinion in the nonaligned world. At the time, Lodge had remarked that pleased reactions at the United Nations came from the most unlikely directions. "Krishna Menon [the Indian foreign minister, noted for frequent and violent attacks upon the United States] has just praised the Puerto Rico statement! His first pro-US statement since I have been here!"[20]

The second and third parts of Lodge's program, however, were bound to cause trouble. In order to place as much distance as possible between American policy and that of the colonialists, Lodge asserted that the United States ought to avoid any three-way sponsorship, with Britain and France, of resolutions in the UN; further, the president ought publicly to call on the Europeans to announce, within ten years, timetables for decolonization. Lodge recognized that these actions would agitate London and Paris, but he thought the administration could manage Anglo-French objections if it explained the new policy correctly.[21] Regarding timetables for decolonization, Lodge urged Eisenhower to cite the precedent by which the United States had announced in 1934 that the Philippines would achieve independence in 1946 and had followed through on schedule. He argued that the administration could assuage French annoyance regarding Algeria by pointing out that the ten-year grace period would allow France plenty of opportunity to settle its dispute with the North African colony/province one way or the other. Lodge claimed that although Britain and France would complain at receiving, simultaneously, unsolicited advice on imperial affairs and a cold shoulder in the UN, they would survive the shock. After all, Lodge contended, "It is in their interest for us to have good standing in areas where they cannot have it." Besides, what could they do? "The colonial powers have really nowhere else to go."[22]

Lodge offered these suggestions one month before Egypt nationalized the Suez canal; he soon received the distancing from the colonialists he desired, though it came in an unanticipated manner. Despite the fact that the Suez crisis caused the administration, Lodge included, a great deal of difficulty, he managed in the aftermath to appreciate the salutary effect Eisenhower's handling of the affair had on American relations with Asian and African states. At the end of 1956, he wrote from the UN to the president, "I continue to get enthusiastic reactions from Afro-Asian nations about your policy here in the Near East crisis. They feel it was 'an honorable act performed in a big and clean cut' way . . . and that it was in the best American traditions of the Declaration of Independence and Abraham Lincoln."[23] A short time later Lodge reported, "The standing of the United States—notably among the Asian powers—is at a brand new high."[24]

Lodge addressed his remarks to Eisenhower, but he had a second audience as well. At the State Department, some career officers thought Lodge went too far in detecting a silver lining in the cloud over Suez. Lodge's case seemed typical of a diplomat stationed too long at one post and beginning to think like the natives. Robert Murphy commented knowingly that Lodge was "laboring under this Afro-Asian influence."[25]

Suez wound down as Lodge completed his fourth year in office, and he found time to summarize his activities and his estimate of the position of the United States in the UN. "The admission of all these new members," Lodge wrote, "has made the United Nations a harder place in which to work." As one example, Lodge described the difficulty he had encountered assembling a two-thirds majority to condemn the Soviet invasion of Hungary.[26] But changes in the operating procedure of the American delegation, which he had been introducing during the administration's first term, were yielding results. "We no longer engage in any 'arm-twisting,' which was a favorite phrase and a favorite technique of the Truman Administration, notably with Latin Americans," Lodge said. "We try to work through persuasion, with the result that we may receive slightly fewer votes on unimportant matters. but we have much more real leadership and respect (and in some cases liking) than was true before—and we get solid support on the big things."[27]

Progress in another direction resulted less from Lodge's actions than from the force of world events, but it was progress just the same. In a reference to the wrenching effect of Suez on the Western alliance, Lodge wrote, "We are no longer forced to act on a tripartite basis with the United Kingdom and France. This was very hampering and did us a great deal of harm—and very little good." He concluded, "We are now free to team up with countries of our choice whenever it suits our interest to do so. . . . Such a strategy gives us greater flexibility and influence."[28]

After Suez, charges of collaboration with the colonialists diminished. Another indictment, however, which was equally potent, continued to be brought against the United States. Many people in the third world, Lodge said, considered Americans racists; this fact threatened ill consequences for administration diplomacy. "At the United Nations General Assembly, you see the world as a place in which a large majority of the human race is non-white. The non-white majority is growing every year, as more African states gain their independence." Lodge warned that if Americans were not careful they might, at some time in the not too distant future, be classed with the authors of apartheid in South Africa[29]—an association that would do severe damage to American interests. Lodge considered the opinion of black Africans, even where they lacked political rights, very important. Africans, Lodge asserted, had "the future in front of them." To impress them with America's good will would benefit the United States "for the long pull."[30]

Not surprisingly, Lodge was dismayed when news of violent opposition to school desegregation in Little Rock flashed around the world in 1957. In the middle of the Arkansas crisis, he wrote to Eisenhower, "Here at the United Nations I can see clearly the harm that the riots in Little Rock are doing to our foreign relations. More than two-thirds of the world is non-white and the reactions of the representatives of these people is easy to see."[31] Though most of the injury to the prestige of the United States occurred when the riots hit the front pages, Lodge appreciated Eisenhower's steadfastness in dealing with the situation, and he thought that in terms of damage control the president's actions had a good effect. Following the dispatch of federal troops to Little Rock, Lodge noted that at least one Asian leader, the prime minister of India, had complimented the administration. "I was delighted," Lodge told Eisenhower, "to see Nehru . . . openly praise what you had done in Arkansas. That goes a long way."[32]

Lodge believed the administration could improve its image on the race issue in ways that required little more than forethought and sensitivity. Commenting that he encountered the opinion at the UN that Americans were "forever lecturing" and that they often assumed "an attitude of insufferable superiority" in their relations with Africans and Asians, Lodge suggested that Eisenhower encourage brief good-will visits by high-ranking officials and spouses to less-developed countries. It was especially important, Lodge contended, that these be more than business trips, for most of the good feelings that would result would be the product of time spent "drinking, dining, dancing and laughing." Certainly, such contacts would yield useful information about Asian and African leaders. "But the main point, "Lodge declared, "would be simply to be agreeable and to make them feel that *we* think *they* are attractive."[33]

Along the same lines, and in response to a specific query from Eisenhower as to how the United States could restore its reputation after the troubles at Little Rock, Lodge urged that American representatives around the world, and not only in nonwhite countries or at the United Nations, make a sustained effort to "extend hospitality to distinguished colored people." He added, "I know from experience here how much it means."[34]

Lodge must have guessed that in an administration as conservative in racial matters as Eisenhower's, and with as strong a Southern influence, few top officials would leap at the opportunity to go junketing around Asia, Africa, and Latin America. He must have realized, too, that some other advice he had to offer would not get much support within an administration that drew so heavily from the Fortune 500. Lodge was disturbed at brusque treatment accorded envoys from Latin America, and he warned Eisenhower, "There is no doubt that the so-called 'big business' approach to Latin-American diplomats has extremely unfortunate and damaging results. With no people, as you well know, are tact and persuasion more important." Lodge thought the administration placed too much emphasis on efficiency and not enough on personal contacts. Referring to the significance of Latin America's twenty votes in the United Nations—without which, he asserted, "the whole question of whether we could afford to stay in the United Nations at all would call for close examination"—Lodge said, "It would certainly be a pity if we lost these votes because of talking to them as though they were corporations instead of people."[35] Lodge also considered it a mistake for the administration to promote "capitalism" as such. The word, if not the concept, he declared beyond rehabilitation in the third world.[36]

And always there was the question of money: foreign economic aid. A chronic sore spot with the budget balancers in the administration and on Capitol Hill, foreign aid funding came hard enough when directed to declared allies of the United States. When Lodge and others attempted to loosen the purse strings for the benefit of neutralists, some serious explaining had to be done to assure critics that Uncle Sam was not being taken for a ride by closet communists. To Lodge's way of thinking, economic assistance had the potential for attracting third world nations toward the West, but it also brought the possibility of antagonizing countries that felt that American generosity did not match American resources.

Lodge advocated two changes in the Eisenhower administration's aid program—two changes that seemed contradictory, but both of which, in fact, were designed to achieve the same end: the enhancement of the standing of the United States among nonaligned countries. First, Lodge urged the administration to sponsor a number of high-profile projects to counter Soviet activities in Asia and Africa. He mentioned a notorious example from Afghanistan in which a well-advertised Russian-built storage silo had been filled with unadvertised American grain. As a consequence, Moscow got the credit for feeding the Afghans while Washington got the bill.[37] In like vein, Lodge recounted a story he had heard in Geneva regarding "immense tips" Russian diplomats always gave to taxi drivers and hotel employees, resulting in a Soviet reputation for largess. A similar tale from Libya concerned a member of the Russian embassy who emptied his pockets and told his cab driver, "I have two pounds and I split them with you—one for you and one for me." Saying that these examples had been described to him as illustrations of "diabolical Soviet cleverness," Lodge argued that the United States should learn a lesson from them. He did not contend that the administration ought to cut back on necessary projects just because they did not receive a big play in the local press. "But we should have every now and then a so-called 'flashy' project which does create some favorable talk for the United States and we should not be in the position of being a 'Mother Superior' who is always trying to make the little boy swallow some medicine he doesn't like."[38]

Lodge's second suggestion for using aid to enhance American prestige and to offset Soviet economic assistance nearly contradicted his advocacy of highly visible, obviously made-in-the-U.S.A. projects. Lodge recommended a channeling of American funds, in the form of challenge grants, through the UN. The result would be a multilateral, more or less anonymous program of assistance to needy countries. Lodge spent considerable effort pushing this scheme, which he dubbed "UN Multilateral." At different times he offered at least a dozen arguments explaining why the administration ought to adopt it.

For one thing, it would diminish the auction effect that resulted when a prospective aid recipient managed to get the United States and the Soviet Union into a bidding contest.[39] Lodge cited the Suez affair, which followed a flap over the funding of the Aswan dam, as an instance of the dangers inherent in economic escalation. A second argument for UN Multilateral was that when aid requests had to be turned down, as many inevitably would, it would be preferable if the United Nations did the refusing. "Handling economic aid on a multilateral basis takes us 'off the spot,' " Lodge wrote. "The most destructive political position is that of saying 'No' all the time. It is better for us to have the UN or some other organization say 'No.' "[40] Third, the matching aspect of Lodge's proposal would make American dollars go further than they would if unmatched by foreign funds.[41]

Lodge's fourth argument was his ace in the hole for winning over tight-fisted opponents like Treasury Secretary George Humphrey. Lodge premised the entire UN Multilateral program on the willingness of the Soviets, specifically, to match American contributions dollar for dollar, and not ruble, or some other nonconvertible currency, for dollar. If the Russians rejected the idea—as Lodge thought likely—the United States would win a significant diplomatic victory. "If the Soviet Union refused, we would have scored an immense advantage in the cold war," claimed Lodge, "and when nations made requests of us in the future they could be constantly reminded of the fact that the Soviet Union refused to help. It would bring all exaggerated ideas about the U.S. Treasury down to earth."[42]

This last line of reasoning raises the question of whether Lodge actually sought to implement UN Multilateral. As Lodge well knew, the Russians would look suspiciously on any proposal suggesting a radical departure from their aid program. The Soviet economic offensive was going well; why else would the Americans offer such a scheme to counteract it? Lodge's analysis of two earlier administration initiatives helps elucidate his thinking on foreign aid. Speaking of the Atoms for Peace and Open Skies proposals, Lodge wrote, "Both were tremendously effective because they were affirmative, they took the initiative, and they *challenged the Soviets*."[43] What Lodge did not say, because it did not require saying, was that these initiatives had elicited cool responses from the Kremlin, to no one's great surprise.[44] A similar reaction most likely awaited UN Multilateral.

Lodge was not entirely disingenuous in forwarding such a program, but he certainly was hedging his bets. To Lodge, UN Multilateral seemed a winning proposition either way: the United States would benefit whether the Russians went along or not. One point that Lodge's comments on assistance to third world nations makes clear is the extent to which he viewed relations with the nonaligned countries against a backdrop of superpower rivalry. "Economic aid is today the most crucial field in which we are contesting with the Russians," Lodge told Eisenhower at the beginning of 1958. "Because it is the most direct way into men's minds, we should do whatever is necessary to win this contest."[45]

Eventually the administration adopted a multilateral approach to foreign aid, though the form it took differed from what Lodge had suggested.[46] Through the end of his term in office, Lodge continued to press on Eisenhower the importance of economic assistance and to lobby for improvements in that area. But other matters required his attention as well.

Lodge spent a great deal of time defending and promoting the general idea of the United Nations. The UN, of course, provided a favorite target for conservatives and latent—and not so latent—isolationists, especially as American control declined with the admission of new members who were unresponsive to American pressure. Lodge felt compelled to engage in a continuing task of selling to the American people the idea that the UN was a worthwhile organization and that American membership brought measurable benefits to the United States.

The most prominent feature of Lodge's sales pitch was his oratorical jousting with communist delegates. Certainly Lodge enjoyed this aspect of his work; no doubt his attacks on communism and his defense of the American way of life expressed sincere convictions. But Lodge knew that good theater made good politics. Year after year, he kept track of popular opinion regarding American participation in the UN, and he proudly reported to Eisenhower that public support kept going up. A typical letter of October 1957 included the results of a recent Gallup poll placing American satisfaction with the UN at an all-time high.[47] Lodge, of course, could not claim full credit for this growing approval. Nor did he; always the diplomat, he attributed it to Eisenhower. Yet Lodge, who was probably the administration's most popular figure after the president, deserved the majority of credit for convincing Americans of the positive value of the UN.

Lodge jealously guarded the hard-won support for the United Nations, and he resisted anything that might diminish it. He stood firmly against the admission of China, partly out of conviction but mostly because he recognized that all the gains in prestige the UN had made in America might evaporate in a day if the administration dropped its opposition to the Beijing government.[48] Lodge paid particular attention to the actions and statements of influential China-resisters like William Knowland, the so-called senator from Formosa. While Republican leader in the Senate, Knowland vowed that if the administration countenanced China's admission, he would resign the Senate leadership and mount a campaign to pull the United States out of the UN.[49] Knowland was an extremist—Eisenhower sometimes wondered whose side he was on[50]—but his attitude toward China reflected the opinions of millions of Americans.

Lodge carefully kept track of Knowland's blasts at the United Nations, which came with fair regularity. The senator not only threatened American participation in the UN by inflaming the China issue; as an influential member of the Senate Appropriations Committee he could make American participation in the UN problematic. For this double reason, Lodge took care to rebut, courteously but firmly, Knowland's charges that the UN had become a nest of neutralists and a one-sided soapbox for the dissemination of Moscow's line. Knowland elaborated the communist propaganda theme in a 1955 letter to Lodge. The California Republican specifically complained that while communist speeches at the UN could be read and heard throughout the United States, American responses received no coverage in the Soviet bloc. In a transparent proposal that revealed his basic hostility to the UN, Knowland urged the administration to demand equal time behind the Iron Curtain; if the Soviets and their allies refused, they ought to be denied use of the UN's forum.[51]

In answering Knowland's charges, Lodge did not mention the obvious fact that even if the United States could engineer the expulsion of the communists—which it couldn't—the effort would wreck the UN. Lodge admitted the organization's propaganda value for the communists, but he contended that the American delegation scored public relations hits of its own. American speeches, said Lodge, had an impact among American allies and especially in neutral nations that more than outweighed communist rhetoric. Lodge carried his defense of the UN so far as to say that the presence of the communists positively served American interests by allowing American delegates and like-thinking representatives from other countries to refute communist allegations at once. "It is clearly advantageous to us to be able to put them on the spot and for others to put them on the spot." Lodge especially appreciated support from nonaligned diplomats who took America's side in debates. Citing a particular example, Lodge told Knowland, "When, as has happened, an Indian representative . . . defends the United States foreign aid program against Soviet attack, it is a victory for us." Lodge went on to describe "some terribly powerful stories that got tremendous coverage in the free world and in the neutralist world," and he reminded Knowland of the number of times—more than twenty—that the Chinese had failed to gain admission. These failures Lodge characterized as a "defeat and humiliation" for the communists.[52]

Knowland was not alone among influential critics of the United Nations, though voices of protest did tend to come from his end of the political spectrum. Like Knowland, Henry Luce often seemed to have China on the brain; like Knowland, he distrusted the UN and went out of his way to make American membership precarious. In early 1957, *Life* flayed Lodge and the UN for failing to take a sufficiently forceful position against the Soviet invasion of Hungary a few months before. The editorial contained enough errors of fact regarding UN operating procedures— errors that could have been corrected, as Lodge wrote in an indignant

reply to Luce, by "a two minute telephone call"—to suggest willful ignorance. Nevertheless, Lodge, who at times must have felt that he did nothing but explain what the UN could and could not do, patiently composed a
point-by-point refutation. When Lodge insisted that his rebuttal be published with prominence equal to that of the original editorial, Luce, to his
credit, agreed, and the magazine ran a slightly shortened version of
Lodge's side of the story.[53]

While fighting a rear guard action against the likes of Luce and Knowland,
protecting his flanks against charges of colonialism and racism, and promoting an economic counteroffensive against the Soviets, Lodge realized
that the most effective weapon in the Eisenhower administration's arsenal
for use in the third world was the president himself.

From the first year of Eisenhower's term in office, Lodge saw that most
of the world liked Ike as much as America did. Two days after the president's 1953 Atoms for Peace speech at the UN, Lodge reported that the
address had elicited "enthusiastic comment by everybody." Among delegates from nonaligned states, Eisenhower's appearance had had an especially significant effect. India's prickly Krishna Menon—with whom
Lodge, in fact, got along rather well—had called Lodge at home late at
night, waking him and demanding to see him right away. Menon would
not be put off, and when he arrived, "in a state of tremendous excitement," according to Lodge, he described Eisenhower's speech as "a tremendously important declaration . . . a new turning point in human affairs." Lodge remarked in a postscript, "It is typical of what your speech
did to the neutralists."[54] In a later letter, Lodge explained that the messen-
ger as much as the message had evoked the favorable response at the UN.
The president, Lodge said, had impressed the representatives with his
"encyclopedic knowledge of world events" and his "effectiveness as a
world statesmen." Referring specifically to diplomats from nonaligned
countries, Lodge added, "You also flattered them tremendously by making them feel that they were really 'in the club.' "[55]

Throughout Eisenhower's two terms, Lodge continued to comment on
the appeal the president had for people from all around the world. Following Eisenhower's heart attack in 1955, Lodge described to the convales-
cent an "outpouring of friendly feelings" at the United Nations. "You have

undoubtedly been prayed for in all Christian churches and in the Moslem, Buddhist, Hindu and Jewish faiths as well!" He remarked further, "The world, in all truth, not only admires you and regards you as essential; the world truly *loves* you."[56]

Several months later, as the election of 1956 approached, Lodge attended a UN reception at which the Indian representative asserted that he had made a canvass of delegates and that by a large majority they hoped Eisenhower would win. (Actually, the Indian representative said the sentiment was unanimous, but Lodge thought this improbable.) "They all feel," Lodge quoted the Indian diplomat, "that President Eisenhower has *the touch*." Lodge appended his own assessment: "This is but one further proof of the unique situation which you hold in the world today."[57]

Comments like these strongly suggest that there was a purpose behind Lodge's repeated and often effusive reports of the power Eisenhower wielded over the minds and affections of the mass of humanity, especially in the neutral nations. One suspects flattery. Lodge seems to have been seeking to draw the president's attention to the third world by intimating that great popular victories awaited him there. Lodge did not often suggest direct presidential initiatives in diplomacy toward the nonaligned states. Instead, he worked by indirection.

In his memoirs, Eisenhower described his thoughts as his second term drew to a close. "In September 1959, I began seriously to consider the feasibility of a personal visit to the Mediterranean area and the Middle East. The general idea of such a trip had been in my mind for some time. . . . I realized that internationally I enjoyed a measure of good will."[58] Eisenhower probably could not have identified the factors that eventually led him to conclude that traveling to Asia, North Africa, and Latin America would be a splendid idea; broad impressions like this often have obscure causes. Nevertheless, Lodge ranks as perhaps the most important, and certainly the most persistent, influence affecting Eisenhower's decision to become his own diplomat to the third world. That the president realized that he "enjoyed a measure of good will" in many countries owed largely to the fact that Lodge had been telling him just that for six years. If Eisenhower believed that personal visits would improve American relations with nonaligned states, that belief reflected Lodge's repeated emphasis on the personal element in relations with lesser powers. In 1956, the president had responded to a suggestion by Lodge that American officials take time for friendly visits to neutral nations, by saying that the idea made "good sense."[59] As Eisenhower's time in office ran out, it seemed to make even better sense.

In some ways, Eisenhower's journeys in 1959 and 1960 across Asia, Africa, and Latin America represented the successful culmination of Lodge's efforts to push relations with those regions to the front burner of American foreign policy. Eisenhower, who was quite moved by his reception in places like New Delhi and Casablanca, probably wished he had been talked into making such trips earlier.[60]

Yet there was more to the story. At the same time that Eisenhower pondered a third-world tour, Lodge did some traveling of his own. For two weeks in September 1959, he escorted Soviet leader Khrushchev on a journey across America.[61] The decision to invite Khrushchev had not been Lodge's, of course; it came from the White House. And as part of a general easing of tensions with the Russians, it had causes transcending anything Lodge had done at the UN. But Lodge's role in this opening to the East, though indirect and largely unintentional, had not been insignificant.

When old hands at the State Department claimed that Lodge was beginning to think like the delegates from Asia and Africa, they were right. They certainly hit the mark with respect to Lodge's heightened sensitivity to colonialism and racism, and probably also regarding his assessment of the nature of the communist threat. When Lodge took office in 1953, his anticommunist convictions were unsurpassed within the administration. Through nearly eight years of close association with the representatives of neutral states, however, Lodge gained a greater appreciation for their perspective. He never lost his belief in the implacable opposition of communism to democracy, but he did imbibe something of the neutralists' ability to view communism in detached, objective fashion.

Near the end of his expedition with Khrushchev, Lodge wrote the memorandum that appears at the beginning of this chapter. Typical of its genre, the sketch reveals as much about its author as about its subject. Especially worth noting in the present context is the appreciation Lodge demonstrates for the individuality and humanness of Khrushchev. Lodge's ideology shows through, in his comments on Khrushchev's "crazy" and "fatuous" political beliefs. But he is willing to set aside ideology to gain a better understanding of Khrushchev as a person. To argue ideological matters would avail little; it would be "like talking to a man about his religion and should not be done."

It is no coincidence that this tendency to gloss over ideological differences summarized nonalignment philosophy in the 1950s. Ideology, whether Marxist, capitalist, or otherwise, often seemed a dangerous distraction to countries newly independent and struggling to survive, since ideology obscured basic human problems and might lead to war. As Lodge rubbed shoulders with representatives of the nonaligned states, some of their philosophy rubbed off.

While it is difficult to determine the extent to which Lodge's attitudes influenced administration policy, it *is* clear that by late 1959 the Eisenhower administration had adopted a less confrontational stance toward the Soviet Union. Khrushchev visited the United States, making a considerable and largely favorable impression. Eisenhower planned to reciprocate the following year.

The president did not make it to Moscow; the downing of an American spy plane in the spring of 1960 got in the way. Though Lodge—of course—did not give an inch in the debates over the U-2 incident at the United Nations,[62] he must have been disappointed. The previous February, he had made a dry run to the Soviet Union for Eisenhower and had encountered great enthusiasm from the Russian people.[63] In pretrip briefings, Lodge may have come across a statement attributed to Lenin that the road between Moscow and the West passed through Beijing and Calcutta. Lodge may have reflected that Lenin had a point. China remained off limits to American diplomats, but for Lodge, if not for Eisenhower, the journey to Moscow *had* included India and other parts of the third world.

IV
Dead Center

9

Dwight Eisenhower and
the Baggage of War

"Irrespective of their ages," C. D. Jackson wrote in 1954, "some people move 'old'; some people move 'young'." Eisenhower, Jackson continued, moved "young":

It is noticeable in the spring of his walk as he enters a room. It is noticeable in the flashlike speed in which he moves from sitting to striding in his office in the middle of an interview. It is noticeable in meetings when, with youthful effortlessness, he will swing from a slouch that must put at least his fifth vertebra on the seat of his chair to bolt upright.

In other respects as well, the president's appearance and presence belied his years.

His color, despite what the camera does to him, is excellent. And if he has to look tired, which most mortals must at some time or other, the only time his features seem to sag is when he is bored. But even that is only momentary, because his almost fantastically patient courtesy comes into play almost instantly in order to give the bore the impression that he is being listened to with interest.

Jackson took pains to refute the conventional wisdom that Eisenhower lacked culture and the ability to put his thoughts into words:

This just isn't so. He is highly literate, and cultured well beyond innate gentlemanliness. His classical, Biblical, and mythological allusions come tumbling out when he is working with words. Even Emmet H[ughes] would have to agree that his capacity for unscrambling an involved paragraph and fixing it so that it says what it was supposed to say in the first place, is sometimes uncanny.

Jackson stopped short of declaring the president an intellectual omnivore. "He is definitely not equally interested in or excited about everything or everybody." If a visitor failed to engage his attention, Eisenhower would nod politely even while drifting off mentally. But when a conversation or a memo aroused his curiosity, he reacted quite differently. "He will instantly go from neutral to high gear, and remain in high as long as is necessary, which is frequently longer than the other person's capacity to stay in high."[1]

In 1954, Jackson had known Eisenhower for more than a decade. Eventually, the psychological warrior's impressions of the president would lose some of their glow; to a certain degree, he would join the doubters who wondered how completely Eisenhower understood the world. But at the beginning of the administration's second year in office, the honeymoon continued. To Jackson, the president remained very much the victorious general, the hero he had served during the war.

World War II made Dwight Eisenhower's career. It raised him from obscurity; it set him before the eyes of the nation and the world; it opened the door to the White House. His journey from the beaches of North Africa to the banks of the Potomac was one long and triumphant, if occasionally interrupted, procession. Had there been no war, Eisenhower would have retired to oblivion; as it was, he died one of the most famous men of his time.

The rewards that came Eisenhower's way after the war occasioned little surprise, and the general's decision to parlay war-won popularity into political success seemed entirely natural in a country where military heroes have often considered the presidency part of their booty; but the leap from army service to politics did not come easily. If it had, Eisenhower might well have been president by 1949, with cold war consequences that can only be imagined. Instead, Eisenhower hesitated. Touted by some for the presidency even before the war ended, he became the focus of speculation by pundits of all persuasions, especially since no one quite knew his party or preferences. As the years passed, interest in his future increased; heightened interest inevitably drove his political stock higher. Yet still he held back, yielding only in 1952 to a concerted effort to convince him that he alone held the keys to a secure and prosperous American future.

To some, Eisenhower's diffidence appeared merely a draft seeker's disguise and his denials of presidential aspirations simply trial balloons in camouflage netting. Undoubtedly, calculation played a part. But to disregard Eisenhower's disclaimers misses the sincerity of his doubts in trying to decide between remaining a soldier and launching a political career. In private comments even more than in public remarks, Eisenhower displayed a deep and genuine distaste for the tumult of politics. Repeatedly, he expressed his belief that the race for place brought out the worst in people. "Politics . . . ," he told a friend in 1951, "excites all that is selfish and ambitious in man."[2] To another, he said that a political career was one he could contemplate "only with the utmost reluctance, even repugnance."[3] He told E. E. Hazlett, a boyhood companion from Abilene, "I cannot conceive of any set of probable circumstances that would ever convince me that it was my duty to enter such a hectic arena."[4] In his diary, he described his "dread" that he might feel compelled to take up a political burden.[5]

These are not pro forma renunciations; Eisenhower really was struggling. And with good reason, for despite America's penchant for promoting victorious generals to commander in chief, a career soldier campaigning for office violated a cherished army principle: the separation of military from political affairs. Eisenhower especially felt the weight of the principle, for he had served under his era's most notorious exception to the rule.

Eisenhower's association with Douglas MacArthur began in Washington, where the senior officer commanded the military force that routed the Bonus Army of 1932. At the time, Eisenhower had objected that getting involved in what amounted to a political question was "highly inappropriate" for a soldier of MacArthur's rank. But MacArthur had ignored his aide's dissent.[6] From Washington, Eisenhower followed MacArthur to the Philippines, at the latter's insistence. The change of scenery did not diminish MacArthur's affinity for politics, nor did it lessen Eisenhower's unease. Eisenhower later commented:

Most of the senior officers I had known always drew a clean-cut line between the military and the political. Off duty, among themselves and close civilian friends, they might explosively denounce everything they thought was wrong in Washington and the world, and propose their own cure for its evils. On duty, nothing could induce them to cross the line they, and old Army tradition, had established. But if General MacArthur ever recognized the existence of that line, he usually chose to ignore it.[7]

Thirty years after the fact, Eisenhower particularly remembered one event that drove home in a personal way the unseemliness of mixing politics with military affairs—an incident, he said, that "chilled the warm relationship" he had had with MacArthur to that point. MacArthur, then military adviser to the president of the Philippines, thought it would be a good move politically to stage a demonstration of the progress he had made in building up the country's armed forces. Eisenhower differed, contending that the funds required for the military review could better be spent on weapons, ammunition, and training. But MacArthur insisted, and Eisenhower reluctantly began the planning. Shortly thereafter, Eisenhower received a call from President Quezon, asking what all the unusual troop movements were about. Eisenhower was more than a little surprised to learn that MacArthur had failed to inform the president of the upcoming demonstration. He was taken aback further, and greatly miffed, when MacArthur, upon hearing of Quezon's demand that the review be cancelled, denied that he had ordered his staff to arrange it. Eisenhower later recalled feeling "considerable resentment" at being made MacArthur's scapegoat; he added, "Never again were we on the same warm and cordial terms."[8]

If MacArthur demonstrated the vices a soldier ought to shun, George Marshall embodied the virtues he should seek. While Eisenhower distrusted MacArthur, he considered Marshall the greatest American he had ever met.[9] Marshall, of course, was known for observing a rigid separation between the military and political spheres. Eisenhower found Marshall's reserve on political matters as commendable as he considered MacArthur's ambitious meddling objectionable. In this area, as in most aspects of professional life, Marshall served as Eisenhower's model. Stephen Ambrose, Eisenhower's foremost biographer, declares of Marshall, "He set the standards Eisenhower tried to meet."[10]

For Eisenhower to enter politics transgressed the code of a lifetime, and it made him out to be a MacArthur rather than a Marshall. Even worse, it forced him to confront the fact that the acclaim he enjoyed owed fully as much to the sacrifices of the men he had led as to anything he himself had done. While agonizing over the question of a political career, Eisenhower probably confided more intimately in Milton than in anyone else—as he did on most subjects. Milton later described his brother's thoughts: "He earnestly believed that it would be wrong to take advantage of the wave of popularity and affection that resulted from military victory, won by the toil and blood of men under his command."[11]

Faced with these arguments against crossing the line into politics, Eisenhower nevertheless chose to toss his general's cap into the ring. Why? Ambition, principally. Eisenhower was capable, and he knew it. He had achieved all he could expect to accomplish in the military; the only higher position to which he could aspire was the presidency. He had too much energy to retire. He considered himself to be as qualified for the White House as any other likely candidate. And he realized that he could win.

But Eisenhower could not simply act on his ambition. To do so would smack of Caesarism, or at least MacArthurism, and it would betray, in a sense, the hundreds of thousands of ordinary soldiers who had fought and died to preserve freedom, not to put Dwight Eisenhower in the White House. As a means of resolving the dilemma, Eisenhower fell back, not quite consciously, on another principle fundamental to the soldier's conception of self: the call of duty. As the prospective candidate wrestled with his desire to accept the office the American people seemed eager to bestow, he emphasized more and more the notion of duty. In telling Hazlett that he neither sought nor desired a political career, Eisenhower said that he could not foresee circumstances "that would convince me that it was my duty" to enter politics.[12] After an interview with some prominent Republicans encouraging him to run, he noted in his diary that he could follow their advice only if he became convinced that "refusal to do so would always thereafter mean to me that I'd failed to do my duty."[13] As the pressure mounted for him to announce, he confided to a close associate, "I hope always to do my duty by my country; but I cannot conceive of circumstances that could convince me that I had a duty to enter politics."[14]

And how would he recognize the call of duty? In democratic America, when he heard the voice of the people. At the end of 1951, following futher visits from promoters of an Eisenhower candidacy, he remarked in his diary, "I believe the presidency is something that should never be sought, just as I believe, of course, that it could never be refused. . . . I would consider the nomination of which they speak, if accomplished without any direct or indirect assistance or connivance on my part, to place upon me a transcendent duty."[15] A few months later he wrote to Christian Herter, later Dulles' successor as secretary of state, in a similar tone. Eisenhower began by describing the importance of his current position as commander of the Allied forces in Europe, and he asserted that he could not lightly abandon his task. "My own personal inclinations, the advice of loyal associates and warm friends, the possibilities that lie ahead—none of these can be permitted to outweigh an inescapable and present duty." Yet he admitted one argument he would not be able to resist. "There is no question in my mind concerning the propriety of answering a clear-cut call to another and higher duty, a call that is traditionally and universally recognized as the voice of the American people speaking through a national convention. Such a call imposes an obligation of citizenship on the man so honored."[16]

Though it may be difficult to take all this seriously—Eisenhower seems so like many others who have played hard to get—Eisenhower *was* serious. The idea of a soldier's duty meant a great deal to him. He could not lightly put down the burden of a life's work just because the White House beckoned; he really did believe he could abandon his post only if called to a higher duty.

Those persons trying to push Eisenhower into politics caught on quickly. They arranged demonstrations of popular enthusiasm, the best-orchestrated of which was a rally at Madison Square Garden in February 1952. To ensure that the general clearly recognized the voice of the people, the organizers recorded the event on film. Within hours, their agent flew to Paris to restage the show for Eisenhower's benefit.

The effect was immediate—and it underlines the sincerity of Eisenhower's struggle. On viewing the film and hearing a description of the rally, Eisenhower was overwhelmed; in his diary he characterized his reaction as "a real emotional experience." "I've not been so upset in years. Clearly to be seen is the mass longing of America for some kind of reasonable solution for her nagging, persistent, and almost terrifying problems. It's a real experience to realize that one could become a symbol for many thousands of the hope they have." He added, "I can't help it; the performance at the Garden is not only something to make an American genuinely proud—it is something to increase his humility, his sense of his own unworthiness to fulfill the spoken and unspoken desires and aspirations of so many thousands of humans."[17]

For Eisenhower, the rally at Madison Square Garden constituted a breakthrough. It allowed him to reconcile ambition with conscience. He never forgot that he owed his political opportunity to the efforts and lives of those who had served under him during the war; he never overcame his conviction that soldiers did not normally belong in politics. But in answering the call of the people, as demonstrated by outbursts of enthusiasm like that at the Garden, he remained the good soldier. Of course, he never could admit that he enjoyed politics. Throughout his presidency, he continually protested that he disliked his job, that only a sense of duty kept him from laying down his burdens and going fishing. Even as he decided in favor of a second term, arguing to himself that his tour of duty was not yet at any end, he continued to complain. To his brother Edgar he wrote in early 1956, "For my part, my attempt to do something for my country in the post I now occupy has cost me a lot in health, much in wear and tear on mind and disposition, to say nothing of some hundreds of thousands of dollars."[18]

The call of duty, in the voice of the people, liberated Eisenhower from the constraints of the war hero's conscience; but, at the same time, it confined him. As president, Eisenhower became a prisoner of his popularity. On a number of occasions, when national interest demanded strong leadership and a willingness to risk contention, Eisenhower backed away. Recognizing the length of the nerve McCarthy had touched, the president refused to denounce the Wisconsin senator publicly, thereby damaging American credibility abroad and limiting his capacity for conducting foreign policy. He delayed and obfuscated on arms control, letting his own doubts, Dulles' opposition, and a fear of stirring up those who would soon claim a "missile gap" kill any hope of containing the arms race before it got out of control. Stephen Ambrose, who on the whole describes Eisenhower in laudatory terms, concedes the president's failure of leadership on disarmament. "Eisenhower not only recognized better than anyone else the futility of an arms race; he was in a better position than anyone else to end it. His prestige, especially as a military man, was so overwhelming that he could have made a test ban with the Russians merely on his own assurance that the agreement was good for the United States." But he did not. Ambrose concludes, "The great tragedy here is opportunity lost."[19]

On subjects like these, some of Eisenhower's caution might be attributed to an honest judgment, or misjudgment, regarding what congressional politics and public opinion would bear; but more is involved. Eisenhower's reluctance to take decisive action reflects what Robert Divine calls the president's "most glaring weakness, a sensitivity to criticism." Eisenhower, Divine explains, wanted "to be liked by everyone." His desire for popular approval repeatedly blocked potentially controversial decisions that many of his advisers judged necessary. "In the White House," Divine says, "instead of using his popularity to advance the interests of his administration, he came more and more to hoard it, placing a greater premium on his adulation by the American people than on any specific achievement."[20]

Eisenhower's need for popular approval surfaced perhaps most clearly in November 1956, while the returns of the presidential election came in. Even as reports indicated a fifty percent increase from 1952 in the size of his winning margin, Eisenhower could not relax. Turning to Emmet Hughes, he said,

You remember that story of Nelson—dying, he looked around and asked, "Are there any of them still left?" I guess that's *me*. . . . I want to win the whole thing. . . . Six or seven states we can't help. But I don't want to lose any more. Don't want any of them "left"—like Nelson. That's the way I feel.[21]

Every politician dreams of a clean sweep, but for Eisenhower the desire "to win the whole thing" went to the heart of his self-image. Eisenhower did not step from the military world to politics until he had convinced himself that the people were calling him to a higher duty. He could sustain such a conviction only so long as he remained popular. Every state, every vote even, that was "left" contradicted this conviction and implicitly denied his right to be in politics. The contradiction left Eisenhower to confront the unacceptable possibility that he was simply another ambitious politician, that he was more like MacArthur than Marshall, that he had used the lives and deaths of those he had commanded for his own ends.

Popularity was the cloak that concealed Eisenhower's ambition from himself. With each dissenting vote, with each contentious decision, the cloak unraveled a bit. Eisenhower rejected the notion of using public acclaim to put his ideas into action. He refused to take forthright stands on many divisive issues. He declined to mount the bully pulpit. To do so would threaten his popularity, and if popularity fell away he would stand revealed—most damningly to himself—as a soldier who had forsaken the true and noble call of duty for the base allure of political ambition.

There was, of course, more to Eisenhower's impedimenta from World War II than the burden of popularity. The war, as well as a career in the army, had accustomed him to a military way of doing things. The armed forces did not lack their own bureaucratic idiosyncrasies, to be sure; but the political world proved far more complex and refractory. At times, Eisenhower reflected longingly on the life he had led before moving into the White House. After a year in office, he told Hazlett of the difficulty of effecting changes in the operation of the government. In a broader sense, his remarks reveal a wistfulness for the more straightforward approach of the military.

One of the features of service life that I miss in this job is an "Inspector General's" service. Visitors here—usually meaning to be helpful—are quite apt to leave me with a hint that something is wrong here or wrong there, and sometimes these allegations are of a grave nature.

In the Army it was so simple to turn to a properly trained and dedicated group for any inspection job ranging from suspected peculation to plain incompetence, and it never occurred to me that a similar or equivalent agency would not be available in the Federal government. But there is no readily available agency to look into hints of this character. Even when they are referred to the interested departments of government, they are very likely to be handled in a lackadaisical manner for the simple reason that people are not accustomed to the standards of administrative accounting and responsibility that prevailed in the Armed Services.[22]

Observers in the administration noted Eisenhower's difficulty in making the transition from the military world to the political. C. D. Jackson, in the memo cited above describing the spring in the president's step and his facility at untangling speeches, expressed reservations about Eisenhower's fluency in the idiom of politics:

Although he is an infinitely more professional and skillful politician than he was on January 20, 1953, he is still mystified in a sincere and uncomplicated way at the maneuvers of politicians, and if he is given to musing with Mamie after a hard day with the gentlemen from the Hill, the words would be something like this: "With all that there is to be done for this country, for the American people, for the whole world, how can any responsible man in public life afford to waste God's time in being a conniving bastard!"[23]

Jackson hoped and probably expected that Eisenhower would learn to deal with "the conniving bastards" of the political world. But he was disappointed, and throughout the president's two terms Jackson privately lamented that for all his skill as a general Eisenhower had failed to master the art of political command. To be sure, some of Jackson's disappointment followed from the president's rejection of his advice regarding psychological warfare. Yet Jackson never ceased admiring Eisenhower personally, and his comments reflect a basically sympathetic attitude. For this reason, they are all the more telling, as when Jackson noted in his diary in 1958:

The President: Lovable as always, with many sense-making flashes and a really unerring sense for what should not be in a speech. But not a national or political leader. He can sprint a few yards, but he tires quickly, and while he can become momentarily fascinated by individual pieces of the international jigsaw puzzle, he does not seem to be able to see what the picture would look like when all the pieces were put together. This impression amply confirmed by inside White House family when hair down.[24]

Staff Secretary Andrew Goodpaster, an even more sympathetic observer than Jackson, also commented on Eisenhower's inability to keep the puzzle pieces straight. Goodpaster described a meeting at which Eisenhower shook his head in wonderment at the administration's failure to reduce American troop levels in Europe. "I just don't seem to be making any progress in getting those troops out," the president complained. "Our policy—the national policy established—is to cut those troops down." Goodpaster hesitated for a moment before politely informing his boss that that such in fact was not American policy. "Well, that just can't be," Eisenhower objected. "I don't believe it. I don't believe it. I won't accept it. . . . I just don't have any doubt in my mind at all. Foster Dulles is coming over here this afternoon. I'll check this with him." A few hours later Dulles arrived. Eisenhower pointed his finger at Goodpaster. "Foster, I want you to tell him he's wrong." Dulles pondered the situation, then replied in his most diplomatic tone, "Well, Mr. President, it isn't just as simple as that. As a matter of fact, I'll have to say he's right."[25]

Eisenhower's lapse in this case might have happened to anyone; Goodpaster cited it as an exception to what he considered a typically capable performance. Still, the kind of leadership required for peacetime politics differed from the style of command Eisenhower had learned in the military during the war, and the president sometimes stumbled over the discrepancy. In 1953, John Foster Dulles hoped Eisenhower would come in and shake up the bureaucracy; the candidate's sweeping victory at the polls buoyed Dulles' expectations. But the president failed to throw his personal momentum against the inertia of the system, and the bureaucracy defied change. Dulles described his disappointment to Jackson in the spring of 1956:

I wish there were some way to solve this problem of government. Arthur Vandenberg told me that the real reason that he was praying that Eisenhower would become President was that the Government of the United States had become so tremendous, so unwieldy, so practically unworkable, that Vandenberg thought it would require someone with the prestige and personality and drive, and above all, the popular mandate, of Eisenhower, to come in and reorganize it and re-invigorate it—and of course that has not happened. The President let the early precious months go by, those months when he did have the leverage of a popular personal mandate. And anyhow, he never was, and is not today, a student of politics in the sense that Vandenberg meant. He doesn't understand, and he is not particularly interested.[26]

The most importance consequence of the war, though, was its effect on Eisenhower's understanding of the world. Like most Americans of his generation, Eisenhower emerged from the conflict convinced of America's moral preeminence—understandably so, considering the nature of the enemies America had fought. Most great countries have traditions of national rectitude; the United States is no exception. But during World War II, the notion flourished as never before. Hitler and his allies seemed indisputably evil, all the more when the full magnitude of Nazi crimes came to light. The United States, if not perhaps all of *its* allies, was unarguably on the side of good. To a greater degree than any earlier conflict, this war was a hothouse for American self-confidence, for an ideology of unquestioning righteousness.

At the same time, though, the war reminded Americans, especially those charged with directing the military effort, of the limits of ideology as a guide to practical policy. Power, in the form of guns, tanks, airplanes, and ultimately atomic weapons, was no respecter of principle; Germany and Japan had bowed to force, not to ideals. Eisenhower would not have denied the significance of ideology in sustaining the will to fight; but all the will in the world, and all the moral superiority, would have meant nothing had the balance of military power not favored America.

The aftermath of the war had reinforced the war's lessons. With most of his contemporaries in the United States, Eisenhower had discovered a new menace in the world. Communism, not fascism, was evil's latest face; Moscow, not Berlin and Tokyo, its present fountainhead. But the issues were hardly less clear-cut than before, and the lines of demarcation were no less distinct. If anything, the Manichean tendencies the war had nurtured grew more pronounced as the "free world" faced off against the countries of the Iron Curtain. The United States had done all it could to demonstrate its peaceful intentions for the postwar period: it had demobilized, it had sought cooperation in the UN, it had offered to share its atomic monopoly. But the communists had persisted in their aggressive designs. From Berlin to Beijing, from Prague to Pusan, they had probed, subverted, threatened, and attacked. Wearily, America had rearmed; reluctantly, Americans had resumed the struggle against aggression that they so recently thought they had won.

Such was the American perception of the origins of the cold war. Eisenhower knew the world well enough to recognize that things were not quite so simple as the myth allowed, but in all essentials he subscribed unhesitatingly. America's superiority, he felt, rested on its claim to a higher spiritual and political morality. In a 1947 letter to Hazlett, Eisenhower outlined his convictions:

I believe fanatically in the American form of democracy—a system that recognizes and protects the rights of the individual and that ascribes to the individual a dignity accruing to him because of his creation in the image of a supreme being and which rests upon the conviction that only through a system of free enterprise can this type of democracy be preserved.[27]

Although blameless itself, this peace-loving, free enterprise democracy had come under attack by the forces of communism. As long as communism existed—and Eisenhower did not anticipate its imminent end—the United States faced a deadly threat. Shortly after writing to Hazlett, Eisenhower confided to his diary:

I believe that democracy has entered its decade (perhaps quarter century) of greatest test. . . . I most earnestly believe that unless those that now live in freedom begin, en masse, to look this world in the face, and begin voluntarily and energetically to meet the issues placed before us, then we are doomed—rather, the system, as we know it, is doomed.[28]

In Eisenhower's opinion, the pressing question of world politics was whether the armies and agents of totalitarianism would vanquish the forces of freedom:

The main issue is dictatorship versus a form of government only by the consent of the governed, observance of a bill of rights versus arbitrary power of a ruler or ruling group. That the issue is with us needs no argument—the existing great exponent of dictatorship has announced its fundamental antagonism to all sorts of capitalism (essential to democracy) and that it will strive to destroy it in the world.

The Soviet Union, in Eisenhower's view, was an implacable foe. In his diary, he continued:

Because of Russia's increased power, territory, and world importance as a result of World War II, it is now pushing the issue more determinedly than ever before. Its pronouncements, dating back to Lenin, are more and more guiding its daily operations. . . . Everywhere the sullen weight of Russia leans against the dike that independent nations have attempted to establish, and boring from within is as flagrantly carried on as is obstructionism in the UN. Russia is definitely out to communize the world—where it cannot gain complete control of territory, as it has in Bulgaria, Poland, Rumania, Yugoslavia, and the Baltic States, it promotes starvation, unrest, anarchy, in the certainty that these are breeding grounds for the growth of their damnable philosophy.[29]

Eisenhower reached these conclusions—the quintessence of American cold war ideology—shortly after World War II, and through the course of his presidency, indeed until he died in 1969, he never found reason to alter them. In the second volume of his memoirs, published in 1965, he wrote:

Despite difficulties that have intermittently arisen in recent history among free nations, the truly virulent problems in international affairs spring from the persistent, continuing struggle between freedom and Communism. . . . Communists embrace every kind of tactic to gain their fundamental objective, the domination of the earth's peoples.[30]

As a consequence, Eisenhower believed that the United States must consistently and actively oppose communism; but, at the same time, he suffered no illusions that America could stamp out communism in the foreseeable future or even effect a significant decrease in its influence. As a military man, he too thoroughly respected the balance of forces in the world to think that the United States could do more than hold its own in the struggle with the Soviets. Victory in the cold war he knew to be out of the question; an uneasy truce was the most he expected.

Eisenhower's skepticism regarding military action against the Russians lay behind his refusal to countenance ambitious schemes like those C. D. Jackson kept promoting. When Jackson urged a forceful response to Moscow's invasion of Hungary in 1956, the president rejected the notion out of hand. "To annihilate Hungary . . . ," he told Jackson, "is in no way to help her."[31] Eisenhower stated his views on the limits of force in relations with Moscow even more clearly in a conversation with Syngman Rhee in the summer of 1954. The South Korean president had come to Washington seeking support for a plan to solve the Korean problem once and for all by an assault on North Korea. In turning Rhee down, Eisenhower asked him to consider the implications of his request:

What you are in effect suggesting is that there can be no peace in the world until the head of the Communist octopus is destroyed. That means Russia is destroyed. . . . When you say we should deliberately plunge into war, let me tell you that if war comes, it will be horrible. Atomic war will destroy civilization. It will destroy our cities. There will be millions of people dead. War today is unthinkable with the weapons which we have at our command. If the Kremlin and Washington ever lock up in a war, the results are too horrible to contemplate. I can't even imagine them.[32]

From personal experience, Eisenhower understood the consequences of modern war. He realized that he had seen the last general conflict the United States could hope to win. As a result, he refused to put his country in a position where a direct confrontation with the Kremlin was a serious possibility. He did not categorically rule out military action; in Lebanon, for example, where the likelihood of a meaningful Soviet challenge seemed slight, he had no qualms about sending troops. Similar considerations lay behind this use of the CIA in Iran, Guatemala, the Congo, and elsewhere. In peripheral countries like these, Moscow would probably not react strongly to American meddling; if it did, the deniability implicit in covert operations allowed a discreet withdrawal involving little damage to American prestige or credibility.

Eisenhower's ideology—his conviction of America's moral hegemony in a necessary struggle with communism—placed him and his administration at the center of the most encompassing consensus of twentieth-century American history. Eisenhower's predecessors created the cold war consensus, or at least attended its creation. In doing so, they summoned into existence forces that led to their political downfall. Eisenhower's successors pushed the consensus to its logical, or perhaps illogical, conclusions. In the process, they contributed materially to its demise. But during the Eisenhower years, the consensus reigned, effectively unchallenged.

That it did so was no accident, and the outcome owed as much to the pragmatism that tempered Eisenhower's ideology as to the ideology itself. Eisenhower's unremitting anticommunism afforded proof against all but the wildest conservative assaults; opponents found it nearly impossible to turn the administration's right flank. At the same time, the president's practical flexibility preserved the country from most of the excesses implicit in the ideology; as it did, it warded off challenges from the left. Lapses occurred, to be sure, from an early excessive deference to the McCarthyites, which, among other things, essentially ruled out any creative policy toward East Asia, to the foolhardy continuance of spy flights right up to the summit of 1960, which helped derail an incipient detente with the Soviets. For the most part, however, Eisenhower succeeded in defending the middle ground, and the measure of his success was the fact that the cold war consensus held as firmly when he departed the White House as it did when he arrived.

Therein, though, lay the problem. Eisenhower could hold the consensus, but he could not hold the world. The bipolar model of international relations that informed Eisenhower's ideology approximated reality passably well in the late 1940s, when much of Europe remained in ruins and most of Asia and Africa still bore the colonial yoke. A decade later, however, the revival of Europe and, more importantly, the explosion of third world nationalism had rendered the model obsolescent and dangerous.

Eisenhower was perceptive enough to realize that the world his generation had inherited at the end of the war—the world they had helped shape during the war—was changing. He recognized that American interests would face a greater challenge from indirect attack in the third world than from an assault over the top of the trenches in Europe. His search for military alliances from the Middle East to Indochina, his use of the CIA in countries from Iran to the Congo, his show of force in Lebanon, his approval of increased economic aid for Latin America and Asia, and his own personal diplomacy in nonaligned states all indicate an appreciation of the shift in the focus of the struggle for global influence.

Nonetheless, Eisenhower could never quite free himself from his belief that the conflict with communism was the only one that really mattered. He promoted collective security pacts to contain Russia. He turned the CIA loose in Iran and elsewhere because he feared that local leftists would ally with the Kremlin. He landed troops in Lebanon to deter Nasser, who seemed to be playing the Soviets' game. He approved increased foreign aid in order to blunt Moscow's economic offensive. He visited Asia, Africa, and Latin America to demonstrate that the United States cared as much about those regions as the communists did. As stopgap measures, these reactions sufficed. They enabled the United States to survive the 1950s—and Eisenhower to get out of office—in reasonably good shape. But they provided no basis for long-term stability, as continuing upheavals and increased American commitments throughout the third world demonstrated.

The trouble was in the ideology. The product of a conflict in which the world divided neatly into camps of good and evil, it failed to provide direction in an era when most of humanity rejected the notion of camps, especially those defined by the great powers. Eisenhower caught glimpses of the growing irrelevance of the cold war, but he failed to act consistently and effectively on this insight. He managed to stretch his war-born ideology, at times remarkably far. But in the end, his convictions lacked the life necessary to allow them to adapt to the new world that was emerging.

Conclusion

World War II had less spectacular effects on the careers of Eisenhower's advisers than on his own, but it propelled them forward as well. In terms of political influence, three of the eight—Bedell Smith, Robert Murphy, and C. D. Jackson—owed such clout as they later acquired to the war and to their personal connections to Eisenhower. Smith, even more than Eisenhower, would have retired in obscurity had there been no war. He almost certainly would not have become ambassador to Moscow, nor director of the CIA, nor undersecretary of state. Murphy might have climbed the rungs of the Foreign Service and the State Department, but without a friend in the White House the ascent would have been slower and more difficult, and his ad hoc adventures certainly would have been fewer. Jackson would have pestered only Henry Luce, rather than the president of the United States, with his bright ideas; as a consequence, he quite likely would have enjoyed greater success in selling his schemes, since they would have had narrower consequences in the world of print than in the realm of nations. A fourth adviser, Milton Eisenhower, had made a modest name for himself in Washington before Pearl Harbor, but the war, by rocketing Ike to fame and eventually to political office, transformed Milton from an occasional consultant to an intimate insider. A fifth, Allen Dulles, probably would have languished on Wall Street, boring friends with stale stories of intrigue from the Great War, rather than replenishing his repertoire with fresh material. What would have become of the other three is harder to say. Perhaps the professional politicians—Henry Cabot Lodge and Harold Stassen—would have latched onto another Republican and gained access to the Oval Office that way. The semipro, John Foster

Dulles, had been constructing a political base for years. His appointment as secretary of state resulted primarily from his own stature in the party. But even for Dulles, as for Lodge and Stassen, knowing a war hero could only improve one's prospects.

As it affected their perceptions of the world, the war did not reorient all the advisers so markedly as it did Lodge, whose conversion to international-alism was scarcely less dramatic than Saul's embracing of Christianity, but it touched them nonetheless. With Eisenhower, they came to believe in America's ethical superiority over the forces of totalitarianism; with him, they learned to shun anything vaguely hinting at appeasement. They ac-quired the moral self-confidence of the generation that fought and defeated the fascists—the self-confidence that allowed Eisenhower, once he had discerned in communism the new face of aggression, to characterize Ameri-ca's struggle as "a war of light against darkness, freedom against slavery, Godliness against atheism."[1] At the same time, however, their experience of the war forced them to recognize that blameless hearts would not guaran-tee success and that, given the nature of modern war, even victory in another general conflict might be disastrous. Against a determined and well-armed adversary, they would have to find methods other than war to pursue America's goals.

Although World War II did not impress everyone caught in its coils with the dangers of repeating the exercise—one need search no further than Douglas MacArthur to find an individual whose belief in the efficacy of force survived Hiroshima—it did put the stamp of caution on Eisenhow-er's advisers. Foster Dulles thundered about massive retaliation and going to the brink, but when he actually had the chance to advocate military intervention in Indochina, he so circumscribed the option politically as to render it nearly impossible. Allen Dulles' practice of the black arts of diplomacy—and Eisenhower's inclination to call on the spymaster's talents—reflected an admission that covert warfare was about the only kind that remained safe in the nuclear age. Bedell Smith urged the adminis-tration to recognize, and openly admit, that the West had suffered a defeat in Indochina and that the United States had no intention of resuming France's fight there. Milton Eisenhower argued for support of reform in Latin America, claiming that repressive violence would simply stoke the boiler for a future explosion. Henry Cabot Lodge made much the same case regarding the third world generally. Harold Stassen promoted arms control as a means of lessening tension with the Soviet Union. Even C. D. Jackson, for all his failure to recognize the boundary between psychological war and real war, understood that the reason for pushing the former was the necessity of avoiding the latter.

The common reluctance of these men to act forcefully on their shared ideology—the caution that shaded most of their policies gray, even as their convictions and rhetoric painted the world in black and white—certainly had broader origins than World War II. One person almost never does something for a single reason; even less do nine individuals do many things from a solitary cause. Foster Dulles, remembering how Korea had entangled Acheson, sought to avoid anything similar in Indochina. Harold Stassen, in stumping for disarmament, was campaigning for president. At the United Nations, Henry Cabot Lodge absorbed some of the third world's tendency to deemphasize ideology. The list of additional considerations extends readily.

But the explanation of broadest applicability leads back to the first: all the advisers had to keep step with the president. They might venture a pace or two ahead; they could afford to lag slightly behind. But as long as they hoped to retain influence, they had to match their recommendations and actions to what Eisenhower might conceivably accept. And because Eisenhower, understanding the consequences of another general war, displayed no intention of pushing his anticommunist convictions to that point, neither did they.

Foster Dulles demonstrated the greatest sensitivity to which way the winds off the Rose Garden were blowing. In Dulles' case, the struggle with Stassen for direction of the administration's arms control policy indicated most clearly the keenness of his weather eye. The secretary of state disliked disarmament and distrusted Stassen. He preferred an arms race to arms control, for the time being at least, believing the former more likely to wring political concessions from the Soviets. But when Eisenhower spoke in favor of Open Skies, the secretary silenced his doubts and changed course. Through his entire tenure, Dulles demonstrated a mastery of the art of sticking close to his source of power. His anxiety at the possibility of being cut off lay behind his efforts to keep Stassen, Smith, Jackson, Lodge, or anyone else from coming between him and the president, and it led him to tailor his advice to Eisenhower's requirements. An eminently practical man, Dulles realized that he would sooner achieve his goals through persuasion, and tactical retreat when necessary, than by dramatic disagreement.

Dulles was not the only trimmer in the group. Stassen exhibited similar tendencies in modifying and remodifying one disarmament proposal after another, trying to hit on something Eisenhower would buy. Allen Dulles, if undeterred by Eisenhower's obvious disapproval, probably would have argued for greater support for the Hungarian rebels in 1956. C. D. Jackson certainly did, but even Jackson could see that the president was set against going beyond diplomatic protests at the Soviet invasion. If Jackson had thought Eisenhower might accept such advice, he doubtless *would* have recommended airlifts of those recoilless rifles. Henry Cabot Lodge would have made a stronger pitch for action on the domestic race issue, realizing the importance of this matter to his third world colleagues at the UN, had he not recognized Eisenhower's backwardness and diffidence on the subject.

But this need to confine proposals to what the president might listen to did not create significant difficulties for the advisers, because it reinforced and directed attitudes they already shared with Eisenhower. They moved with the president not simply because he held the reins, but because they were going in his direction anyway.

In another sense, Eisenhower and his eight advisers fit a single pattern. With minor exceptions, the president and his advisers were a remarkably unreflective lot. At a critical point in their lives—the war years—they had learned a basic lesson: dictatorship intended the destruction of democracy. Rarely afterward did they stop to question whether they had got the lesson just right, or to ask whether it still applied. For them, the transition from world war to cold war required only transferring what they had learned about Hitler and the fascists to Stalin and the communists. Hitler had aimed for world conquest; so, therefore, must Stalin. Conciliation had failed with the former; it would succeed no better with the latter. Occasionally, one or another among the group asked whether the Munich paradigm covered all contingencies. Milton Eisenhower differed with Allen Dulles over the influence of communism in Bolivia; Henry Cabot Lodge suggested a broader view in dealing with the third world. On the whole, however, they held tenaciously to the one big truth the war had taught them. They might dispute minor points of interpretation, but they never seriously doubted its continued validity. The learning had cost their generation, and their country, too much.

War collapses time. In geopolitical terms, it crushes old empires and spits forth new ones in what amounts to the twinkling of an eye. For individuals, it compresses the generational process, dividing those who come of age before the war from those who mature after; and it separates both groups from persons caught in the middle.

Eisenhower's was the generation of the middle, the generation of the war itself. Not physically or emotionally, of course: Eisenhower and his advisers entered adulthood years before America joined the fight against fascism. But from the perspective of responsibility for the safety of their country, they only came to the fore in the period between 1941 and 1945, and they owed their emergence to the pressurized atmosphere of the global struggle.

By contrast, Truman's foreign policy team mostly comprised individuals who acceded to power either before the war or by means incidental to the conflict. George Marshall was well settled into his job as chief of staff long before Japan attacked Hawaii. Dean Acheson became undersecretary of the treasury in 1933, a rank he would not surpass in the State Department until 1947. James Forrestal inherited the job of secretary of the navy in 1944 on the death of his predecessor. Harry Truman followed a similar route to the presidency the following year. Just as important, each spent the war years in Washington. The Battle of the Potomac was significant, but it lacked the immediacy of North Africa and Normandy. To order troops into action from half a world away is one thing; to share a smoke and good wishes with men who will die before another day passes is something else.

Beyond the divide, the generation that came after Eisenhower's—the generation that accompanied John Kennedy to office—participated in the war, but principally as junior officers. War, for the most part, is something that happens *to* lieutenants. Like a tremendous hurricane, the war certainly shaped the later lives of Kennedy and the others. But in the trenches or on the PT boats, they could have had little more sense of materially altering its course than they had of deflecting a storm. When Kennedy,

Bundy, Rusk, McNamara, and the rest took over in 1961, they remained novices at deciding great issues of war and peace. In pressing to the edge of the abyss over Cuba, and in committing American forces to Southeast Asia, they were learning on the job. Eisenhower ended his first day as president by remarking that the cares and troubles of his new post, serious as they were, seemed "like a continuation of all I've been doing since July 1941."[2] Even at the discount appropriate to an old and world-weary soldier, the comment rings true. One cannot imagine Kennedy writing words at all similar.

To be sure, the generational argument must not be pushed too far. Generations never divide cleanly: people are born every day, not just every twenty years. Eisenhower's administration, like Truman's and Kennedy's, included individuals of widely varying ages. Moreover, what does one do with a person like Averell Harriman, who occupied important posts under both Truman and Kennedy? And who would seriously contend that Harold Stassen felt the impact of the war more directly than George Marshall?

For all the exceptions and caveats, however, it *does* make sense to speak in generational terms in dealing with Eisenhower's administration, for the reasons elaborated above, but also because of Eisenhower's style of leadership. Eisenhower did not rely on one or two advisers alone. Rather, he deliberately spread responsibility and brought several individuals into the process of making and implementing decisions. As a consequence, the policies that emerged reflected the influence of a variety of people—of a generation of policymakers.

To John Foster Dulles, of course, Eisenhower delegated the greatest authority. The president had only a passing acquaintance with the secretary of state when the two joined forces in 1953, and although Eisenhower took care to prevent Dulles' monopolizing the lines of communication to the Oval Office—causing the secretary fits at times—he almost immediately came to respect Dulles' expertise and to follow his advice. Occasionally Eisenhower overruled the secretary, as he essentially did in deciding to go to Geneva in 1955. And he certainly assumed a less bellicose public posture than Dulles adopted. At times, the president thought Dulles got carried away with his provocative rhetoric; when the *Life* article describing "brinkmanship" appeared, the president confided to White House aides his "astonishment" at the secretary's choice of words.[3] On the whole, however, and on the substance of nearly every issue of importance, Eisenhower and Dulles saw eye to eye. As a consequence, the president had no qualms about granting Dulles a great deal of leeway in shaping and enunciating administration policy.

Milton Eisenhower played an entirely different role. Although his reports on Latin America received greater attention coming from the president's brother than they would have otherwise, Milton's efforts as a spokesman counted far less than his role as sounding board and devil's advocate. Ike recognized that Milton could speak more freely, and offer more penetrating criticism of proposed policies, than could individuals who owed their livelihoods to the president. Much of Milton's usefulness lay in his ability to disagree with his brother, for his objections kept alive alternatives that mere bureaucrats might have given up for dead. Regarding Latin America, Milton's persistence eventually paid off.

In certain respects, and depending on whom one believes, Allen Dulles may have wielded the greatest independent influence of any of Eisenhower's advisers. Left to his own preferences, the president probably would not have chosen Allen Dulles to head the CIA; Eisenhower would have been just as happy leaving Bedell Smith in charge. But Foster Dulles wanted Smith out and Allen in, and Eisenhower humored the secretary of state. As an intelligence briefer, Allen Dulles struck the president as uninspired and long-winded. And Dulles' notion of an administrator's task grated, to say the least, on one accustomed to a military conception of order. But as a spy-runner and director of covert operations, Dulles had undeniable gifts. In handling the administration's dirty work, he allowed the president to keep his hands clean. Eisenhower probably did not know the details of certain covert operations, particularly the more sordid and controversial ones like the attempted assassination of Lumumba. He did not want to know. Especially after Dulles' early successes in Iran and Guatemala, the president had confidence in Dulles' ability to carry out assignments without direct supervision. It sufficed for Eisenhower to indicate that he wanted Lumumba removed from power. Dulles could handle the specifics of the job. If anything went wrong, Eisenhower needed to be able to deny, believably, that his administration employed hit men. Allen Dulles was expendable. The president was not.

Bedell Smith served principally as an expediter of policy. Eisenhower had commanded complicated operations during the war, and he recognized that the best-planned policy could fall flat if not executed properly.

As chief of staff, Smith had impressed Eisenhower as a man who ran a tight organization and knew how to get things done. Deciding for political reasons that Smith should not take a position in the White House, Eisenhower was content to see him go to the State Department to give that troubled organization the Smith treatment and, at the same time, to keep Foster Dulles on his toes. Eisenhower could not help respecting Smith's analytical abilities. The administration's response to the Geneva accords of 1954 reflected Smith's advice at least in part. But the president considered Smith more a doer than a thinker.

Robert Murphy held a similar position, although Murphy's particular gifts tended to the personal rather than the organizational. Murphy's repeatedly demonstrated skills at soothing, cajoling, and persuading had come in handy during the war, and Eisenhower counted on them again during his presidency. Eisenhower listened carefully to Murphy's opinions on matters of policy implementation, especially on the crucial issue of how to keep soldiers from having to fight. On broader questions of policy formulation, the president turned to others.

C. D. Jackson remained on the fringes of power long past the time when Eisenhower gave up on Jackson's more ambitious psychological warfare plans, partly because Jackson could write a good speech, and partly because he had ties to influential groups that Eisenhower preferred not to offend. In addition, Jackson symbolized a course of action that Eisenhower wished to pursue, yet knew he could not. No less than Jackson, the president ardently desired the liberation of Eastern Europe. But his broader responsibilities and clearer sense of the stakes involved prevented him from acting on this desire. Still, Eisenhower was reluctant to admit despair of progress on the central front in the struggle with the Soviets. Jackson represented the hope, albeit slim and distant, that the situation might improve; in keeping Jackson around, Eisenhower kept the candle flickering. Finally, Eisenhower valued Jackson as a designated dissenter, as one who tested the policy machinery by challenging accepted wisdom and conventional ways of conducting business. The president might have paid a higher price for encouraging Jackson's unsettling activities—as he did in Stassen's case—had Jackson not possessed such an engaging personality. Actually, though, a large part of Jackson's ability to avoid bruising feelings lay in the fact that his opponents generally recognized him to be a relative lightweight. Had they taken him more seriously, he might have caused greater problems.

As for Harold Stassen, nearly everyone in the administration could sense his presidential ambitions from afar; not a few wondered why Eisenhower suffered him as long as he did. The explanation here resembles that in the Jackson case. Though Eisenhower could not quite bring himself to accept most of Stassen's proposals, he considered them a worthwhile corrective to the tendency of the State Department and the Pentagon to smother new ideas at birth. Further, the president believed, accurately, that Stassen's reputation as "secretary of peace" improved the image of the administration on arms control at a time when that image needed all the help it could get. Eisenhower probably underestimated the personal element in Stassen's desire for an agreement with the Soviets; he was surprised and embarrassed by the developments that led to Stassen's fall. But Eisenhower did not ignore the risks involved in working with Stassen. He simply thought that the dangers of appearing intransigent on arms control were greater.

Like Stassen, Henry Cabot Lodge served in what amounted to a public relations position. Eisenhower himself believed firmly in the idea of the United Nations, but he realized that American support for that organization, especially after the Korean War when the United States shouldered by far the greatest part of the UN's fighting burden, might easily slip away. Lodge, appointed to the UN post in payment for a political debt, proved an inspired choice with his well-publicized and popular blasts at the communists. Although Lodge held a nominal seat in the cabinet, and although he did not hesitate to air his views in administration debates, he played a limited role in formulating policy. In fact, the point of his being elevated to cabinet rank was not to amplify his voice at the White House, but to enhance his stature at the UN and to signify the administration's commitment to that organization. Unexpectedly, Lodge came to acquire an interest in the affairs of the third world, and before long he was representing the nonaligned states to the administration. His lobbying met relatively little success, however. The president found it easier to accept Lodge's cosmetic recommendations than to follow his substantive advice. Nonetheless, at a time when Foster Dulles usually acted as spokesman for the administration, and when Dulles was winning few popularity contests in the third world, Eisenhower valued Lodge's ability to get along with the likes even of India's Krishna Menon.

In bringing, at various levels and in different areas, these several individuals into the decision-making process, Eisenhower sought to ensure that the policies that the administration put into action reflected a diversity of opinions and beliefs. And so they did, within a common philosophical framework. Occasionally, the mixture proved unstable, as in the Dulles-Stassen feud. On the whole, however, the strategy worked reasonably well, and Eisenhower avoided much of the infighting and downright sabotage that has afflicted some other presidents. In part, this stability owed to the strength of the Eisenhower-Dulles axis and to the tenacity of the secretary of state in repelling challengers. In part, it resulted from the president's insistence on keeping the big decisions—regarding intervention in Indochina or the Middle East, aid to Latin America and the rest of the third world, responses to Soviet activities in Eastern Europe, arms control, and other matters—indisputably in his own hands. More than anything else, however, it followed from a fundamental consensus within the administration regarding the nature of the challenge facing America and the character of the required response. On the issues that really told, Eisenhower and his advisers all thought essentially alike.

Eisenhower may not have recognized the degree to which his administration represented a different generation from that which had gone before, but his successor, speaking of the next administration, certainly did. With John Kennedy's inauguration, the torch did indeed pass to a new generation. Of the nine men described in the preceding chapters, only Henry Cabot Lodge retained anything like the influence he enjoyed during Eisenhower's presidency, serving first as Kennedy's and then Lyndon Johnson's representative in South Vietnam. For the rest, the 1960s and after were twilight years. John Foster Dulles was dead. C. D. Jackson and Walter Bedell Smith did not long survive him. Allen Dulles was forced out of the CIA after the Bay of Pigs fiasco. Robert Murphy resurfaced now and then as one of the "wise men" of American diplomacy, but he was strictly a per diem expert and made his living in private industry. Although Milton Eisenhower kept in touch with the White House, Johns Hopkins claimed most of his energy. Harold Stassen returned to the practice of law, emerging quadrennially to reenact the days of his youth when people took his political hopes seriously. Dwight Eisenhower remained interested and active in political affairs, but with advancing years and growing infirmity he became ever more a symbol of an earlier age.

Eisenhower and his advisers left their successors a legacy at once of excess and of deficiency. By their insistence on containing communism and their enthusiasm for collective security, they passed along a debt of commitments that would outstrip American capabilities. By their willingness to wage the cold war by covert and admittedly repugnant means, they created a record of intrusion into the affairs of other nations that would haunt America's conscience and eventually damage America's interests. By their failure to take serious steps toward disarmament, they encouraged, or at least acquiesced in, an arms race that has grown to proportions they could scarcely imagine. By their tardy and half-hearted efforts to accept the challenge of third world nationalism, they placed the United States on the wrong side of revolutions that were reshaping the globe.

More tellingly, they left too much ideology and too little experience. The young Turks who took office with Kennedy yielded nothing ideologically to their predecessors; their pay-any-price, bear-any-burden attitude made Eisenhower's crew seem pikers by comparison. But the new wielders of power lacked the firsthand knowledge of responsibility during war that had sobered Eisenhower and his generation. Sam Rayburn regretted that none of Kennedy's bright men had run for sheriff;[4] he might better have wished that they had lived with the consequences of sending thousands to their deaths. Perhaps then they would have adopted a less ambitious course and spared the country a decade of division and defeat.

The ideology, it turned out, was transferrable; the experience was not. And the experience counted for everything, for it indicated the limits of the ideology as a blueprint for policy. The cold war defined Eisenhower's world and that of his advisers—defined it too narrowly. But his and their memories of the greatest conflict humanity had ever seen made them walk cautiously through that world. Another war might have come during their watch, in Indochina in 1954, in the Formosa Strait in 1955, in Eastern Europe in 1956, or on various other occasions. But they recognized the location of the brink, and for all their tough talk they stayed well away. As a consequence, they managed to guide their country safely through a dangerous time. They might have done better, but they might also have done far worse.

Notes

Introduction

1. Immerman, "Eisenhower and Dulles."
2. Among the clearest statements of the traditional view of the Eisenhower-Dulles relationship are Drummond and Coblentz, *Duel at the Brink;* and Goold-Adams, *The Time of Power.* Early, but essentially suggestive, reinterpretations are Kempton, "The Underestimation of Dwight D. Eisenhower"; Wills, *Nixon Agonistes,* passim; Rovere, "Eisenhower Revisited," pp. 14–15, 54–59, 62. In the recent scholarly revisionist vein are Immerman, "Eisenhower and Dulles"; Divine, *Eisenhower and the Cold War;* Cook, *The Declassified Eisenhower;* Greenstein, *The Hidden-Hand Presidency;* and Ambrose, *Eisenhower,* vol. 2.
3. Eisenhower, *Crusade in Europe,* p. 22.
4. Ambrose, *Eisenhower,* 1:36.
5. Goodpaster Oral History.

1. John Foster Dulles: Speak Loudly and Carry a Soft Stick

1. Lansing to Dulles, February 19, 1920, Box 3, John Foster Dulles Papers, ML.
2. Murphy Oral History, ML.
3. O'Connor Oral History.
4. Quoted in Pruessen, *John Foster Dulles,* p. 10.
5. Notes for speech by Allen Dulles to the Whig-Cliosophic Society, December 6, 1966, Box 4, Allen W. Dulles Papers.
6. Pruessen, *Dulles,* pp. 24, 78.
7. Lansing to Dulles, February 19, 1920, Box 3, John Foster Dulles Papers, ML.
8. Vandenberg to Dulles, July 2, 1948, in Vandenberg, ed., *The Private Papers of Senator Vandenberg,* p. 447.

9. Murphy Oral History, ML.

10. The best account of foreign policy in the 1948 election is Divine, *Foreign Policy and U.S. Presidential Elections*, chs. 5–7.

11. Robert Murphy had met Dulles in the mid-1930s, and he later said he thought Dulles had had his eye on the secretaryship even in that early period. Murphy Oral History, ML.

12. Pruessen, *Dulles*, pp. 400–401.

13. Dulles to Murphy, December 19, 1949, Box 42, John Foster Dulles Papers, ML.

14. Dulles to Angelopoulos, December 30, 1949, Box 42, *ibid.*

15. Transcript of address on CBS, March 1, 1951, Box 54, *ibid.*

16. Dulles to World Affairs Council of Seattle, September 18, 1952, Box 59, *ibid.*

17. Hughes, *The Ordeal of Power*, p. 70.

18. John Foster Dulles, "A Policy of Boldness."

19. Rusk to Dulles, March 11, 1952, Box 63, John Foster Dulles Papers, ML.

20. From Emmet Hughes interview, cited in Hoopes, *The Devil and John Foster Dulles*, p. 128.

21. The story of Eisenhower's dinner at the Dulles house, and his suggestion regarding what would become Dulles' book, was related to me by John W. F. Dulles (Dulles' son) in an interview on September 11, 1984.

22. In his memoirs, Eisenhower declared that the selection of Dulles was "an obvious one," based on Dulles' heritage, training, character, and diplomatic views (*Mandate for Change*, p. 86). Townsend Hoopes writes of a report that Eisenhower considered John McCloy for the job but backed away after hearing of resistance in the Taft wing of the Republican party (*Devil and Dulles*, pp. 135–136). Leonard Mosley mentions as others considered—in some cases only by themselves—to be in the running Henry Luce, Thomas Dewey, Paul Hoffman, and Walter Judd (*Dulles: A Biography of Eleanor, Allen, and John Foster Dulles*, p. 292). Mosley's book is full of interesting details not available elsewhere, but like many works relying on unattributed sources it must be handled with care.

23. Johnson Oral History.

24. Bohlen, *Witness to History*, pp. 309–310.

25. George F. Kennan, *Memoirs*, chs. 7–8.

26. Bohlen, *Witness*, p. 310.

27. Bohlen Oral History, EL.

28. Johnson Oral History.

29. Bohlen Oral History, ML.

30. In 1957, Dulles replaced Bohlen as ambassador to the Soviet Union in a manner that Bohlen considered less than honest. The story can be followed in the Bohlen Papers at the Library of Congress.

31. Quoted in Guhin, *Dulles: A Statesman and His Times*, p. 188.

32. Bohlen Oral History, ML. See Hoopes, *Devil and Dulles*, pp. 153–155, for

Dulles' treatment of Vincent and Davies. Dulles' appeasement of the Republican right was noted by contemporaries beyond the State Department. A persistent critic on this point was Hans J. Morgenthau, author of several articles in *The New Republic*—see especially "What the President and Mr. Dulles Don't Know"; and "John Foster Dulles," in Graebner, ed., *An Uncertain Tradition*, ch. 15.

33. Dulles to Luce, February 24, 1950, Box 48, John Foster Dulles Papers, ML.

34. Dulles to John W. F. Dulles, February 20, 1948, John W. F. Dulles Papers.

35. *New York Times*, December 15, 1953.

36. Dulles, "A Policy of Boldness."

37. See "The 'New Look' of 1953," in Schilling, Hammond, and Snyder, *Strategy, Politics, and Defense Budgets*. See also Gaddis, *Strategies of Containment*, chs. 5–6.

38. U.S. Department of State, *Department of State Bulletin*, January 25, 1954.

39. Criticism of Dulles' speech and the policy it described is discussed in Guhin, *Dulles*, p. 229 ff.; Hoopes, *Devil and Dulles*, pp. 199–201; and Peeters, *Massive Retaliation*, chs. 4–7.

40. Shepley, "How Dulles Averted War."

41. Reston quoted in Hoopes, *Devil and Dulles*, p. 311.

42. *Department of State Bulletin*, June 18, 1956.

43. Notes on Dulles address of May 6, 1948, John W. F. Dulles Papers.

44. Dulles to Eisenhower, January 30, 1957, Box 6, Dulles-Herter Series, Eisenhower Papers as President (Ann Whitman File).

45. Malik Oral History.

46. Hoopes, *Devil and Dulles*, pp. 178–180.

47. See Robert A. Divine, *Eisenhower and the Cold War*, pp. 29–31.

48. On Operation Vulture, see Prados, *The Sky Would Fall*. The best recent account of administration decision making on Dien Bien Phu is Herring and Immerman, "Eisenhower, Dulles, and Dienbienphu."

49. Dulles to Eisenhower, March 23, 1954. *FRUS 1952–1954*, 13:1141.

50. Memorandum of conversation, April 5, 1954, *ibid.*, 1224–1225.

51. See Herring and Immerman, "Eisenhower, Dulles, and Dienbienphu," p. 353.

52. Memorandum of conversation at 192d NSC meeting, April 6, 1954, *FRUS 1952–1954*, 13:1254.

53. *Ibid.*

54. Eisenhower to Dulles, April 15, 1952, Box 36, Eisenhower Pre-Presidential Papers.

55. Dulles to Jackson, August 24, 1954, Box 40, Jackson Papers.

56. See James C. Hagerty diary entry for June 23, 1954, in Robert H. Ferrell, ed., *Diary of James C. Hagerty*, pp. 73–74.

57. Smith Oral History.

58. Wiley Oral History.

59. Murphy Oral History, ML.
60. Goodpaster Oral History.

2. Milton Eisenhower and the Coming Revolution in Latin America

1. Milton Eisenhower Oral History, EL. Also, for general background on Milton Eisenhower, see his *The President Is Calling*.

2. See his memorandum to Roosevelt upon departing the WRA, in *The President Is Calling*, pp. 123–124. An interim report to Congress, dated April 20, 1942, can be found in Box 32, Henry A. Wallace Papers.

3. In addition to Milton Eisenhower's own account of his work in connection with the Darlan deal in *The President Is Calling*, pp. 133–143, see Ambrose, *The Supreme Commander*, ch. 9; and Murphy, *Diplomat Among Warriors*, pp. 150–151. The quoted statement to Murphy is from the latter.

4. Milton Eisenhower to Wallace, April 24, 1943, Box 32, Wallace Papers.

5. Milton Eisenhower's activities in higher education are the subject of Ambrose and Immerman, *Milton S. Eisenhower: Educational Statesman*.

6. See Milton Eisenhower, *The Wine Is Bitter*, pp. 4–6.

7. Milton Eisenhower Oral History, ML.

8. Diary entry for May 14, 1953, in Ferrell, ed., *The Eisenhower Diaries*, p. 238.

9. Milton Eisenhower Oral History, EL.

10. Milton Eisenhower, *The President Is Calling*, p. 247.

11. Entry for May 14, 1953, in Ferrell, *The Eisenhower Diaries*, p. 238. Ike did have one reservation regarding Milton's fitness for the presidency: his less than robust health. "I do not think he is physically strong enough to take the beating," Ike wrote to Swede Hazlett. December 24, 1953, Box 4, DDE Diary Series, Eisenhower Papers as President (Ann Whitman File). This file will be cited hereafter as AWF.

12. Ambrose, *Eisenhower*, 1:75–78.

13. Milton Eisenhower, *Wine*, p. 187.

14. *Department of State Bulletin*, April 20, 1953.

15. The quoted phrase is from a cable from the ambassador in Guatemala, John Peurifoy, to State, December 17, 1953, *FRUS 1952–1954*, 4:1093.

16. For administration involvement in the removal of Arbenz, see Immerman, *The CIA in Guatemala;* Schlesinger and Kinzer, *Bitter Fruit;* and Cook, *The Declassified Eisenhower*.

17. Milton Eisenhower to Dwight Eisenhower, April 17, 1953, Box 12, Name File, AWF.

18. Dulles to Stassen, September 2, 1953, *FRUS 1952–1954*, 4:535.

19. Milton Eisenhower to Dwight Eisenhower through State, July 13, 1953, Box 12, Name Series, AWF.

20. Milton Eisenhower to Dwight Eisenhower, July 24, 1953, Box 12, Name Series, AWF.

21. Milton Eisenhower to Allen Dulles, November 27, 1953, Box 56, Allen W. Dulles Papers; Allen Dulles to Milton Eisenhower, November 30, 1953, *ibid.*

22. Dulles to embassy in Argentina, March 3, 1953, *FRUS 1952–1954*, 4:436.

23. Ambassador in Argentina (Albert Nufer) to State, February 5, 1953, *ibid.*, p. 432. Somewhat later, Peron made a rather more sweeping claim regarding his grip on the Communist party in Argentina. He told Henry Holland, then assistant secretary of state for inter-American affairs, that fifty thousand Argentine Communists and fellow travelers had been placed under the surveillance of personal monitors, who reported on the leftists' movements and who had orders to liquidate their charges in the event of war or other crisis. Memorandum of conversation by Holland, September 19, 1954, *ibid.*, p. 473.

24. Dulles to Eisenhower, June 18, 1953, *ibid.*, pp. 440–441; O'Connor to Dulles, June 18, 1953, *ibid.*, p. 441, note 4.

25. Milton Eisenhower, *Wine*, pp. 64–66.

26. Milton Eisenhower to Dwight Eisenhower, no date, Box 13, Name Series, AWF.

27. Milton Eisenhower, "United States–Latin American Relations: Report to the President," *Department of State Bulletin*, November 23, 1953.

28. *Ibid.*

29. *Ibid.*

30. *Ibid.*

31. Milton Eisenhower to Dwight Eisenhower, October 9, 1953, Box 12, Name Series, AWF. The "International" bank was the International Bank for Reconstruction and Development, commonly called the World Bank. The "Ex-Im" bank was the United States Export-Import Bank.

32. Milton Eisenhower to Dwight Eisenhower, October 9, 1953, *ibid.*

33. Milton Eisenhower, "United States–Latin American Relations." For the story of the evolution of the foreign aid policy of the Eisenhower administration, see Kaufman, *Trade and Aid;* and Rostow, *Eisenhower, Kennedy, and Foreign Aid.*

34. Dulles to Dwight Eisenhower, November 19, 1953, Box 1, Dulles-Herter Series, AWF.

35. Dwight Eisenhower to Milton Eisenhower, October 31, 1953, Box 14, Milton Eisenhower Papers.

36. Dwight Eisenhower to Milton Eisenhower, November 3, 1953, Box 3, DDE Diary Series, AWF.

37. Kaufman, *Trade and Aid*, pp. 29–31.

38. Milton Eisenhower to Dwight Eisenhower, November 25, 1953, Box 12, Name Series, AWF.

39. Milton Eisenhower to Dwight Eisenhower, January 14, 1954, *ibid.*

40. Minutes of cabinet meeting, February 26, 1954, *FRUS 1952–1954*, 4:301.

41. See memorandum of 189th NSC meeting, March 18, 1954, *ibid.*, pp. 304–306.

42. Milton Eisenhower telephone conversation with Dulles, October 27, 1954, Box 3, Telephone Calls Series, John Foster Dulles Papers, EL.

43. Milton Eisenhower to Dwight Eisenhower, October 22, 1954, Box 12, Name Series, AWF.

44. Dwight Eisenhower to Milton Eisenhower, October 25, 1954, Box 8, DDE Diary Series, AWF.

45. Memorandum of 224th NSC meeting, November 15, 1954, *FRUS 1952–1954*, 4:344–352.

46. Milton Eisenhower to Dwight Eisenhower, no date (late October or early November 1954), Box 12, Name Series, AWF.

47. Dwight Eisenhower telephone conversations with Milton Eisenhower, October 30, 1954, and November 19, 1954, Box 7, DDE Diary Series, AWF.

48. Milton Eisenhower to Dwight Eisenhower, November 30, 1954, Box 12, Name Series, AWF.

49. Dwight Eisenhower to Milton Eisenhower, December 1, 1954, Box 14, Milton Eisenhower Papers.

50. See Milton Eisenhower to Dwight Eisenhower, September 7, 1954, Box 12, Name Series, AWF. See also Milton Eisenhower, *Wine*, pp. 203–204.

51. Not surprisingly, the uncertain state of the president's health and frequent visits by Milton sparked speculation that the younger brother was being groomed to catch the falling scepter. Milton was in something of a quandary as to how to deal with the situation. To say nothing might increase the rumors; to deny that he was interested in the presidency "would smack of effrontery." At about the same time, Ike commented to Swede Hazlett that reports of a dynasty in the making were totally unfounded. "In fact, it is my own private opinion that if ever there is a fight to develop in this world between my kid brother and myself, it will be when and if he ever finds out that I would like to see him shoved into politics in this fashion." Milton Eisenhower to Dwight Eisenhower, October 23, 1955, Box 14, Milton Eisenhower Papers; Dwight Eisenhower to Hazlett, October 26, 1955, Box 11, DDE Diary Series, AWF.

52. Milton Eisenhower, "United States-Latin American Relations, 1953–1958," *Department of State Bulletin,* January 19, 1959,

53. The dangerous nature of the "ferment" in Latin America had been brought home to the administration by the violence that had greeted Vice President Richard Nixon on a trip to South America in the first half of 1958. So threatening had the situation in Venezuela seemed that Dwight Eisenhower had ordered a contingent of airborne troops flown to the Caribbean, in preparation for a rescue attempt. See Eisenhower, *Waging Peace,* pp. 519–520; Nixon, *RN: The Memoirs of Richard Nixon,* pp. 185–193. Nixon also told the story, with more dramatic effect, in *Six Crises,* ch. 4.

54. Eisenhower, "United States-Latin American Relations, 1953–1958."

55. This report was a public document; needless to say, there were no references to American intervention in Guatemala in 1954.

56. Eisenhower, "United States-Latin American Relations, 1953–1958."

57. *Ibid.*

58. *Ibid.*
59. Milton Eisenhower to Dwight Eisenhower, no date, Box 13, Name Series, AWF.
60. *Ibid.*
61. *Ibid.*
62. For Dwight Eisenhower's account of his journey, see *Waging Peace*, pp. 525–533.
63. Milton Eisenhower's assessment of these events is in *Wine*, pp. 249–254. Dwight Eisenhower's is in *Waging Peace*, pp. 537–539.
64. Milton Eisenhower to Dwight Eisenhower, October 18, 1960, Box 13, Name Series, AWF.
65. Eisenhower, *Wine*, p. xi.

3. Allen Dulles and the Overthrow of Clausewitz

1. Grandfather John W. Foster served briefly under Benjamin Harrison; uncle Robert Lansing would serve under Woodrow Wilson; brother John Foster Dulles would be Eisenhower's chief diplomatic adviser.
2. A copy of the book is in Box 3 of the Allen W. Dulles Papers. Allen's financial gesture toward the Boers turned out not to be quixotic. His proud father had the book published; it sold for fifty cents a copy and, enjoying something of a vogue in Washington, it brought in two thousand dollars. It also gained for Allen standing as a published author. Eighteen years later, when Allen was courting his wife-to-be, Clover Todd, the young lady's father, a professor at Columbia, wanted to know something about his daughter's suitor. Professor Todd went to the library catalog and was pleased to discover that Clover was interested in an intellectual man, a historian. But he was somewhat taken aback at the publication date (1902) of *The Boer War*. Not yet having met Allen Dulles, Professor Todd wondered if Dulles was a bit too old for his daughter. See Allen M. Dulles (father) to Allen Dulles, March 21, 1902, Box 3, Allen Dulles Papers, and especially Eleanor Lansing Dulles, *Chances of a Lifetime*, pp. 80–81.
3. See Mosley, *Dulles: A Biography of Eleanor, Allen, and John Foster Dulles*, p. 26.
4. Described in Allen Dulles to Frantz, July 31, 1964, Box 3, Allen Dulles Papers.
5. Allen Dulles Oral History.
6. See Allen Dulles to Mrs. Robert Lansing, October 9, 1914, Box 3, Allen Dulles Papers; and various letters from Allen Dulles to his mother, 1915, *ibid.*
7. Notes for speech before Whig-Cliosophic Society, December 6, 1966, Box 4, *ibid.* See also Robert Lansing to Allen Dulles, April 18, 1917, *ibid.*
8. Allen Dulles to John Foster Dulles, July 16, 1918, Box 5, *ibid.*
9. Allen Dulles to Robert Lansing, January 17, 1918, *ibid.*

10. Allen Dulles to John Foster Dulles, January 28, 1918, *ibid.*

11. Murphy, *Diplomat Among Warriors*, p. 9.

12. Allen Dulles, address to the American Gas Association, October 20, 1963, reported in *New York Times*, October 21, 1963.

13. Allen Dulles to Lansing, April 27, 1921, Robert Lansing Papers.

14. Allen Dulles to Lansing, January 31, 1921, *ibid.*

15. Allen Dulles to Lansing, February 13, 1922, *ibid.*

16. Allen Dulles, *The Craft of Intelligence*, p. 2.

17. See the biographical resume of Allen Dulles in a brief history of the CIA, no date, Name Files, Post-Presidential Files, Harry S. Truman Papers.

18. Allen Dulles to Mrs. Allen Dulles, May 1, 1932, Box 12, Allen Dulles Papers; memorandum of conversation with Hitler, April 8, 1933, *ibid.*

19. Allen Dulles, *The Secret Surrender*, pp. 10–11.

20. *Ibid.*, pp. 12–15.

21. See Allen Dulles, ed., *Great Spy Stories from Fiction* and *Great True Spy Stories*.

22. See the citation accompanying Dulles' Medal of Merit award, July 18, 1946, copy in Box 1046, Official File, Truman Papers.

23. See Allen Dulles, *Germany's Underground* and *Secret Surrender*.

24. Donovan to Roosevelt, November 18, 1944, Box 13, Allen Dulles Papers.

25. At Donovan's suggestion, a group called Veterans of Strategic Service was formed to promote the idea of a peacetime intelligence organization. See Smith, *The Shadow Warriors*, pp. 410–412.

26. Richard Helms to Allen Dulles, October 30, 1946, Box 25, Allen Dulles Papers.

27. See Donovan to Allen Dulles, June 29, 1946, Box 24, *ibid.*, and Allen Dulles to Donovan, July 8, 1946, *ibid.* See also biographical information on Dulles in a memorandum on the background of the CIA, no date, Box 25, Name Files, Post-Presidential Files, Truman Papers.

28. See, for example, Allen Dulles to Donovan, December 16, 1946, Box 24, Allen Dulles Papers; Allen Dulles to Donovan, April 25, 1947, Box 29, *ibid.*

29. Truman to Wayne Morse, February 22, 1963, Name Files, Post-Presidential Files, Truman Papers.

30. Dulles received the Medal of Merit in July 1946.

31. Generally known as the Dulles-(William) Jackson-(Mathias) Correa report.

32. The Dulles-Jackson-Correa report was summarized and critiqued in NSC-50, July 1, 1949, Box 206, President's Secretary's File, Truman Papers.

33. Allen Dulles' remarks to meeting of Practicing Law Institute, October 15, 1958, Box 35, Allen Dulles Papers.

34. Allen Dulles to Stephenson, September 5, 1951, Box 49, *ibid.*

35. Richard Bissell Oral History, ML.

36. Robert Kennedy Oral History.

37. Meyer, *Facing Reality*, pp. 80–81.

38. Bissell Oral History, ML.

39. Transcript of "Town Meeting of the Air," April 6, 1948, Box 34, Allen Dulles Papers.

40. Memorandum of conversation with Acheson, March 23, 1949, Box 41, *ibid;* Allen Dulles to Byrd, October 5, 1949, Box 41, *ibid.*

41. Interview for National Broadcasting Company, October 1, 1950, Box 45, *ibid.*

42. Allen Dulles to Jackson, November 16, 1957, Box 13, Administration Series, Eisenhower Papers as President (Ann Whitman File) This file will be cited hereafter as AWF.

43. Allen Dulles to Jackson, March 31, 1959, Box 40, Jackson Papers.

44. Allen Dulles to Truman, January 7, 1964, Name Files, Post-Presidential Files, Truman Papers.

45. Robert Amory Oral History.

46. Richard Bissell Oral History, ML.

47. Roger Hilsman Oral History.

48. Allen Dulles, *Craft of Intelligence*, pp. 6–7.

49. Smith, *Shadow Warriors*, p. 403.

50. Quotation excerpted from *Washington Post*, December 28, 1963, Box 25, Name Files, Post-Presidential Files, Truman Papers.

51. Speech to the Practicing Law Institute, October 15, 1958, Box 35, Allen Dulles Papers.

52. Briefing, April 3, 1953, Box 56, *ibid.*

53. Memorandum of conversation, October 19, 1954, Box 13, Administration Series, AWF.

54. *Ibid.*

55. *Ibid.*

56. Eisenhower quoted from a classified CIA history in United States Senate, *Supplementary Detailed Staff Reports on Foreign and Military Intelligence*, p. 62.

57. Allen Dulles, *Craft of Intelligence*, p. 82.

58. Thomas Powers, *The Man Who Kept the Secrets*, p. 80; Mosley, *Dulles*, pp. 376–377. Powers (p. 323, note 5) includes the most judicious assessment of these, and other, conflicting reports of the acquisition of Khrushchev's speech. See also Ambrose and Immerman, *Ike's Spies*, pp. 236–237.

59. Powers, *The Man Who Kept the Secrets*, p. 81; Colby and Forbath, *Honorable Men*, p. 133. See also Cline, *Secrets, Spies, and Scholars*, pp. 162–164.

60. Richard Bissell, the head of the U-2 project, described it, bureaucratically speaking, as "a moderately bloody affair." Bissell Oral History, EL.

61. Eisenhower, *Waging Peace*, p. 551; Eisenhower press conference, May 11, 1960, in *Public Papers of the Presidents: Dwight D. Eisenhower, 1960*, pp. 403–404. The most recent telling of the U-2 tale is Beschloss, *Mayday*.

62. On Iran, see Rubin, *Paved with Good Intentions;* and Roosevelt, *Countercoup*. On Guatemala, see Immerman, *The CIA in Guatemala;* Schlesinger and Kinzer, *Bitter Fruit;* and Cook, *The Declassified Eisenhower*. On both, see Ambrose and Immerman, *Ike's Spies*, chs. 14–16.

63. Those who did hope that Stalin's death—of natural causes—would lead to turmoil in the satellite states, quickly found themselves in a minority. See chapter 7, on the work of C. D. Jackson.

64. Eisenhower gave the order for the training of anti-Castro exiles on March 17, 1960. See Eisenhower, *Waging Peace*, p. 533.

65. J.C. King, memorandum to Allen Dulles, December 11, 1959, quoted in United States Senate, *Alleged Assassination Plots Involving Foreign Leaders*, p. 92. Henceforth this reference will be cited as "Church committee hearings," after committee chairman Frank Church.

66. Special group minutes, January 13, 1960, quoted in *ibid.*, p. 93.

67. Memorandum for the record, March 9, 1960, *ibid.*

68. Memorandum for the record, March 15, 1960, *ibid.*

69. Bissell testimony to Church committee, June 9, 1975, *ibid.*, pp. 94–95.

70. Consult *ibid.* (p. 95 ff.), for example, for details of post-Eisenhower attempts to assassinate Castro.

71. CIA cable, Leopoldville to Director, August 18, 1960, quoted in *ibid.*, p. 14.

72. Minutes of NSC meeting, July 21, 1960, *ibid.*, p. 57.

73. Minutes of NSC meeting, August 18, 1960, *ibid.*, p. 58.

74. *Ibid.*, p. 15.

75. In the original cable, a code word was used to refer to Lumumba. The translation was provided to the Church committee by the CIA. *Ibid.*, p. 15, note 3.

76. CIA cable, Dulles to Station Officer in Leopoldville, August 26, 1960, quoted in *ibid.*, p. 15.

77. Dillon testimony to Church committee, September 20, 1975, *ibid.*, 63.

78. Minutes of NSC meeting, September 21, 1960, *ibid.*, p. 62.

79. CIA cable, Dulles and Tweedy to Leopoldville, September 24, 1960, *ibid.*, p. 63.

80. CIA cable, Leopoldville to Director, September 20, 1960, *ibid.*, p. 18.

81. Joseph Scheider testimony before Church committee, October 7, 1975, and October 9, 1975, *ibid.*, pp. 20–21.

82. Scheider testimony before Church committee, October 7, 1975, *ibid.*, p. 25.

83. Hedgman testimony before Church committee, August 21, 1975, *ibid.*, p. 25.

84. CIA cable, Station Officer to Tweedy, November 14, 1960, *ibid.*, p. 33.

85. CIA cable, Leopoldville to Director, January 12, 1960, *ibid.*, p. 49.

86. CIA cable, Leopoldville to Director, January 13, 1960, *ibid.*, p. 49.

87. CIA cable, Elisabethville to Director, January 19, 1961, quoted in *ibid.*, p. 51. For more details on the events surrounding Lumumba's death, see Kalb, *The*

Congo Cables; Weissman, *American Foreign Policy in the Congo;* and Mahoney, *JFK: Ordeal in Africa.*

88. U.S. Senate, *Supplementary Reports,* pp. 52–53, note 9.

89. For a discussion of how much Eisenhower knew, see Church committee hearings, pp. 51–70; Ambrose and Immerman, *Ike's Spies,* pp. 294–296, 304–306; and Ambrose, *Eisenhower,* 2:588–589.

4. Walter Bedell Smith and the Geneva Conference on Indochina

1. Quoted in Mosley, *Dulles: A Biography of Eleanor, Allen, and John Foster Dulles,* p. 270. The speaker did not wish to be identified.

2. Kirkpatrick was chief executioner on the "Murder Board," Smith's instrument for organizational housecleaning. Kirkpatrick, *The Real CIA,* pp. 91, 135.

3. A nickname Smith seemed not to mind; he used stationery with a pale blue embossed beetle as a letterhead. See the Walter Bedell Smith Papers.

4. Ambrose, *Eisenhower,* 1:187–188.

5. Dulles to Bidault, May 3, 1954, *FRUS 1952–1954,* 16:677.

6. Memorandum of meeting with Mendès-France et al., July 13, 1954, *ibid.,* 16:1352. At an NSC meeting on July 15, 1954, Dulles said that the administration could not get into the "Yalta business" of guaranteeing Soviet conquests. *Ibid.,* 13:1835.

7. Kirkpatrick, *The Real CIA,* p. 91.

8. Philby in Mosley, *Dulles,* pp. 270, 283.

9. Allen Dulles Oral History.

10. Ambrose, *Eisenhower,* 1:187–188. On Smith's role during the war, see Snyder, "Walter Bedell Smith."

11. Eisenhower to Hazlett, March 13, 1946, Box 17, Name Series, Eisenhower Papers as President (Ann Whitman File). This file will be cited hereafter as AWF.

12. Diary entry for May 14, 1953, in Ferrell, ed., *The Eisenhower Diaries,* p. 237.

13. Diary entry for December 6, 1943, *ibid.* See also Ambrose, *Eisenhower,* 1:274.

14. Eden, *Full Circle,* p. 125.

15. Eisenhower, *Mandate for Change,* p. 142.

16. Churchill quoted in Hoopes, *The Devil and John Foster Dulles,* p. 221.

17. Eisenhower to Cutler, September 21, 1954, Box 8, DDE Diary Series, AWF.

18. Smith deposition in Benton-McCarthy case, September 29, 1952, Smith Papers.

19. "Evaluation of Present Kremlin International Policies," November 5, 1947, *FRUS 1947,* 4:612.

20. Eisenhower to Smith, November 28, 1947, in Galambos, ed., *The Papers of Dwight David Eisenhower,* 9:2084–2085.

21. See Eisenhower, *Mandate for Change*, pp. 88–89, 367; Hoopes, *Devil and Dulles*, pp. 145–146; Kirkpatrick, *Real CIA*, pp. 91–92; Mosley, *Dulles*, pp. 293–297.

22. Murphy Oral History, ML. See also Murphy Oral History, EL.

23. Johnson Oral History.

24. Smith to Morgan, February 18, 1953, Box 5, Smith Papers.

25. Smith quoted in Mosley, *Dulles*, p. 194.

26. See Smith to Adler, January 12, 1953, Box 5, Smith Papers.

27. Memorandum by Hanes, August 17, (no year, probably 1953), Box 6, Subject Series, John Foster Dulles Papers, EL.

28. The best works to date on the Geneva conference are Randle, *Geneva 1954;* and Devillers and Lacouture, *End of a War.*

29. Smith to State, May 19, 1954, *FRUS 1952–1954*, 16:856.

30. Smith to State, May 20, 1954, *ibid.*, pp. 864–865.

31. Memorandum of coversation by Smith, May 10, 1954, *ibid.*, pp. 755–756.

32. Press briefing in Smith to State, June 2, 1954, *ibid.*, p. 1007.

33. Smith to State, May 23, 1954, *ibid.*, pp. 895–899.

34. *Ibid.*

35. Smith to State, June 5, 1954, *ibid.*, p. 1039.

36. The Russians also hoped, said Smith, to render more difficult approval of the European Defense Community by the French Assembly. Smith to State, June 19, 1954, *ibid.*, p. 1193; memorandum of meeting, June 23, 1954, Box 1, Legislative Meetings Series, AWF.

37. Memorandum of conversation by Smith, June 7, 1954, *FRUS 1952–1954*, 16:1060.

38. Smith to State, June 19, 1954, *ibid.*, pp. 1189–1191.

39. *Ibid.*, p. 1193.

40. See, for example, record of Dulles-Smith-Eden meeting in secretary to State, May 2, 1954, *ibid.*, pp. 648–649. See also, Eden, *Full Circle*, p. 122.

41. Churchill in United Kingdom House of Commons *Parliamentary Debates*, vol. 527 (May 17, 1954), columns 1691–1692.

42. Eden, *Full Circle*, p. 135.

43. See Health to Bonsal, July 4, 1954, *FRUS 1952–1954*, 16:1281.

44. Robertson Oral History.

45. Eden, *Full Circle*, p. 126.

46. *Ibid.*, pp. 125–127.

47. Memorandum of 199th NSC meeting, May 27, 1954, *FRUS 1952–1954*, 16:943; *Dulles to Smith*, July 18, 1954, *ibid.*, pp. 1429–1430.

48. Eden, *Full Circle*, pp. 124–125.

49. Robertson to Dulles, June 1, 1954, Box 3, General Correspondence and Memoranda Series, John Foster Dulles Papers, EL. See also, Heath to Bonsal, July 4, 1954, *FRUS 1952–1954*, 16:1281.

50. Smith to State, May 7, 1954, *FRUS 1952–1954*, 16:711.

51. Dulles to Smith, May 20, 1954, *ibid.*, pp. 869–870.

52. Smith to State, May 22, 1954, *ibid.*, pp. 886–887.

53. See, for example, Smith to State, May 10, 1954, *ibid.*, pp. 749–751; Smith to State, May 12, 1954, *ibid.*, p. 785; Smith to State, May 26, 1954, *ibid.*, p. 924; Smith to State, June 14, 1954, *ibid.*, p. 1143.

54. See, for instance, Smith to State, May 25, 1954, *ibid.*, p. 930–931.

55. Dulles to Smith, May 6, 1954. *ibid.*, pp. 705–706.

56. Smith to State, May 16, 1954, *ibid.*, p. 821; Smith to State, May 20, 1954, *ibid.*, p. 864.

57. Memorandum of 193d NSC meeting, April 13, 1954, *ibid.*, 13:1326. See also memorandum of conversation, May 24, 1954, *ibid.*, 16:905–906.

58. Smith to State, June 9, 1954, *ibid.*, 16:1084.

59. *Department of State Bulletin,* July 12, 1954.

60. Eisenhower to Gruenther, April 26, 1954, Box 4, DDE Diary Series, AWF.

61. Smith to George Kennan, July 1, 1948, Box 28, Kennan Papers.

62. Smith to Kennan, June 11, 1948, *ibid.*

63. Smith to Marshall, June 8, 1948, *ibid.*

64. Eisenhower quoted in James Hagerty diary entry for June 23, 1954, in Ferrell, ed., *The Diary of James C. Hagerty,* p. 74.

65. Smith to State, May 26, 1954, *FRUS 1952–1954,* 16:936.

66. Memorandum of conversation, April 4, 1954, *ibid.*, 13:1234.

67. Smith to State, May 8, 1954, *ibid.*, 16:712–713.

68. Summary of staff meeting, April 23, 1954, *FRUS 1952–1954,* 13:1366.

69. Smith to State, May 24, 1954, *FRUS 1952–1954,* 13:902.

70. Bidault, *Resistance,* pp. 198–199.

71. Ferrell, *Eisenhower Diaries,* p. 296.

72. See Smith's addition to memorandum accompanying Dillon to State, May 13, 1953, *FRUS 1952–1954,* 13:563, note 1.

73. Memorandum of meeting of special committee, January 29, 1954, *ibid.*, p. 1003.

74. Memorandum of 194th NSC meeting, April 29, 1954, *ibid.*, pp. 1443–1444.

75. Smith to State, June 12, 1954, *ibid.*, 16:1126–1127. Smith to State, June 15, 1954, *ibid.*, p. 1152.

76. For Eisenhower's view of the Laniel government, see Eisenhower, *Mandate for Change,* p. 343.

77. Smith to State, May 26, 1954, *FRUS 1952–1954,* 16:936. Similarly, Smith to State, May 9, 1954, *ibid.*, p. 741; Smith to State, May 24, 1954, *ibid.*, pp. 900–901; Smith to State, June 7, 1954, *ibid.*, p. 1055.

78. Smith to State, May 4, 1954, *ibid.*, pp. 689–690.

79. Smith to State, May 24, 1954, *ibid.*, pp. 902–903.

80. Hagerty diary entry for July 18, 1954, in Ferrell, *Diary of Hagerty,* pp. 93–94.

81. Eisenhower, *Mandate for Change*, p. 343.

82. Eisenhower to Gruenther, April 26, 1954, Box 4, DDE Diary Series, AWF.

83. Eisenhower, *Mandate for Change*, p. 364. Perhaps Eisenhower was rewriting history in the interest of American diplomacy. His memoirs were published while de Gaulle was president of France.

84. Memorandum of meeting, June 23, 1954, Box 1, Legislative Meetings Series, AWF; Eisenhower diary entry for January 10, 1955, in Ferrell, *Eisenhower Diaries*, p. 291.

85. See Smith to State, May 15, 1954, *FRUS 1952–1954*, 16:807.

86. *Ibid.*

87. Smith to State, June 16, 1954, *ibid.*, pp. 1154–1155.

88. William Jenner, April 20, 1954, in U.S. Congress, *Congressional Record*, vol. 100, part 4, p. 5322.

89. See minutes of cabinet meeting, July 9, 1954, Cabinet Series, Staff Secretary Records, Eisenhower Papers; minutes of cabinet meeting, July 9, 1954, Cabinet Series, AWF; James Hagerty diary entries for July 8 and 9, 1954, in Ferrell, *Diary of Hagerty*, pp. 86–87.

90. Smith to Dulles, June 23, 1954, *FRUS 1952–1954*, 13:1733–1734.

91. Eisenhower, *Public Papers of the Presidents 1954*, p. 642.

92. *Ibid.*

5. Robert Murphy and the Middle East Crisis of 1958

1. See *FRUS 1952–1954*, vol. 12, passim.

2. Bedell Smith was the one who suggested that Murphy was the logical person to deal with Tito. See Eisenhower to Smith, September 4, 1954, Box 8, DDE Diary Series, Eisenhower Papers as President (Ann Whitman File). This file will be cited hereafter as AWF.

3. See summary report by Murphy, March 12, 1958, Box 5, Subject Series, Staff Secretary Records, Eisenhower Papers; and other reports in the same location.

4. Murphy, *Diplomat Among Warriors*, pp. 66–70.

5. See memorandum by the Division of Near Eastern Affairs, February 5, 1942, State Department decimal file 851R.00/2-542, Record Group 59, National Archives, Washington, D.C.

6. Murphy, *Diplomat*, p. 81.

7. Marshall to Eisenhower, September 3, 1942, in Chandler and Ambrose, eds., *The Papers of Dwight David Eisenhower*, 1:545, note 2.

8. Eisenhower to Marshall, September 19, 1942, *ibid.*, p. 562.

9. Address by Vice Admiral Raymond Fenard, Chief of French Naval Mission to the United States, August 17, 1943, State Department decimal file 851R.00/8-1743, Record Group 59, National Archives, Washington, D.C.

10. On the Darlan deal, see Murphy, *Diplomat*, ch. 9; Eisenhower, *Crusade in Europe*, pp. 104–109; Ambrose, *The Supreme Commander*, ch. 9.

11. Eisenhower to Combined Chiefs of Staff, November 14, 1942, in Chandler and Ambrose, *Papers of Eisenhower*, 2:708.

12. Roosevelt to Eisenhower, December 15, 1942, President's Official File 5197, Roosevelt Papers.

13. Eisenhower to Murphy, November 9, 1942, Box 84, Eisenhower Pre-Presidential Papers.

14. Eisenhower to Murphy, November 9, 1943, Box 84, Eisenhower Pre-Presidential Papers.

15. See Early to Hassett, September 2, 1944, President's Official File 5197, Roosevelt Papers; Carter to Roosevelt, September 4, 1944, *ibid.;* Pomener to Roosevelt, September 6, 1944, *ibid.;* Cullen to Roosevelt, November 14, 1944, *ibid.*

16. Roosevelt to Murphy, November 25, 1943, *ibid.* Murphy was happy to be back with Eisenhower, but he was not so thrilled about working again with some other members of Eisenhower's staff. Murphy had met C. D. Jackson in North Africa, and like many persons trained in the Foreign Service and the State Department, Murphy was ill at ease with the psychological warfare that was Jackson's specialty. As the war in Europe neared its end, Murphy was especially worried about the way in which Jackson and his British colleague Richard Crossman were obscuring in their propaganda toward Germany one of the basic tenets of American policy: unconditional surrender. In January 1945, Murphy complained to his friend H. Freeman Matthews that Jackson and Crossman had been "wobbling around lately on the subject of Unconditional Surrender." Murphy to Matthews, January 10, 1945, State Department decimal file 740.00119/1-1045, Record Group 59, National Archives, Washington, D.C.

17. Entry for July 15, 1943, in Macmillan, *War Diaries*, p. 151.

18. Diary entry for March 23, 1944, *ibid.*, p. 393.

19. Diary entry for June 29, 1944, *ibid.*, p. 477.

20. Diary entry for August 20, 1944, *ibid.*, p. 505.

21. Macmillan, *The Blast of War*, p. 188.

22. Murphy, *Diplomat*, p. 317.

23. Correspondence for this period between Murphy and Eisenhower is in Box 84, Eisenhower Pre-Presidential Papers.

24. Murphy, *Diplomat*, p. 356.

25. O'Connor Oral History.

26. Eden, *Full Circle*, pp. 476–477.

27. Eisenhower, *Waging Peace*, p. 37.

28. Murphy, *Diplomat*, p. 379.

29. *Ibid.*

30. Macmillan, *Riding the Storm*, p. 105.

31. Eisenhower, *Waging Peace*, p. 38.

32. "Political Crisis in Lebanon," Report 7784, April 15, 1958, State Department Office of Intelligence Research and Analysis Records, Record Group 59, National Archives, Washington, D.C.

33. *Ibid.*

34. *Ibid.*

35. *Ibid.*

36. McClintock to State, May 10, 1958, reproduced in *Declassified Documents Reference System* (hereafter *DDRS*) (76) 99D.

37. Eisenhower, *Waging Peace*, pp. 266–267.

38. McClintock to State, June 20, 1958, *DDRS* (76) 100C.

39. McClintock to State, June 24, 1958, *ibid.* (76) 100I.

40. McClintock to State, July 12, 1958, *ibid.* (76) 101C.

41. The best accounts of activity at the American embassy during the Lebanon crisis are McClintock, "The American Landing in Lebanon"; and Thayer, *Diplomat*, chs. 1–3. Thayer served on the embassy staff during the latter part of the crisis. See also Eveland, *Ropes of Sand*, chs. 26–27.

42. Memorandum of conference, Eisenhower et al., July 14, 1958, Box 3, Subject Series, Staff Secretary Records, Eisenhower Papers; Allen Dulles briefing, July 14, 1958, Box 11, *ibid.* The context of the coup in Baghdad is described in Mosley, *Power Play*, p. 278 ff.; and Stookey, *America and the Arab States*, p. 148 ff.

43. Malik Oral History.

44. Chamoun Oral History. See also Allen Dulles briefing, July 14, 1958, Box 11, International Series, Eisenhower Staff Secretary Records.

45. Memorandum of discussion, July 14, 1958, *DDRS* (R) 628H.

46. Eisenhower, *Waging Peace*, p. 270.

47. Cutler, *No Time for Rest*, pp. 363–364.

48. Ambrose, *Eisenhower*, 2:470.

49. Memorandum of conference, July 14, 1958, Box 11, International Series, Eisenhower Staff Secretary Records.

50. *Ibid.*

51. Eisenhower, *Waging Peace*, p. 273.

52. Murphy Oral History, ML. See also Murphy telephone conversation with Dulles, May 11, 1958, Box 8, Telephone Calls Series, John Foster Dulles Papers, EL.

53. Dulles telephone conversation with Murphy, July 16, 1958, *ibid.*

54. Dulles telephone conversation with Nixon, July 15, 1958, *ibid.*

55. Eisenhower, *Waging Peace*, p. 279.

56. Dulles telephone conversation with Murphy, July 16, 1958, Box 8, Telephone Calls Series, John Foster Dulles Papers, EL.

57. Macmillan, *Riding the Storm*, p. 512.

58. Murphy, *Diplomat*, p. 398. See also Murphy Oral History, ML.

59. Eisenhower had originally intended that Chamoun be given no more than ninety minutes advance notice of the landing, but the president later agreed to a three-hour warning. Memorandum of conversation, Eisenhower and Dulles, July 15, 1958, Box 3, Subject Series, Eisenhower Staff Secretary Records.

60. McClintock to State, July 16, 1958, *DDRS* (77) 64D. A fuller and more

dramatic account of the near-battle is in Thayer, *Diplomat,* pp. 33–34. See also McClintock, "The American Landing in Lebanon"; and Hadd, "Orders Firm But Flexible." Colonel Hadd was the commander of the American tank column. In addition, see Bodron, "US Intervention in Lebanon—1958."

61. Memorandum of conversation, July 21, 1958, Box 7, White House Memoranda Series, John Foster Dulles Papers, EL.

62. Chamoun Oral History.

63. Murphy, *Diplomat,* p. 405.

64. McClintock to State, July 16, 1958, *DDRS* (77) 64D.

65. Murphy Oral History, ML.

66. Chamoun Oral History.

67. Murphy Oral History, ML; Murphy, *Diplomat,* pp. 407–408.

68. Murphy Oral History, ML.

69. Memorandum of conference, July 14, 1958, Box 11, International Series, Eisenhower Staff Secretary Records,

70. Murphy, *Diplomat,* pp. 411–412.

71. Memorandum of conference, July 14, 1958, Box 11, International Series, Eisenhower Staff Secretary Records,

72. Murphy, *Diplomat,* pp. 414–415.

73. *Ibid.,* pp. 412–414.

74. Eisenhower, *Waging Peace,* p. 266.

75. Memorandum of conference, July 20, 1958, Box 3, Subject Series, Eisenhower Staff Secretary Records,

76. Murphy, *Diplomat,* p. 414.

77. Before the Iraqi coup, Nasser had supported Chehab as an acceptable successor to Chamoun. See Copeland, *The Game of Nations,* p. 237.

78. Murphy, *Diplomat,* pp. 414–418; Dulles telephone conversation with Eisenhower, August 12, 1958, Box 7, White House Memoranda Series, John Foster Dulles Papers, EL.

79. Eisenhower, *Waging Peace,* p. 490.

80. Murphy, *Diplomat,* pp. 333–338. See chapter 4 for more on the Eisenhower administration and Lumumba.

6. C. D. Jackson: Psychological Warriors Never Die

1. Roderic O'Connor, a State Department aide who played a role in the rejection of many of Jackson's plans in a later period, described his unsinkable nature: "He would come up with an idea at a staff meeting—or four or five ideas—and he would get shot down, and he'd say, 'Well, I'll go back to my typewriter and think up some more.' Completely relaxed about it." O'Connor Oral History. Background information on Jackson, here and below, comes from a lengthy obituary article circulated in *FYI, Time*'s house organ, on September 25, 1964. A copy of this article accompanies the Jackson Papers at the Eisenhower Library.

2. Jackson to Emeny, January 14, 1947, Box 40, Jackson Papers.

3. See Steinhardt to Jackson, September 5, 1946, Box 50, Laurence Steinhardt Papers. Steinhardt was the American ambassador in Prague.

4. Jackson to Steinhardt, March 30, 1948, Box 57, Steinhardt Papers.

5. Jackson to Steinhardt, May 5, 1948, *ibid.*

6. Jackson to McClure, April 25, 1950, Box 60, Jackson Papers.

7. Jackson to Steinhardt, June 12, 1948, Box 57, Steinhardt Papers.

8. Jackson to Elliot, February 7, 1951, Box 40, Jackson Papers; Smith to Jackson, March 11, 1952, Box 78, *ibid.;* Jackson to Eisenhower, December 17, 1952, Box 41, *ibid.* For more on the NCFE-RFE-CIA link, see Cook, *The Declassified Eisenhower,* pp. 129–130. Cook presents Jackson as an influential, somewhat mysterious, but basically shallow promoter of private enterprise. "For Jackson, the world was crudely simple: The United States was the 'all-important part' of the world. Business was the 'all-important part' of the United States; and 'businessmen are the important men in the U.S.—Q.E.D.' " (p. 124). Cook expands her theme in "First Comes the Lie: C. D. Jackson and Political Warfare." The present argument differs from Cook's in ascribing greater depth and different motives to Jackson. Regarding the passage quoted, Cook fails to allow sufficiently for the fact that Jackson's cited phrases were directed at audiences of businessmen, and for the fact that when Jackson was striving to make a point, whether in a broadcast to Eastern Europe or in a speech to the St. Louis Advertising Club, one of his cardinal principles was to state the message in as stark and simple terms as possible. On the air or on a podium, Jackson knew how to play to the prejudices of his audience. That was what psychological warfare was all about.

9. See "Summary of Psychological Warfare Arrangements Within the U.S. Government Since World War II," no date, Box 3, NSC Series, Special Assistant for National Security Affairs Records.

10. Jackson to Eisenhower, December 17, 1952, Box 41, Jackson Papers.

11. Jackson to Adams, January 24, 1953, Box 7, Jackson Records.

12. Jackson to Hauge, February 23, 1953, Box 48, Jackson Papers.

13. Executive order establishing the Operations Coordinating Board, August 10, 1953, Box 1, Jackson Records.

14. Jackson to Cutler, March 4, 1953, Box 2, *ibid.*

15. *Ibid.*

16. For example, Jackson to Eisenhower, December 17, 1952, Box 41, Jackson Papers.

17. Jackson to Cutler, March 4, 1953, Box 2, Jackson Records.

18. Emmet John Hughes, *The Ordeal of Power,* pp. 101–102.

19. See "Probable Consequences of Death of Stalin," CIA memo of March 10, 1953, Box 1, Jackson Records.

20. Kyes to Jackson, March 9, 1953, *ibid.* Roger Kyes was deputy secretary of defense.

21. Smith to Jackson et al., March 11, 1953, *ibid.*

22. On the origins of the "Chance for Peace" address, see Eisenhower, *Mandate for Change*, pp. 144–147; and Hughes, *Ordeal of Power*, p. 100 ff. For an interesting insider's account of the events in Washington in the month after Stalin's death, see Rostow, *Europe After Stalin*.

23. See Rostow, *Europe After Stalin*, pp. 35–39.

24. Rostow to Jackson, June 28, 1953, Box 10, Jackson Records.

25. Jackson to Speer, August 4, 1953, Box 1, *ibid.*

26. *Ibid.*

27. Langelaan to Jackson, June 15, 1953, Box 4, Jackson Records.

28. The most recent authorities on the Rosenberg case, Ronald Radosh and Joyce Milton, in *The Rosenberg File*, give no indication that Brownell considered following Jackson's suggestion.

29. Jackson to Brownell, February 23, 1953, Box 2, Jackson Records.

30. Jackson to Taylor, June 22, 1953, Box 6, *ibid.*

31. Jackson to Dulles, June 13, 1955, Box 40, Jackson Papers.

32. Dulles's aide Roderic O'Connor later said, "Jackson fitted in perfectly." O'Connor Oral History.

33. Smith to Jackson, with Jackson's marginal comment, December 24, 1953, Box 6, Jackson Records.

34. Kennan to Jackson, September 15, 1953, Box 4, *ibid.*

35. Jackson to Lodge, May 20, 1953, *ibid.*

36. Jackson to Eisenhower, September 21, 1953, Box 41, Jackson Papers.

37. Jackson to Eisenhower, August 13, 1954, *ibid.*

38. On "Atoms for Peace," see Ambrose, *Eisenhower*, vol. 2, ch. 6. See also Eisenhower, *Mandate for Change*, pp. 251–255.

39. "Suggested Check List for Presidential Speech Implementation," November 30, 1953, Box 1, Jackson Records. "Operation Wheaties," no date, Box 7, *ibid.*

40. Jackson to Hauge, November 17, 1954, Box 48, Jackson Papers.

41. Jackson to Dulles, April 9, 1954, Box 68, *ibid.*

42. *Ibid.*

43. See Millikan to Jackson, November 12, 1954, Box 64, Jackson Papers. See also Kaufman, *Trade and Aid*, pp. 49–51; Cook, *Declassified Eisenhower*, p. 298 ff; Rostow, *Eisenhower, Kennedy, and Foreign Aid*, ch. 6.

44. Jackson to Dulles, August 3, 1954, Box 2, General Correspondence and Memoranda Series, John Foster Dulles Papers, EL.

45. Jackson to Smith and Allen Dulles, January 13, 1954, Box 1, Jackson Records.

46. Jackson to Rockefeller, November 10, 1955, Box 66, Jackson Papers.

47. For more details, see Kaufman, *Trade and Aid*, chs. 4–8; and Rostow, *Eisenhower, Kennedy, and Foreign Aid*, chs. 7–8.

48. Jackson to Allen Dulles, November 24, 1954, Box 40, Jackson Papers.

49. Jackson to William Jackson, November 17, 1956, Box 52, *ibid.* William Jackson occupied C. D. Jackson's former position at the White House.

50. Jackson to William Jackson, November 5, 1956, *ibid.*

51. Jackson to Smith and Allen Dulles, January 13, 1954, Box 1, Jackson Records.

52. Jackson to William Jackson, November 5, 1956, Box 52, Jackson Papers.

53. Jackson to William Jackson, November 17, 1956, *ibid.*

54. Eisenhower to Jackson, November 19, 1956, Box 20, DDE Diary Series, Eisenhower Papers as President (Ann Whitman file). This file will be cited hereafter as AWF.

55. Jackson to Hadley, November 30, 1956, Box 48, Jackson Papers.

56. Jackson to Allen Dulles, June 22, 1957, Box 40, *ibid.*

57. See Eisenhower to Jackson, December 6, 1958, Box 37, DDE Diary Series, AWF. See also Eisenhower to Dulles, November 6, 1958, *ibid.*

58. Jackson to Allen Dulles, December 11, 1957, Box 40, Jackson Papers.

59. For more on Dulles' motivation, see chapter 4.

60. Jackson to Allen Dulles, February 24, 1959, Box 40, Jackson Papers.

61. Eisenhower to Jackson, January 28, 1958, Box 30, DDE Diary Series, AWF; Eisenhower telephone conversation with Dulles, April 9, 1958, Box 31, *ibid.;* Dulles telephone conversation with Jackson, January 18, 1958, Box 8, Telephone Calls Series, John Foster Dulles Papers, EL.

62. Jackson to Eisenhower, July 10, 1959, Box 43, DDE Diary Series, AWF.

63. Eisenhower to John Foster Dulles, October 24, 1953, Box 41, Jackson Papers.

7. Harold Stassen and the Perils of Disarmament

1. Eisenhower to Jackson, December 31, 1953, Box 4, DDE Diary Series, Eisenhower Papers as President (Ann Whitman File). This file abbreviated hereafter as AWF.

2. Eisenhower to Grenville Clark, quoted in Eisenhower to John Cowles, October 27, 1953, Box 3, *ibid.*

3. For the story of the nuclear test ban debate, see Divine, *Blowing on the Wind.* A brief survey of Eisenhower's attempts at disarmament is Soapes, "A Cold Warrior Seeks Peace." The best overall survey of disarmament negotiations during this period is Bechhoefer, *Postwar Negotiations for Arms Control.*

4. See Eisenhower dictation, December 17, 1958, Box 38, DDE Diary Series, AWF.

5. Stassen Oral History. For more background on Stassen, see Barbara Stuhler, *Ten Men of Minnesota,* pp. 145–159.

6. Though Nixon added the qualifier, "except when blinded by ambition." Nixon, *RN: The Memoirs of Richard Nixon,* p. 174.

7. See Eisenhower to Lucius Clay, December 18, 1958, Box 37, DDE Diary Series, AWF. See also John Foster Dulles memorandum of conversation with Eisenhower, September 27, 1957, Box 5, White House Memoranda Series, John Foster Dulles Papers, EL.

8. See Kaufman, *Trade and Aid*, p. 52.

9. Eisenhower to Stassen through Scott, March 1, 1955, Box 34, Administration Series, AWF.

10. Kaufman, *Trade and Aid*, pp. 52–54.

11. *Ibid.*

12. Murphy Oral History, ML.

13. *Ibid.*

14. According to Kaufman (*Trade and Aid*, p. 223, note 83), Dulles had found the relationship between the State Department and Stassen's FOA to be satisfactory, and he would have been content to leave that relationship alone. Considering what happened later, perhaps Dulles thought Stassen would create fewer problems at the FOA than elsewhere.

15. "Memorandum on Limitation of Armament," June 29, 1955, Box 4, Subject Series, John Foster Dulles Papers, EL.

16. *Ibid.*

17. *Ibid.*

18. For a record of the meeting, see memorandum for the record by A. J. Goodpaster, July 25, 1955 (meeting of July 20, 1955), Box 1, International Meetings Series, AWF.

19. Eisenhower stated that the concept of aerial inspection had been discussed casually for a number of years. Eisenhower, *Mandate for Change*, p. 519. A more detailed accounting of the immediate genesis of the plan presented at Geneva is in Rostow, *Open Skies*. Rostow describes the important role played by Nelson Rockefeller, C. D. Jackson's replacement as Eisenhower's psychological warfare expert, in convincing Stassen of the benefits of aerial inspection.

20. Eisenhower's account of the events surrounding the presentation of the Open Skies plan is in *Mandate for Change*, pp. 519–522.

21. Memorandum for the record by A. J. Goodpaster, July 25, 1955 (meeting of July 20, 1955), Box 1, International Meetings Series, AWF.

22. See Bechhoefer, *Postwar Negotiations*, p. 305.

23. This view, in particular, was challenged by others in the administration. Robert Murphy spoke for many when he said he was "shocked" at what he described as Stassen's opinion that the United States had an "enormous margin" of safety. Murphy Oral History, ML.

24. Minutes of 271st NSC meeting, December 22, 1955, Box 7, NSC Series, AWF.

25. *Ibid.*

26. Memorandum of telephone conversation, Dulles and Anderson, February 9, 1956, Box 11, Telephone Calls Series, John Foster Dulles Papers, EL.

27. "Memorandum on Limitation of Armament," June 29, 1955, Box 4, Subject Series, *ibid.*

28. Stassen to Eisenhower, February 1, 1956, with attachments, Box 35, Administration Series, AWF.

29. Memoranda of telephone conversations, Dulles and Radford, February 3,

1956, and February 9, 1956, Box 11, Telephone Calls Series, John Foster Dulles Papers, EL.

30. NSC Record of Action 1513, February 15, 1956, Box 2, NSC Series, AWF.

31. Memorandum of conference, March 1, 1956, Box 13, DDE Diary Series, AWF.

32. *Ibid.*

33. *Ibid.*

34. Stassen to Eisenhower, February 1, 1956, Box 35, Administration Series, AWF.

35. On the establishment and early work of the disarmament subcommittee, see Bechhoefer, *Postwar Negotiations*, p. 208 ff.

36. Stassen to Eisenhower, April 9, 1956, Box 35, Administration Series, AWF.

37. Eisenhower, *Waging Peace*, p. 471, note 5.

38. Memorandum of conference, July 12, 1956, Box 34, Administration Series, AWF.

39. Memorandum of telephone conversation, May 21, 1956, Box 4, Subject Series, John Foster Dulles Papers, EL.

40. Memorandum of telephone conversation, September 7, 1956, Box 5, Telephone Calls Series, *ibid.*

41. See Eisenhower, *Waging Peace*, p. 10; and Nixon, *Memoirs*, pp. 173–176.

42. Memorandum of conversation, September 8, 1956, Box 1, General Correspondence and Memoranda Series, John Foster Dulles Papers, EL.

43. Memorandum of telephone conversation, September 12, 1956, Box 11, Telephone Calls Series, *ibid.* The issue of disarmament, especially as it related to nuclear testing, in the 1956 election campaign is described in Divine, *Blowing on the Wind*, ch. 4.

44. Stassen to Eisenhower, November 7, 1956, Box 34, Administration Series, AWF.

45. Memorandum of telephone conversation, Eisenhower and Dulles, December 21, 1956, Box 11, Telephone Calls Series, John Foster Dulles Papers, EL; memorandum of conversation, Eisenhower and Dulles, January 30, 1957, Box 6, White House Memoranda Series, *ibid.*

46. See memorandum of conversation, Eisenhower and Dulles, September 27, 1957, Box 5, White House Memoranda Series, *ibid.*

47. See, for instance, memorandum of telephone conversation, Eisenhower and Herbert Hoover, Jr., September 15, 1955, Box 11, DDE Diary Series, AWF.

48. Eisenhower to Bion East, September 12, 1957, Box 26, *ibid.*

49. Memorandum of telephone conversation, December 17, 1956, Box 11, Telephone Calls Series, John Foster Dulles Papers, EL.

50. Memorandum of conversation, December 20, 1956, Box 6, White House Memoranda Series, *ibid.*

51. Memorandum of conversation, January 30, 1957, *ibid.*

52. Memorandum of conversation, February 11, 1957 (conversation of Febru-

ary 9, 1957), Box 1, General Correspondence and Memoranda Series, John Foster Dulles Papers, EL.

53. Draft memoranda by Stassen for Henry Cabot Lodge, January 10, 1957, Box 35, Administration Series, AWF.

54. Minutes of 315th NSC meeting, March 6, 1957, Box 8, NSC Series, AWF.

55. *Ibid.*

56. Pre-press conference briefing, April 10, 1957, Box 6, Press Conference Series, AWF.

57. Stassen to Eisenhower, April 13, 1957, Box 35, Administration Series, AWF.

58. For more on the May 25 decision in favor of a test ban, see Divine, *Blowing on the Wind*, pp. 143–145.

59. Memorandum of telephone conversation, Eisenhower and Dulles, June 4, 1957, Box 12, Telephone Calls Series, John Foster Dulles Papers, EL; Dulles to Stassen, June 4, 1957, Box 35, Administration Series, AWF.

60. Murphy Oral History, ML.

61. Memorandum of telephone conversation, Dulles and Adams, June 10, 1957, Box 12, Telephone Calls Series, John Foster Dulles Papers, EL.

62. Memorandum of conversation, Eisenhower and Dulles, June 4, 1957, Box 6, White House Memoranda Series, *ibid.*

63. Memorandum of telephone conversation, Eisenhower and Dulles, June 11, 1957, *ibid.*

64. Dulles to Stassen, June 12, 1957, Box 7, Dulles-Herter Series, AWF; memorandum of telephone conversation, Eisenhower and Dulles, June 12, 1957, Box 12, Telephone Calls Series, John Foster Dulles Papers, EL.

65. The other scientists were Ernest Lawrence and Mark Mills. The meeting is described in Divine, *Blowing on the Wind*, pp. 148–150.

66. Stassen to Dulles, July 2, 1957, Box 35, Administration Series, AWF.

67. Stassen to Dulles, September 23, 1957, Box 5, White House Memoranda Series, John Foster Dulles Papers, EL.

68. Dulles to Stassen, September 27, 1957, *ibid.*

69. *Ibid.*

70. Strauss to Dulles, September 28, 1957, *ibid.;* Twining to Dulles, September 30, 1957, *ibid.;* Quarles to Dulles, September 30, 1957, *ibid.;* Dulles to Eisenhower, September 29, 1957, *ibid.;* Dulles to Eisenhower, October 1, 1957, *ibid.*

71. Dulles to Eisenhower, September 28, 1957, *ibid.*

72. Memorandum of telephone conversation, Dulles and Adams, October 1, 1957, Box 12, Telephone Calls Series, John Foster Dulles Papers, EL.

73. Memorandum of telephone conversation, Dulles and Adams, October 4, 1957, *ibid.*

74. Memorandum of conversation, Eisenhower, Dulles, and Stassen, October 8, 1957, Box 5, White House Memoranda Series, John Foster Dulles Papers, EL.

75. Memorandum of conversation, Dulles and Stassen, October 20, 1957, Box 1, General Correspondence and Memoranda Series, *ibid.*

76. Reported by Adams in telephone call to Dulles, January 16, 1958, Box 12, Telephone Calls Series, *ibid.*

77. Murphy Oral History, ML.

78. Stassen Oral History.

79. Divine (*Blowing on the Wind*, p. 177) suggests that one reason for Stassen's dismissal in February 1958 was that Eisenhower, contemplating a shift on the testing issue in the direction Stassen had advocated and Dulles had opposed, hoped to save the secretary some embarrassment. Perhaps such a consideration played a role. As argued above, however, Stassen's fate had been sealed for months. By late 1957, only the moment of parting was in doubt.

80. See Divine, *Blowing on the Wind*, p. 174 ff., for details of the decision for a moratorium, and its consequences.

8. The Discovery of the Third World: Henry Cabot Lodge at the United Nations

1. Henry Cabot Lodge memorandum, September 25, 1959, Henry Cabot Lodge Papers, MHS.

2. Lodge, *The Storm Has Many Eyes*, chs. 1–2.

3. See, for example, Lodge to Roosevelt, October 13, 1943, President's Personal File 6231, Roosevelt Papers

4. "I would do just what you are doing, if I could," wrote Roosevelt to Lodge. "I missed being with the guns in 1917–18. It's too late now. I envy you the opportunity that is yours and I congratulate you upon the decision that you have made." Roosevelt to Lodge, February 1, 1944, *ibid.*

5. Lodge, *Storm*, ch. 2; Miller, *Henry Cabot Lodge*, ch. 11.

6. Memorandum of conversation, November 30, 1950, Lodge Papers, EL; Murphy Oral History, EL.

7. Lodge feared that the national Republican party would become a larger version of what the party already was in the South. As evidence of what this would mean for the integrity of Republicanism, Lodge liked to cite the story of the southern delegate to the 1948 Republican convention who, when asked the preferences of his state's delegation, replied, "Well, some of us is for Dewey and some of us is for Taft, and all of us is for sale." Lodge, *Storm*, p. 76.

8. Memoranda of conversations, June 9, 1950, November 30, 1950, Lodge Papers, EL.

9. Lodge, *Storm*, ch. 3. Lodge believed that his defeat by Kennedy was due, in large part, to the rancor of Taft Republicans who were upset at his management of the Eisenhower campaign. See Lodge Oral History.

10. Eisenhower, *Mandate for Change*, p. 89. See also Lodge, *As It Was*, pp. 55–56.

11. Memorandum of conversation with Eisenhower, no date (1959), Arthur Krock Papers, ML.

12. Robert Murphy Oral History, ML.

13. After castigating capitalists and their stooges for hours in front of the cameras and microphones at the United Nations, Vishinsky often could be found in the delegates' private lounge discussing the most provocative issues with dispassionate good humor. See Murphy, *Diplomat Among Warriors*, p. 366.

14. Lodge to Eisenhower, April 27, 1953, Lodge Papers, MHS.

15. Lodge to Eisenhower, July 30, 1954, Box 24, Administration Series, Eisenhower Papers as President (Ann Whitman File). This file will be cited hereafter as AWF.

16. Lodge to Johnson, June 18, 1957, Box 6, LBJ-A Famous Names File, Johnson Papers.

17. Journal entry, February 5, 1957, Lodge Papers, MHS.

18. Lodge to Eisenhower, March 5, 1956, Box 24, Administration Series, AWF.

19. Lodge to Eisenhower, June 26, 1956, Lodge Papers, MHS.

20. Lodge to Eisenhower, November 28, 1953, Box 23, Administration Series, AWF.

21. Lodge to Eisenhower, June 26, 1956, Lodge Papers, MHS.

22. *Ibid.*

23. Lodge to Eisenhower, December 21, 1956, Box 24, Administration Series, AWF.

24. Lodge to Eisenhower, March 11, 1957, *ibid.*

25. Murphy Oral History, ML.

26. Lodge to Eisenhower, December 21, 1956, Administration Series, AWF.

27. Lodge to Eisenhower, February 4, 1957, Lodge Papers, MHS.

28. *Ibid.*

29. Memorandum, November 6, 1959, *ibid.*

30. Lodge to Dulles, February 15, 1956, Box 4, General Conversations and Memoranda Series, John Foster Dulles Papers, EL.

31. Lodge to Eisenhower, September 25, 1957, Lodge Papers, MHS.

32. Lodge to Eisenhower, October 16, 1957, Box 24, Administration Series, AWF.

33. Lodge to Eisenhower, March 28, 1956, Lodge Papers, MHS. See also minutes of cabinet meeting, April 26, 1956, Box 7, Cabinet Series, AWF.

34. Lodge to Eisenhower, October 15, 1957, Box 24, Administration Series, AWF. The effects of racism in the United States on American relations with other countries continued to be a source of concern to Lodge after he left the United Nations. In 1963, while serving as the Kennedy administration's ambassador to South Vietnam, Lodge had occasion to attempt to persuade the Saigon government to improve its record regarding the human rights of South Vietnamese citizens. His arguments met the response that the United States should hardly

be telling other countries how to manage their affairs on human rights. Paraphrasing Saigon's reply, Lodge cabled to the State Department, "GVN [Government of Vietnam] does not use dogs and cattle prods against its people. Both GVN and and US use special troops, fire hoses, arms and bayonets." Lodge to State, September 20, 1963, Box 200-1, Countries Series, National Security Files, Kennedy Papers.

35. Lodge to Eisenhower, November 22, 1954, Lodge Papers, MHS.

36. Cabinet meeting, November 6, 1959, Box 14, Cabinet Series, AWF.

37. Lodge to Eisenhower, February 21, 1958, Lodge Papers, MHS.

38. Lodge to Eisenhower, March 5, 1956, Administration Series, AWF.

39. Lodge to Eisenhower, May 11, 1956, Box 24, *ibid.*

40. Lodge to Eisenhower, February 21, 1958, Lodge Papers, MHS.

41. Lodge to Eisenhower, May 11, 1956, Box 24, Administration Series, AWF.

42. Lodge to Eisenhower, March 15, 1956, *ibid.*

43. *Ibid.* Emphasis in the original.

44. In 1957, the International Atomic Energy Agency was established. Thus Eisenhower's "Atoms for Peace" speech was not without eventual results of substance. At the time Lodge wrote the letter quoted, however, the Soviets continued to drag their feet regarding the idea of atomic cooperation.

45. Lodge to Eisenhower, March 21, 1958, Lodge Papers, MHS.

46. See Kaufman, *Trade and Aid*, ch. 9. See also Rostow, *Eisenhower, Kennedy, and Foreign Aid*, chs. 8–10.

47. Lodge to Eisenhower, October 16, 1957, Box 24, Administration Series, AWF. See also Lodge to Eisenhower, October 7, 1954, *ibid.*, and Lodge to Eisenhower, August 26, Lodge Papers, MHS.

48. For Lodge's opinions on seating China, consult *FRUS 1952–1954*, vol. 3, passim.

49. *New York Times*, July 2, 1954.

50. Ferrell, ed., *The Eisenhower Diaries*, p. 291.

51. Knowland to Lodge, March 3, 1955, Lodge Papers, MHS.

52. Lodge to Knowland, March 15, 1955, *ibid.*

53. *Life*, March 4, 1957, March 18, 1957; Lodge to Luce, March 4, 1957, Box 56, Jackson Papers.

54. Lodge to Eisenhower, December 10, 1953, Box 24, Administration Series, AWF.

55. Lodge to Eisenhower, November 16, 1954, Lodge Papers, MHS.

56. Lodge to Eisenhower, September 26, 1955, Box 24, Administration Series, AWF.

57. Lodge to Eisenhower, May 25, 1956, Lodge Papers, MHS. Emphasis in the original.

58. Eisenhower, *Waging Peace*, p. 485.

59. Eisenhower to Dulles, March 30, 1956, Box 4, White House Memoranda Series, John Foster Dulles Papers, EL.

60. On Eisenhower's travels, see *Waging Peace*, chs. 21–22.

61. For Lodge's published account of his experiences with Khrushchev, see Lodge, *Storm*, ch. 5.

62. The high point of the debate occurred when Lodge produced a large wooden plaque bearing the seal of the United States. The ornament had been presented as a gift to America from the Soviet Union and had hung in the Moscow embassy for fifteen years—electronically bugged. Miller, *Lodge*, pp. 317–318.

63. *Ibid.*, pp. 310–311.

9. Dwight Eisenhower and the Baggage of War

1. "Notes on Ike," January 4, 1954, Box 41, C. D. Jackson Papers.

2. Ambrose, *Eisenhower*, 1:519.

3. Eisenhower to Humphrey, July 29, 1957, Box 3, DDE Diary Series, Eisenhower Papers as President (Ann Whitman file). This file will be cited hereafter as AWF.

4. Eisenhower to Hazlett, October 29, 1947, Box 56, Eisenhower Pre-Presidential Papers.

5. Ferrell, ed., *The Eisenhower Diaries*, p. 164.

6. Eisenhower, *At Ease*, p. 216; Lisio, *The President and Protest*, p. 193.

7. Eisenhower, *At Ease*, p. 213.

8. *Ibid.*, pp. 225–226.

9. Eisenhower to Hazlett, December 8, 1954, Box 18, Name Series, AWF.

10. Ambrose, *Eisenhower*, 1:135.

11. Eisenhower, *The President Is Calling*, p. 241.

12. Eisenhower to Hazlett, October 29, 1947, Box 56, Eisenhower Pre-Presidential Papers.

13. Ferrell, *Eisenhower Diaries*, p. 164.

14. *Ibid.*, p. 186.

15. *Ibid.*, pp. 203–204.

16. Eisenhower to Herter, March 10, 1952, Box 19, Name Series, AWF.

17. Ferrell, *Eisenhower Diaries*, p. 214.

18. Eisenhower to Edgar Eisenhower, January 18, 1956, Box 11, Name Series, AWF.

19. Ambrose, *Eisenhower*, 2:621.

20. Divine, *Eisenhower and the Cold War*, p. 9.

21. Hughes, *The Ordeal of Power*, pp. 227–228.

22. Eisenhower to Hazlett, April 27, 1954, Box 56, Name series, AWF.

23. "Notes on Ike," January 4, 1954, Box 41, Jackson Papers.

24. Jackson log, August 12, 1958, Box 56, Jackson Papers.

25. Goodpaster Oral History.

26. Dulles quoted in Jackson to Luce, April 16, 1956, Box 56, Jackson Papers.

27. Eisenhower to Hazlett, July 19, 1947, Box 56, Eisenhower Pre-Presidential Papers.

28. Ferrell, *Eisenhower Diaries*, p. 143.

29. *Ibid.*

30. Eisenhower, *Waging Peace*, pp. 624–625.

31. Eisenhower to Jackson, November 19, 1956, Box 20, DDE Diary Series, AWF.

32. Memorandum of Eisenhower-Rhee meeting, July 27, 1954, *FRUS 1952–1954*, 15:1844.

Conclusion

1. Ambrose, *Eisenhower*, 2:40.

2. Diary entry for January 21, 1953 in Ferrell, ed., *The Eisenhower Diaries*, p. 225.

3. Pre–press conference briefing, January 19, 1956, Box 4, Press Conference Series, Eisenhower Papers as President (Ann Whitman File).

4. Halberstam, *The Best and the Brightest*, p. 41.

Works Cited

Unpublished Collections

Charles Bohlen Papers. Library of Congress, Washington, D.C.

Allen W. Dulles Papers. Seeley G. Mudd Library, Princeton University, Princeton, N.J. (The Mudd Library will be abbreviated hereafter and in the notes as ML.)

John Foster Dulles Papers. Eisenhower Library, Abilene, Kansas. (The Eisenhower Library will be abbreviated hereafter and in the notes as EL.)

John Foster Dulles Papers. ML.

John W. F. Dulles Papers. Humanities Research Center, University of Texas, Austin.

Dwight D. Eisenhower. Pre-Presidential Papers. EL.

Dwight D. Eisenhower. Papers as President (Ann Whitman File). EL.

Dwight D. Eisenhower. Staff Secretary Records. EL.

Dwight D. Eisenhower. Special Assistant for National Security Affairs Records. EL.

Milton S. Eisenhower Papers. EL.

C. D. Jackson Papers. EL.

C. D. Jackson Records. EL.

Lyndon B. Johnson Papers. Johnson Library, Austin, Texas.

George F. Kennan Papers. ML.

John F. Kennedy Papers. Kennedy Library, Boston, Mass.

Arthur Krock Papers. ML.

Robert Lansing Papers. Library of Congress, Washington, D.C.

Henry Cabot Lodge Papers. EL.

Henry Cabot Lodge Papers. Massachusetts Historical Society, Boston, Mass. (The Massachusetts Historical Society will be abbreviated in the notes as MHS.)

Franklin D. Roosevelt Papers. Roosevelt Library, Hyde Park, N.Y.

Walter Bedell Smith Papers. EL.

Harry S. Truman Papers. Truman Library, Independence, Mo.
Laurence Steinhardt Papers. Library of Congress, Washington, D.C.
United States Department of State. Decimal Files. National Archives, Washington, D.C.
United States Department of State. Office of Intelligence Research and Analysis Records. National Archives, Washington, D.C.
Henry A. Wallace Papers. Roosevelt Library, Hyde Park, N.Y.

Oral Histories

Robert Amory. Kennedy Library, Boston, Mass.
Richard Bissell. EL.
Richard Bissell. ML.
Charles Bohlen. EL.
Charles Bohlen. ML.
Camille Chamoun. ML.
Allen Dulles. ML.
Abba Eban. ML.
Milton Eisenhower. EL.
Milton Eisenhower. ML.
Andrew Goodpaster. ML.
Roger Hilsman. Kennedy Library, Boston, Mass.
U. Alexis Johnson. ML.
Robert Kennedy. Kennedy Library, Boston, Mass.
Henry Cabot Lodge. Kennedy Library, Boston, Mass.
Charles Malik. ML.
Robert Murphy. EL.
Robert Murphy. ML.
Roderic O'Connor. ML.
Walter Robertson. EL.
H. Alexander Smith. ML.
Harold E. Stassen. Bancroft Library, Berkeley, Calif.
Alexander Wiley. ML.

Published Works

Ambrose, Stephen E. *Eisenhower*, 2 vols. New York: Simon and Schuster, 1983, 1984.
Ambrose, Stephen E. *The Supreme Commander: The War Years of General Dwight D. Eisenhower*. Garden City, N.Y.: Doubleday, 1970.
Ambrose, Stephen E., with Richard H. Immerman. *Ike's Spies: Eisenhower and the Espionage Establishment*. Garden City, N.Y.: Doubleday, 1981.

Ambrose, Stephen E., and Richard H. Immerman, *Milton S. Eisenhower: Educational Statesman*. Baltimore: Johns Hopkins University Press, 1983.

Bechhoefer, Bernhard G. *Postwar Negotiations for Arms Control*. Washington, D.C.: Brookings Institution, 1961.

Beschloss, Michael R. *Mayday: Eisenhower, Khrushchev, and the U-2 Affair*. New York: Harper and Row, 1986.

Bidault, Georges. *Resistance*. Marianne Sinclair, tr. New York: Praeger. 1967.

Bodron, Margaret M. "US Intervention in Lebanon—1958." *Military Review* (1976), 56(2):66–76.

Bohlen, Charles E. *Witness to History, 1929–1969*. New York: Norton, 1973.

Chandler, Alfred D., and Stephen E. Ambrose, eds. *The Papers of Dwight David Eisenhower*. Baltimore: Johns Hopkins University Press, 1970, vols. 1, 2.

Cline, Ray. *Secrets, Spies, and Scholars*. New York: Acropolis, 1976.

Colby, William, with Peter Forbath. *Honorable Men: My Life in the CIA*. New York: Simon and Schuster, 1978.

Cook, Blanche Wiesen. *The Declassified Eisenhower: A Divided Legacy*. Garden City, N.Y.: Doubleday, 1981.

Cook, Blanche Wiesen. "First Comes the Lie: C. D. Jackson and Political Warfare," *Radical History Review* (1984), 31:42–70.

Copeland, Miles. *The Game of Nations*. New York: Simon and Schuster, 1969.

Cutler, Robert. *No Time for Rest*. Boston: Little, Brown, 1965.

Declassified Documents Reference System. Washington, D.C.: Carrollton Press, 1976–1978.

DeSantis, Vincent P. "Eisenhower Revisionism," *Review of Politics* (1976), 38:190–207.

Devillers, Philippe and Jean Lacouture. *End of a War: Indochina, 1954*. New York: Praeger, 1969.

Divine, Robert A. *Blowing on the Wind: The Nuclear Test Ban Debate*. New York: Oxford University Press, 1978.

Divine, Robert A. *Eisenhower and the Cold War*. New York: Oxford University Press, 1981.

Divine, Robert A. *Foreign Policy and U.S. Presidential Elections, 1940–1948*. New York: New Viewpoints, 1974.

Drummond, Roscoe, and Gaston Coblentz. *Duel at the Brink: John Foster Dulles' Command of American Power*. Garden City, New York: Doubleday, 1960.

Dulles, Allen. *The Craft of Intelligence*. New York: Harper and Row, 1963.

Dulles, Allen. *Germany's Underground*. New York: Macmillan, 1947.

Dulles, Allen. *The Secret Surrender*. New York: Harper and Row, 1966.

Dulles, Allen, ed. *Great Spy Stories from Fiction*. New York: Harper and Row, 1969.

Dulles, Allen, ed. *Great True Spy Stories*. New York: Harper and Row, 1968.

Dulles, John Foster. "A Policy of Boldness," *Life*, May 19, 1952.

Dulles, John Foster. *War or Peace*. New York: Macmillan, 1950.

Dulles, Eleanor Lansing. *Chances of a Lifetime*. Englewood Cliffs, N.J.: Prentice-Hall, 1980.

Eban, Abba. *An Autobiography*. New York: Random House, 1977.

Eden, Anthony. *Full Circle*. Boston: Houghton Mifflin, 1960.

Eisenhower, Dwight D. *At Ease: Stories I Tell to Friends*. Garden City, N.Y.: Doubleday, 1967.

Eisenhower, Dwight D. *Crusade in Europe*. Garden City, N.Y.: Doubleday, 1948.

Eisenhower, Dwight D. *Mandate for Change*. Garden City, N.Y.: Doubleday, 1963.

Eisenhower, Dwight D. *Public Papers of the Presidents: Dwight D. Eisenhower, 1953*. Washington, D.C.: GPO, 1961.

Eisenhower, Dwight D. *Public Papers of the Presidents: Dwight D. Eisenhower, 1954*. Washington, D.C.: GPO, 1960.

Eisenhower, Dwight D. *Public Papers of the Presidents: Dwight D. Eisenhower, 1960*. Washington, D.C.: GPO, 1961.

Eisenhower, Dwight D. *Waging Peace*. Garden City, N.Y.: Doubleday, 1965.

Eisenhower, Milton S. *The President Is Calling*. Garden City, N.Y.: Doubleday, 1974.

Eisenhower, Milton S. *The Wine Is Bitter: The United States and Latin America*. Garden City, N.Y.: Doubleday, 1963.

Eveland, Wilbur Crane. *Ropes of Sand: America's Failure in the Middle East*. New York: Norton, 1980.

Ferrell, Robert H., ed. *The Diary of James C. Hagerty: Eisenhower in Mid-Course, 1954–1955*. Bloomington: Indiana University Press, 1983.

Ferrell, Robert H., ed. *The Eisenhower Diaries*. New York: Norton, 1981.

Gaddis, John Lewis. *Strategies of Containment: A Critical Appraisal of Postwar American National Security Policy*. New York: Oxford University Press, 1982.

Galambos, Louis, ed. *The Papers of Dwight David Eisenhower*, vol. 9. Baltimore: Johns Hopkins University Press, 1978.

Goold-Adams, Richard. *The Time of Power: A Reappraisal of John Foster Dulles*. London: Weidenfeld and Nicolson, 1962.

Guhin, Michael A. *John Foster Dulles: A Statesman and His Times*. New York: Columbia University Press, 1972.

Graebner, Norman A., ed. *An Uncertain Tradition: American Secretaries of State in the Twentieth Century*. New York: McGraw-Hill, 1961.

Greenstein, Fred I. *The Hidden-Hand Presidency: Eisenhower as Leader*. New York: Basic Books, 1982.

Hadd, H. A. "Orders Firm But Flexible," *United States Naval Institute Proceedings* (1962), 88(10):81–89.

Halberstam, David. *The Best and the Brightest*. New York: Random House, 1972.

Herring, George C., and Richard H. Immerman. "Eisenhower, Dulles, and

Dienbienphu: 'The Day We Didn't Go to War' Revisited," *Journal of American History* (1984), 71:343–363.

Hoopes, Townsend. *The Devil and John Foster Dulles*. Boston: Little, Brown, 1973.

Hughes, Emmet John. *The Ordeal of Power: A Political Memoir of the Eisenhower Years*. New York: Atheneum, 1963.

Immerman, Richard H. *The CIA in Guatemala: The Foreign Policy of Intervention*. Austin: University of Texas Press, 1982.

Immerman, Richard H. "Eisenhower and Dulles: Who Made the Decisions?" *Political Psychology* (Autumn 1979), 1:3–20.

Kalb, Madeleine G. *The Congo Cables: The Cold War in Africa—From Eisenhower to Kennedy*. New York: Macmillan, 1982.

Kaufman, Burton I. *Trade and Aid: Eisenhower's Foreign Economic Policy, 1953–1961*. Baltimore: Johns Hopkins University Press, 1982.

Kempton, Murray. "The Underestimation of Dwight D. Eisenhower," *Esquire* (September 1967), 68:108–109, 156.

Kennan, George F. *Memoirs: 1950–1963*. Boston: Little, Brown, 1972.

Kirkpatrick, Lyman B., Jr. *The Real CIA*. New York: Macmillan, 1968.

Lisio, Donald J. *The President and Protest: Hoover, Conspiracy, and the Bonus Riot*. Columbia: University of Missouri Press, 1974.

Lodge, Henry Cabot. *As It Was*. New York: Norton, 1976.

Lodge, Henry Cabot. *The Storm Has Many Eyes*. New York: Norton, 1973.

McClintock, Robert. "The American Landing in Lebanon," *United States Naval Institute Proceedings* (October 1962), 88(10):65–80.

Macmillan, Harold. *The Blast of War*. New York: Harper and Row, 1967.

Macmillan, Harold. *Riding the Storm, 1956–1959*. New York: Harper and Row, 1971.

Macmillan, Harold. *War Diaries: Politics and War in the Mediterranean*. London: Macmillan, 1984.

Mahoney, Richard D. *JFK: Ordeal in Africa*. New York: Oxford University Press, 1983.

Meyer, Cord. *Facing Reality: From World Federalism to the CIA*. New York: Harper and Row, 1980.

Miller, William J. *Henry Cabot Lodge*. New York: Heineman, 1967.

Morgenthau, Hans J. "What the President and Mr. Dulles Don't Know," *The New Republic*, January 17, 1956.

Mosley, Leonard. *Dulles: A Biography of Eleanor, Allen, and John Foster Dulles and Their Family Network*. New York: Dial Press/James Wade, 1978.

Mosley, Leonard. *Power Play: Oil in the Middle East*. New York: Random House, 1973.

Murphy, Robert. *Diplomat Among Warriors*. Garden City, New York: Doubleday, 1964.

Nixon, Richard M. *RN: The Memoirs of Richard Nixon*. New York: Grosset and Dunlap, 1978.

Nixon, Richard M. *Six Crisis*. Garden City, N.Y.: Doubleday, 1962.

Patterson, James T. *Mr. Republican: A Biography of Robert A. Taft*. Boston: Houghton Mifflin, 1972.

Peeters, Paul. *Massive Retaliation: The Policy and Its Critics*. Chicago: Henry Regnery, 1959.

Powers, Thomas. *The Man Who Kept the Secrets: Richard Helms and the CIA*. New York: Knopf, 1979.

Prados, John. *The Sky Would Fall: Operation Vulture: The U.S. Bombing Mission in Indochina, 1954*. New York: Dial, 1983.

Pruessen, Ronald W. *John Foster Dulles: The Road to Power*. New York: Free Press, 1982.

Radosh, Ronald, and Joyce Milton. *The Rosenberg File*. New York: Holt, Rinehart and Winston, 1983.

Randle, Robert F. *Geneva 1954: The Settlement of the Indochinese War*. Princeton: Princeton University Press, 1969.

Reichard, Gary W. "Eisenhower as President: The Changing View," *South Atlantic Quarterly* (1978), 77:265–281.

Roosevelt, Kermit. *Countercoup: The Struggle for the Control of Iran*. New York: McGraw-Hill, 1979.

Rosenau, James N. *The Nomination of "Chip" Bohlen*. New York: Holt, 1958.

Rostow, W. W. *Eisenhower, Kennedy, and Foreign Aid*. Austin: University of Texas Press, 1985.

Rostow, W. W. *Europe After Stalin: Eisenhower's Three Decisions of March 11, 1953*. Austin: University of Texas Press, 1982.

Rostow. W. W. *Open Skies*. Austin: University of Texas Press, 1982.

Rovere, Richard H. "Eisenhower Revisited: A Political Genius?" *New York Times Magazine*, February 7, 1971.

Rubin, Barry. *Paved with Good Intentions: The American Experience and Iran*. New York: Oxford University Press, 1980.

Schilling, Warner R., Paul Y. Hammond, and Glenn H. Snyder. *Strategy, Politics, and Defense Budgets*. New York: Columbia University Press, 1962.

Schlesinger, Stephen, and Stephen Kinzer. *Bitter Fruit: The Untold Story of the American Coup in Guatemala*. Garden City, N.Y.: Doubleday, 1982.

Shepley, James. "How Dulles Averted War," *Life*, January 16, 1956.

Smith, Bradley F. *The Shadow Warriors: OSS and the Origins of the CIA*. New York: Basic Books, 1983.

Snyder, William P. "Walter Bedell Smith: Eisenhower's Chief of Staff," *Military Affairs* (1984), 48:6–14.

Soapes, Thomas F. "A Cold Warrior Seeks Peace: Eisenhower's Strategy for Nuclear Disarmament," *Diplomatic History* (1980), 4:57–71.

Stimson, Henry L., with McGeorge Bundy. *On Active Service in Peace and War.* New York: Harper, 1948.

Stookey, Robert W. *America and the Arab States: An Uneasy Encounter.* New York: Wiley, 1975.

Stuhler, Barbara. *Ten Men of Minnesota and American Foreign Policy, 1898–1968.* St. Paul: Minnesota Historical Society, 1973.

Thayer, Charles W. *Diplomat.* New York: Harper, 1959.

United States Department of State. *Foreign Relations of the United States 1947*, vol. 4. Washington, D.C.: GPO, 1972. (Cited in notes as *FRUS 1947*.)

United States Department of State. *Foreign Relations of the United States 1952–1954*, vols. 3, 4, 12, 13, 15, 16. Washington, D.C.: GPO, 1982. (Cited in notes as *FRUS 1952–1954*.)

United States Senate. *Executive Sessions of the Senate Foreign Relations Committee (Historical Series)*, vol. 5, Washington, D.C.: GPO, 1977.

United States Senate. *Hearings Before the Committee on Foreign Relations on the Nomination of Charles E. Bohlen to be United States Ambassador Extraordinary and Plenipotentiary to the Union of Soviet Socialist Republics.* 83d Cong., 1st Sess. Washington, D.C.: GPO, 1953.

United States Senate. Select Committee to Study Government Operations with Respect to Intelligence Activities (Church committee). *Alleged Assassination Plots Involving Foreign Leaders.* 94th Cong., 1st Sess. Washington, D.C.: GPO, 1975.

United States Senate. Select Committee to Study Government Operations with Respect to Intelligence Activities. 94th Cong., 2d Sess. *Supplementary Detailed Staff Reports on Foreign and Military Intelligence, Book IV.* Washington, D.C.: GPO, 1976.

Vandenberg, Arthur H., Jr., ed. *The Private Papers of Senator Vandenberg.* Boston: Houghton Mifflin, 1952.

Weissman, Stephen. *American Foreign Policy in the Congo. 1960–1964.* Ithaca, N.Y.: Cornell University Press, 1974.

Wills, Garry. *Nixon Agonistes: The Crisis of the Self-Made Man.* New York: New American Library, 1969.

Yergin, Daniel. *Shattered Peace: The Origins of the Cold War and the National Security State.* Boston: Houghton Mifflin, 1977.

Index